Deleuze in Children's Literature

Plateaus – New Directions in Deleuze Studies

'It's not a matter of bringing all sorts of things together under a single concept but rather of relating each concept to variables that explain its mutations.'
Gilles Deleuze, *Negotiations*

Series Editors
Ian Buchanan, University of Wollongong
Claire Colebrook, Penn State University

Editorial Advisory Board
Keith Ansell Pearson, Ronald Bogue, Constantin V. Boundas, Rosi Braidotti, Eugene Holland, Gregg Lambert, Dorothea Olkowski, Paul Patton, Daniel Smith, James Williams

Titles available in the series
Christian Kerslake, *Immanence and the Vertigo of Philosophy: From Kant to Deleuze*
Jean-Clet Martin, *Variations: The Philosophy of Gilles Deleuze*, translated by Constantin V. Boundas and Susan Dyrkton
Simone Bignall, *Postcolonial Agency: Critique and Constructivism*
Miguel de Beistegui, *Immanence – Deleuze and Philosophy*
Jean-Jacques Lecercle, *Badiou and Deleuze Read Literature*
Ronald Bogue, *Deleuzian Fabulation and the Scars of History*
Sean Bowden, *The Priority of Events: Deleuze's Logic of Sense*
Craig Lundy, *History and Becoming: Deleuze's Philosophy of Creativity*
Aidan Tynan, *Deleuze's Literary Clinic: Criticism and the Politics of Symptoms*
Thomas Nail, *Returning to Revolution: Deleuze, Guattari and Zapatismo*
François Zourabichvili, *Deleuze: A Philosophy of the Event* with *The Vocabulary of Deleuze* edited by Gregg Lambert and Daniel W. Smith, translated by Kieran Aarons
Frida Beckman, *Between Desire and Pleasure: A Deleuzian Theory of Sexuality*
Nadine Boljkovac, *Untimely Affects: Gilles Deleuze and an Ethics of Cinema*
Daniela Voss, *Conditions of Thought: Deleuze and Transcendental Ideas*
Daniel Barber, *Deleuze and the Naming of God: Post-Secularism and the Future of Immanence*
F. LeRon Shults, *Iconoclastic Theology: Gilles Deleuze and the Secretion of Atheism*
Janae Sholtz, *The Invention of a People: Heidegger and Deleuze on Art and the Political*
Marco Altamirano, *Time, Technology and Environment: An Essay on the Philosophy of Nature*
Sean McQueen, *Deleuze and Baudrillard: From Cyberpunk to Biopunk*
Ridvan Askin, *Narrative and Becoming*
Marc Rölli, *Gilles Deleuze's Transcendental Empiricism: From Tradition to Difference*, translated by Peter Hertz-Ohmes
Guillaume Collett, *The Psychoanalysis of Sense: Deleuze and the Lacanian School*
Ryan J. Johnson, *The Deleuze-Lucretius Encounter*
Allan James Thomas, *Deleuze, Cinema and the Thought of the World*
Cheri Lynne Carr, *Deleuze's Kantian Ethos: Critique as a Way of Life*
Alex Tissandier, *Affirming Divergence: Deleuze's Reading of Leibniz*
Barbara Glowczewski, *Indigenising Anthropology with Guattari and Deleuze*
Koichiro Kokubun, *The Principles of Deleuzian Philosophy*, translated by Wren Nishina
Felice Cimatti, *Unbecoming Human: Philosophy of Animality After Deleuze*, translated by Fabio Gironi
Ryan J. Johnson, *Deleuze, A Stoic*
Jane Newland, *Deleuze in Children's Literature*

Forthcoming volumes
Justin Litaker, *Deleuze and Guattari's Political Economy*
Nir Kedem, *A Deleuzian Critique of Queer Thought: Overcoming Sexuality*
Sean Bowden, *Expression, Action and Agency in Deleuze: Willing Events*
Andrew Jampol-Petzinger, *Deleuze, Kierkegaard and the Ethics of Selfhood*

Visit the Plateaus website at edinburghuniversitypress.com/series-plateaus-new-directions-in-deleuze-studies.html

DELEUZE IN CHILDREN'S LITERATURE

Jane Newland

EDINBURGH
University Press

Edinburgh University Press is one of the leading university presses in the UK. We publish academic books and journals in our selected subject areas across the humanities and social sciences, combining cutting-edge scholarship with high editorial and production values to produce academic works of lasting importance. For more information visit our website: edinburghuniversitypress.com

© Jane Newland, 2021, **2022**

Edinburgh University Press Ltd
The Tun – Holyrood Road,
12(2f) Jackson's Entry
Edinburgh EH8 8PJ

First published in hardback by Edinburgh University Press 2021

Typeset in 11/13 Sabon LT Std by
Servis Filmsetting Ltd, Stockport, Cheshire

A CIP record for this book is available from the British Library

ISBN 978 1 4744 6667 7 (hardback)
ISBN 978 1 4744 6668 4 (paperback)
ISBN 978 1 4744 6670 7 (webready PDF)
ISBN 978 1 4744 6669 1 (epub)

The right of Jane Newland to be identified as the author of this work has been asserted in accordance with the Copyright, Designs and Patents Act 1988, and the Copyright and Related Rights Regulations 2003 (SI No. 2498).

Contents

Acknowledgements vii
List of Abbreviations ix

1 Introduction: The Paradoxes of Children's Literature; or Making *Sense* of Children's Literature 1
2 Pure Repetition and Aiôn 25
3 Becoming-animal, Becoming-molecular, Becoming-imperceptible 47
4 Lines, Maps and Islands 75
5 Stuttering, Nonsense and Zeroth Voice 105
6 Painting the Imperceptible: Deleuze in Picture-book Form 133
7 Conclusion: Children's Literature on a Witch's Broom 155

References 163
Index 174

For Mum and Dad, with love always

Acknowledgements

This project would never have come about without the support of many people. My thanks go to my friends and colleagues at the Department of Languages and Literatures at Wilfrid Laurier University, in particular to Dr Nathalie Freidel, Dr Simona Pruteanu and Dr Milo Sweedler, to whom I am indebted for their collegiality, mentorship and encouragement. I am truly grateful to Dr Markus Bohlmann for his friendship and for his willingness to read and critique early drafts of this manuscript, and to Dr Tara Collington from the University of Waterloo, whose friendship and generosity opened many doors for me. Thanks are due to Professor Michael Kelly and Dr Loraine Day of the University of Southampton who were so supportive of me when I first discovered Deleuze. I am grateful to Wilfrid Laurier University for allowing me generous research leave to complete this work. I also wish to acknowledge the Children's Literature Association whose Faculty Research grant facilitated my interview work with Jacqueline Duhême in July 2012, which informed my Chapter on *L'Oiseau philosophie*. There are, however, four people without whom this project would never have reached fruition. It is impossible to put into words the depth of my feelings for and gratitude to my parents for their unfailing support and encouragement at every point of this journey; to Franz, my muse in this Deleuzian adventure; and finally, to John, whose lines of flight never cease to amaze me.

List of Abbreviations

For ease of reference, all quotations from works by Deleuze and Deleuze and Guattari are taken from the standard English translations listed below. References include the page numbers of the English translation followed by the corresponding passages of the original French edition, in the form (AO 3E/4F). All other translations in this text are my own, unless noted otherwise, and page numbers refer to the original French editions.

ATP   Deleuze, Gilles and Guattari, Félix (2003), *A Thousand Plateaus: Capitalism and Schizophrenia*, trans. Brian Massumi, London and New York: Continuum.
Deleuze, Gilles and Guattari, Félix (1980), *Capitalisme et Schizophrénie 2: Mille Plateaux*, Paris: Les Éditions de Minuit.

AO   Deleuze, Gilles and Guattari, Félix (2004), *Anti-Oedipus: Capitalism and Schizophrenia*, trans. Robert Hurley, Mark Seem and Helen R. Lane, London and New York: Continuum.
Deleuze, Gilles and Guattari, Félix (1972/3), *Capitalisme et Schizophrénie: L'Anti-Œdipe Nouvelle édition Augmentée*, Paris: Les Éditions de Minuit.

CC   Deleuze, Gilles (1997), *Essays Critical and Clinical*, trans. Daniel W. Smith and Michael A. Greco, Minneapolis: University of Minnesota Press.
Deleuze, Gilles (1993), *Critique et Clinique*, Paris: Les Éditions de Minuit.

C2   Deleuze, Gilles (2013), *Cinema II: The Time-Image*, trans. Hugh Tomlinson and Robert Galeta, London and New York: Bloomsbury.
Deleuze, Gilles (1985), *Cinéma II: L'Image-Temps*, Paris: Les Éditions de Minuit.

D   Deleuze, Gilles and Parnet, Claire (2007), *Dialogues II*, trans. Hugh Tomlinson and Barbara Habberjam, New York: Columbia University Press.

LIST OF ABBREVIATIONS

      Deleuze, Gilles and Parnet, Claire (1996), *Dialogues*, Paris: Flammarion.

DI   Deleuze, Gilles (2004), *Desert Islands and other texts 1953–1974*, ed. David Lapoujade, trans. Mike Taormina, Los Angeles and New York: Semiotext(e).
      Deleuze, Gilles (2002), *L'île déserte et autres textes 1953–1974: Textes et Entretiens 1953–1974*, Paris: Les Éditions de Minuit.

DR   Deleuze, Gilles (2001), *Difference and Repetition*, trans. Paul Patton, London: Continuum.
      Deleuze, Gilles (1968), *Différence et Répétition*, Paris: Presses Universitaires de France.

FB   Deleuze, Gilles (2003), *Francis Bacon: The Logic of Sensation*, trans. Daniel W. Smith, Minneapolis: University of Minnesota Press.
      Deleuze, Gilles (2002), *Francis Bacon: Logique de la sensation*, Paris: Les Éditions de Seuil.

K   Deleuze, Gilles and Guattari, Félix (1986), *Kafka: Toward a Minor Literature*, trans. Dana Polen, Minneapolis: University of Minnesota Press.
      Deleuze, Gilles and Guattari, Félix. (1975), *Kafka: pour une littérature mineure*, Paris: Les Éditions de Minuit.

LOP Deleuze, Gilles, (1997) *L'Oiseau philosophie*. Illus. Jacqueline Duhême, Paris: Les Éditions du Seuil.

LOS Deleuze, Gilles (2004), *The Logic of Sense*, trans. Mark Lester, with Charles Stivale, ed. Constantin V. Boundas, London and New York: Continuum.
      Deleuze, Gilles (1969), *Logique du Sens*, Paris: Les Éditions de Minuit.

N   Deleuze, Gilles (1995), *Negotiations: 1972–1990*, trans. Martin Joughin, New York: Columbia University Press.
      Deleuze, Gilles (2003), *Pourparlers 1972–1990*, Paris: Les Éditions de Minuit.

NP   Deleuze, Gilles (1983), *Nietzsche and Philosophy*, trans. Hugh Tomlinson. New York: Columbia University Press.
      Deleuze, Gilles (1962), *Nietzsche et la philosophie*, Paris: Presses Universitaires de France.

TRM Deleuze, Gilles (2006), *Two Regimes of Madness: Texts and Interviews, 1975–1995*, ed. David Lapoujade, trans. Ames Hodges and Mike Taormina, Los Angeles and New York: Semiotext(e).

List of Abbreviations

      Deleuze, Gilles (2003), *Deux Régimes de Fous: Textes et entretiens 1975–1995*, Paris: Les Éditions de Minuit.
WP   Deleuze, Gilles and Guattari, Félix (1994), *What is Philosophy?*, trans. Graham Burchell and Hugh Tomlinson, London and New York: Verso.
      Deleuze, Gilles and Guattari, Félix (1991), *Qu'est-ce que la philosophie?*, Paris: Les Éditions de Minuit.

1

Introduction: The Paradoxes of Children's Literature; or Making *Sense* of Children's Literature

> 'And now, which of these finger-posts ought I to follow, I wonder?'
> It was not a very difficult question to answer, as there was only one road through the wood, and the two finger-posts both pointed along it. 'I'll settle it,' Alice said to herself, 'when the road divides and they point different ways.'
> But this did not seem likely to happen. She went on and on, a long way, but wherever the road divided there were sure to be two finger-posts pointing the same way. (*Through the Looking-Glass, and What Alice Found There* (Carroll 2008: 158))

> 'Which way, which way?' asks Alice. The question has no answer, since it is the characteristic of sense not to have any direction of 'good sense.' Rather, sense always goes in to both directions at once. (*Logic of Sense* 88–9E/95F)

Gilles Deleuze is known for his somewhat cerebral tastes in literature, and throughout his *œuvre* he makes reference to innumerable authors, playwrights and poets, who he sees as exemplary practitioners of their craft and whose works create such new possibilities for life.[1] Yet, to elaborate his theory of sense in his *Logique du Sens* [*The Logic of Sense*] (1969), Deleuze turns, in part, to the nonsense and paradoxes he finds in Lewis Carroll's children's texts *Alice's Adventures in Wonderland* (1865) and *Through the Looking-Glass, and What Alice Found There* (1871). Whilst these are the only children's texts to which Deleuze explicitly refers, there are, nonetheless, glimpses of an interest in children's literature throughout his work. The series of conversations recorded with Claire Parnet, his former student, broadcast posthumously on Arte in 1995, give a nod to children's literature with their title *L'Abécédaire de Gilles Deleuze*. These conversations reprise the deceptively simple format, typically reserved for children, of the alphabet primer and provide a glimpse into Deleuze's mind at work as he speaks about words and concepts derived from each letter of the alphabet (A is for animal ... Z is for zigzag). The small book published in 1997 by Éditions du Seuil with the whimsical title *L'Oiseau philosophie: Duhême dessine*

Deleuze [The Bird Philosophy: Duhême draws Deleuze] – a homage in the most delightful way from Deleuze's long-time friend and illustrious children's literature illustrator, Jaqueline Duhême – makes a children's picture book of Deleuze and extracts of his thought. More broadly, Deleuze's thought is peopled with a rich imagery of sorcerers and witches, more commonly found in the genre of children's literature itself.

Children's literature is particularly attuned to Deleuzian thought because of a peculiarity it creates within the context of literary studies. The study of literature typically departs from distinct points of origin; the study of particular authors, Shakespeare, Molière or Goethe, for example; or specific periods, such as nineteenth- or twentieth-century literature. The study of children's literature, however, begins 'from the point of *arrival*, the child consumers, [which] feels like Alice's Looking-Glass logic, in which you must select the exact opposite direction in order to get to where you really want to go' (McMaster 2001: 281, original emphasis). Children's literature, unlike any other genre, forces us to consider the slippery idea of an implied child readership from the outset, and in doing so takes us into a Deleuzian looking-glass world of paradox and presumed binaries.

Paradox works against *doxa* or commonly held beliefs or opinions, taking terms which, on the surface, appear straightforward and self-explanatory and showing them to need further investigation. Paradox may trouble us and tempt us: we may feel the need to refute or resolve it. But for Deleuze we should do neither. Instead, we should approach paradox productively and use it to highlight the limitations of common sense and to create anew. The paradoxes of children's literature arise from the possessive apostrophe that links the two parts of the term *children's literature*, provoking in turn the emergence of a binary of what appear to be mutually exclusive terms – child and adult.

Common sense tells us that children's literature is a misnomer: children's literature is not a literature of children, created by children for children. Children do not typically write the texts we find in bookshops and libraries marketed and offered to children, adults do. The texts that children write[2] are rarely considered to be *L*iterature: great, canonical literature, the stuff of university studies; and in some ways, this mirrors the position of the discipline of children's literature itself, which in its infancy was not considered substantial enough for the academy. Children's literature is, then, a literature for children and about children: a literature to be read by children.

The Paradoxes of Children's Literature

Therein lies the paradox of children's literature: it seems almost impossible to talk about children's literature without talking about the adult who writes it, provides it, critiques and reviews it, and therefore also reads it, in juxtaposition to the child for whom it is essentially destined. The challenge of grappling with this paradox is taken up by many eminent scholars of children's literature. Two ground-breaking critiques, laudable for bringing the inherent imbalances of power between the key players of child and adult in children's literature to the fore, are Jacqueline Rose's *The Case of Peter Pan, or The Impossibility of Children's Fiction* (1984) and Karin Lesnik-Oberstein's later text, *Children's Literature: Criticism and the Fictional Child* (1994). Rose gestures towards the paradox of children's literature when, as her title suggests, she describes children's fiction as an impossible undertaking, one which positions the child as passive and external, 'unashamedly, [taken] *in*' (Rose 1994: 2, original emphasis)[3] by a fiction, which purports to be its own but can never be. Whilst Rose posits the presence of a 'real' child existing, 'outside' the book, Lesnik-Oberstein denies any possibility for the existence of a real child outside the text with its own unique agency and voice. 'Children', Lesnik-Oberstein claims, 'in culture and history, have no such voice' (Lesnik-Oberstein 1994: 26):[4] adults create or silence any voice that pertains to be of children. This 'real' child can never be, as that child is always constructed through the discourses that adults control and create. These readings of children's literature are problematic, not only because they promote the somewhat self-perpetuating notions of the voiceless, passive child, but also because they foreground alterity: that the child is other than and different to its adult counterparts; that both child and adult are distinct, knowable entities, neatly organised into discrete categories in binary opposition to each other. Yet, as more recent scholars such as Susan Honeyman (2005), Markus Bohlmann (2012) and Marah Gubar (2013) suggest, both child and adult are much more elusive. Both are knowable and unknowable, 'at once strangely familiar and yet elusively unrepresentable' (Bohlmann 2012: 1); both overlap and pass through each other: the child may play at being grown up; the adult may long to rediscover childhood. The not-yet-adult of the child is co-present with the once-was-child of the adult.

Peter Hunt's *Criticism, Theory, and Children's Literature* (1995) extends the paradox of children's literature to questions of readership. Children's books typically position the reader as a child: a tenable situation for a child reader of a children's text perhaps, but more problematic for an adult reader. Hunt advocates the need to adopt a new criticism when dealing with children's literature, which seeks to make the adult critic of children's literature acknowledge and consider the child's perspective. This criticism he calls childist, thereby sidestepping the often-pejorative suffixes of terms such as 'childish' and 'child-like' and capturing a similar approach to that of, for example, a feminist reading of a text. As Hunt openly admits, however, such an approach is grounded on (im)possibilities: 'childist criticism confronts an unacknowledged impossibility by manipulating probabilities. The impossibility is that the adult can never really know what a book means to a child: the major probability is that a child's reading differs substantially from an adult's' (Hunt 1995: 180). Hunt argues that an adult accepting the implied role and surrendering to the book 'is as close as we can get to reading as a child', but he outlines further complications in the process: 'do you read as the child you were, or as the child you are? on your self-image as a child or the memory of the "feel" of youthful reading? How far can experienced readers forget their adult experience?' (48). Hunt's arguments capture the paradox of an adult reading a text written by another adult, but destined for a child. Whilst Hunt acknowledges there may be traces of the child that remain with the adult, a childist critique of children's literature is, by his own admission, always beyond our reach. For Hunt, as for Rose and Lesnik-Oberstein, child and adult remain different to each other and a child's experience of a children's text remains different from and essentially unknowable to the adult.

More recently, Perry Nodelman, in his *The Hidden Adult: Defining Children's Literature* (2008), addresses this notion of the otherness of the child by referring to what he calls 'the fatal contradiction' in adult perceptions of childhood 'which insist both that children are different from and even opposite to adults and that they are in the process of becoming more adult all the time' (Nodelman 2008: 67). This leads to a situation where children's literature, for Nodelman, paradoxically 'claims to be devoid of adult content that nevertheless lurks within it' (341). David Rudd's *Reading the Child in Children's Literature: An Heretical Approach* (2013) challenges Nodelman's reading of children's literature, however, and views, inversely, the adult as the more visible figure in children's literature, 'unlike the more occluded presence of the child' (Rudd 2013: 102). The paradox of the intertwined presence of child and adult surfaces again: for Nodelman, it is the shadowy presence of the adult that paradoxically pervades literature for children and causes concern; for Rudd, it is the child of children's literature who is more elusive. We return to a looking-glass world where we are being pulled in two opposite directions at the same time.

To read Deleuze in children's literature is not to attempt to resolve these contradictions of children's literature, but to put the paradoxes inherent in it to use to negotiate new pathways through this looking-glass genre. These pathways bring us to two key concepts which recur throughout Deleuze's work: the molecular child and the encounter. The following sections expand upon these concepts as they underpin my readings that follow.

A Molecular Child

The child is a recurrent figure throughout Deleuze's *œuvre*,[5] and in *Capitalisme et Schizophrénie 2: Mille Plateaux* [*A Thousand Plateaus: Capitalism and Schizophrenia*] (1980), Deleuze and Guattari write of '"a" molecular child [which] is produced . . . "a" child coexists with us, in a zone of proximity or block of becoming, on a line of deterritorialization that carries us both off' (ATP 294E/360F). They oppose this molecular child to 'the child we once were, whom we remember or phantasize, the molar child whose future is adult' (ATP 294E/360F). The molar child has already been categorised by the adult world around it: parameters (age, gender, race, nationality and so on) have been 'imposed on it and [. . .] its subsequent actions are made to conform to those prescribed by its assigned category' (Massumi 1992: 55). The molar child is the child constructed, as Lesnik-Oberstein would argue, through the discourses of the adult world around it. It is this molar child who Jacqueline Rose invites into children's fiction. It is the child who Nodelman's hidden adults form and mould. The molar child is the child in children's literature who we think we know and understand, or, at the very least, hope to come to know and understand from reading its fiction.

For the molar child, there is only one prescribed, linear pathway from childhood towards adulthood. It is the molar child who we recall in our childhood memories and who, for Hunt, may colour our adult readings of children's texts. In his E (*Enfance*/Childhood) entry to *L'Abécédaire*, however, Deleuze warns us of the dangers of speaking about childhood: of import is not discussing one's own childhood, but *a* childhood, marked by an indefinite article.[6] Deleuze sees no interest in recalling a personal childhood, rather 'what interests him is discovering the "child emotion" and, through it, "not the child I once was," but rather "*a* child emerging among others, any child whatsoever (*un enfant quelconque*)"' (Stivale 2008: 130, original emphasis). In the encounter of child and adult in the space that is children's literature, another child emerges: a Deleuzian child. This Deleuzian child is any child whatsoever. It has not been subjected to categorisation; it retains 'an experimental body, sexuality and subjectivity' (Beckman 2017: 17). It has not been subjected to the constraints of possession; it is not somebody's child, nor the child somebody once was, nor the child of our memory. Rather, it is an indefinite, impersonal child: a molecular child.

It is not a child who exists purely outside the text waiting to be invited in; nor is it merely a fictional child inside the text waiting to be discovered. Rather the molecular child of children's literature draws from the reader and character alike, bringing both together through reading. The molecular child is not just accessible to the child, but to both adult and child alike. It is not a child longing to be an adult, nor is it an adult attempting to recapture a past childhood. The molecular child captures something of the adult and something of the child within, transforming what it takes from each so that it is both child and adult and yet neither. The molecular child is then what we discover as an adult or a child reader, or simply a reader, of a children's text; or as adult and child come together in a communal reading of a children's story. The molecular child is what emerges through the paradoxical pull of children's literature, in the pull towards both child and adult. The molecular child therefore undoes our traditional perceptions of childhood and adulthood; of two consecutive periods of life accessed in a linear fashion. The molecular child allows for the contiguity of childhood and adulthood. To read Deleuze in children's literature is to seek the emergence of this molecular child through the encounter[7] of children's literature.

An Encounter

To encounter is to come upon or to meet with, perhaps unexpectedly. The encounter inherent in children's literature is, at its very simplest, the coming-together of reader and book. When Deleuze speaks about an encounter however, he considers not only the coming-together of the individual elements comprising the encounter but also what passes between those elements. For Deleuze, this may be a block or a line; a zigzag which captures both parts of the encounter, steals

The Paradoxes of Children's Literature

something of each, and transforms each *and* that which they become. What passes between both parts of the encounter is a lightning-like flash, a Z-like connector which 'draws together creative forces and often incites the spark that unleashes potentials and thought' (Stivale 2008: 22).

The encounter inherent in children's literature is double: it not only involves the coming-together of reader and book, but also, as we have seen, of child and adult in the space of children's literature. When Deleuze, with Guattari, considers the book, it is as such an encounter. They tell us never to 'ask what a book means, as signified or signifier', but only to ask 'what it functions with, in connection with what other things it does or does not transmit intensities' (ATP 4E/10F). Of interest here is the expression 'transmit' (in French *faire passer*): the book functions with and transmits intensities to an external body. Intensity occurs in the flow between parts, in the connection between book and its external observer or reader. With this statement, Deleuze and Guattari are asking us to change, in the most radical way, how we approach literature, and it merits citing at length how Deleuze compares a traditional interpretative method to his encounter with the book:

> there are, you see, two ways of reading a book: you either see it as a box with something inside and start looking for what it signifies, and then if you are even more perverse and depraved you set off after signifiers. And you treat the next book like a box contained in the first or containing it. And you annotate and interpret and question, and write a book about the book, and so on. Or there's the other way: you see the book as a little non-signifying machine, and the only question is 'Does it work, and how does it work?' How does it work for you? If it doesn't work, if nothing comes through, you try another book. The second way of reading's intensive: something comes through or it doesn't. There's nothing to explain, nothing to understand, nothing to interpret. It's like plugging into an electric circuit. (N 7–8E/17F)

The traditional literary method, about which Deleuze is so cynical, creates distance: a gap imposes itself between reader and book, between interpreter and text. Authors can equally accentuate this gap and Deleuze tells us that those authors who allow readers to identify with their characters 'introduce[] a distance which allows [them] and us to observe, to criticize, to prolong. But this is no good' (D 52E/66F). Deleuze's proposed approach is one of proximity. It eliminates this distance, by considering the book as a machine, which connects with something on the outside. In this gesture of connecting, the book, this machine, comes together or is plugged in to its reader. Of import is not whether this reader is child or adult but whether an electric zigzag passes between the two parts. Of import is that a Deleuzian encounter occurs; an assemblage[8] is formed.

In a Deleuzian approach to literature, 'there is no hidden meaning or secret to be interpreted; rather, the text is part of a complex continuum with everything that is external to it. Its interest does not lie in what it contains, because it contains nothing; rather, we should be concerned with how it functions as it engages with the world' (Davis 2010: 62). It could be argued that whilst we are no longer looking for something to interpret in a text, no longer asking what a text means or represents, attempting to understand what a text connects with and how it transmits intensities is nonetheless a form of interpretation. In such an approach to literature, we are not, therefore, dismissing interpretation all together; rather we are shifting the focus of that interpretation, away from 'the empire of signs and the idea of the text as a tissue of signifiers in favour of a vision of the literary work as a machine or practical object composed of asignifying or non-representational particles discernible in blocs, traits and figures' (Buchanan et al. 2015: 2). Literature, then, for Deleuze is not a revelatory process, but a productive process. It is not a critical process, but an intensely creative process, producing assemblages and creating possibilities for molecular transformations of those who read it.

To read Deleuze in children's literature is to read children's literature in an entirely different way. With Deleuze in children's literature, we must relinquish the role of the distanced observer of a text. With Deleuze, we no longer get tangled up in ways of reading children's literature, as adult or child. We no longer need to search for meanings or negotiate questions of ideology or problems of didacticism. Rather, we can focus on the immediacy of reading, on the intense encounter that is reading and how assemblages arising from this encounter may transform us and disrupt the molar structures in our lives that try to contain us. To read Deleuze in children's literature allows us to embrace the molecular child that emerges from the curious and paradoxical sense of children's literature, which never ceases to pull us in two directions at once.

The Paradoxes of Children's Literature

Chapter Overview

Many authors fascinate Deleuze and references to them recur across his *œuvre*, shaping his writings on literature. Of his favoured authors, Miguel Angel Asturias, Lewis Carroll, Jean-Marie Gustave Le Clézio, André Dhôtel, Pierrette Fleutiaux, James Joyce, Eugène Ionesco, Michel Tournier and Virginia Woolf are unusual in that, in addition to their more well-known texts destined for an adult readership, they have also written texts for children. Of these authors, Tournier, Le Clézio and Ionesco could be considered as crossover writers: their texts are not distinguishable by readership and can be enjoyed by both young and adult readers alike. Dhôtel, Fleutiaux, Tournier and Le Clézio write for distinct readerships of children and adults. Despite a vast corpus, Dhôtel is remembered specifically for one particular children's book, *Le Pays où l'on n'arrive jamais*, for which he won the Prix Fémina in 1955. Tournier is renowned for re-writing his texts for adults as texts for children, and many of Le Clézio's children's texts have been adapted from his texts for adults. Ionesco, Joyce and Woolf wrote for specific children, young relatives, whereas Asturias wrote his children's texts for one specific children's literature illustrator, Jacqueline Duhême.

Some of these authors, such as Lewis Carroll or Virginia Woolf, feature prominently in Deleuze's work; others, like Jean-Marie Gustave Le Clézio or Miguel Angel Asturias, only appear more briefly. With the exception of the work of Lewis Carroll, the children's texts of these authors tend to be largely understudied in the field of children's literature and are often poorly known. For that reason, I draw on other more widely known children's texts as illustration where appropriate. In *Deleuze in Children's Literature*, I read the texts specifically written for children (as opposed to those appropriated by or adapted for children) by Deleuze's favoured authors. With the exception of Lewis Carroll's texts, Deleuze does not allude to these children's texts at any point in his work. Yet, the children's texts I study here reveal much of what intrigues Deleuze in literature and point to key tensions and further paradoxes within the genre of children's literature itself. In these children's texts we find stunning examples of repetitions and ritournelles that resonate across time and space, liberating us from linear time. There are curious becomings-animal and -plant that force us to re-evaluate what it means to grow up. There are child cartographers and nomads, who do not simply leave home to return changed but require us to move rhizomatically to access the atemporal landscapes of the molecular child. And of course, there is much (non)sense.

In Chapter 2, I begin my readings of Deleuze in children's literature with repetition – a concept not only key to Deleuze's philosophical project but also to children's literature. For Deleuze, the publication of his *Différence et Répétition* [*Difference and Repetition*] in 1968 marks a turning point in his work, moving him, in some ways, away from the studies of historical figures (Hume, Nietzsche, Kant, Bergson) in philosophy who dominate his early career. *Difference and Repetition* is the text in which Deleuze, as he so unassumingly puts it, first 'tried to do philosophy' (TRM 305E/280F).

In children's literature, repetition is not only ubiquitous, its presence creates a paradox. Young readers often appear to revel in repetition, delightedly returning to the same book over and over or reading something which is quite near to the original apart from minor variations. Traditional approaches to literature in general focus on the concept of comparative difference looking for distinctiveness and uniqueness in a given work. When such difference cannot be demonstrated, the literature concerned is typically rejected as inferior. Children's literature suffers under these conditions because of what children's literature scholars identify as its apparent sameness which, in turn, gives rise to its historically unhappy position in the field of critical theory.[9] Eugène Ionesco's *Contes 1, 2, 3, 4*[10] pop art picture books, illustrated by Étienne Delessert, provide a perfect illustration of the excesses of repetition in children's literature. Whilst Deleuze himself only makes the most fleeting of references to Ionesco in *Deux Régimes de Fous* [*Two Regimes of Madness*],[11] by considering Deleuze's concept of repetition for itself alongside Ionesco's *contes* we can put the paradox of repetition in children's literature to productive use to discover the difference in repetition.

To discuss another facet of repetition, the ritournelle,[12] I turn to Pierrette Fleutiaux's[13] *Trini fait des vagues* [*Trini Makes Waves*] (1997) and its sequel *Trini à l'île de Pâques* [*Trini on Easter Island*] (1999). Fleutiaux admits that, during the 1970s, she was fascinated by Deleuze. In describing Deleuze as 'someone who sent an electric current through your tired or lazy visions. He literally turned you on' (Knapp 1998: 438), Fleutiaux captures the essence of the Deleuzian approach to reading outlined above. Pierrette Fleutiaux's two detective novels, featuring the thirteen-year-old Trini and her police inspector sister Séréna, resemble traditional series fiction to some extent with their use of recurring characters, although they are not as formulaic as, for example, the Nancy Drew series from the Stratemeyer syndicate in the United States or the Famous Five series written by Enid Blyton in England. Fleutiaux's two texts exemplify how a haunting refrain can permeate a work. Her ritournelles drift through her writing for children and adults alike, creating not a pre-classified molar child, but a molecular child who brings together the seemingly disparate periods of childhood and adulthood in one.

Leading on from my discussion of the time of repetition – Aiôn, which simultaneously links all times: past, present and future – in Chapter 3 I focus on the notion of growing up in children's literature and how characters evolve and mature over time. Inherent in the idea of growing up is a linear, uni-directional movement through time towards a greater maturity and towards adulthood. If such linear movement of time is not apparent, then the characters of children's literature appear to stagnate, unable to grow up. Deleuze and Guattari do not deny this movement towards adulthood but create room for other changes or becomings during this progression from child to adult which break with our traditional expectations of growing up. In this chapter, I shift the focus of growing up from evolution and transformation to what Deleuze and Guattari term involution and becoming, specifically the becomings-animal, -plant and -molecular of characters, and the progression to the cosmic formula of becoming: becoming-imperceptible.

To illustrate becomings-animal, I draw firstly on two texts by Virginia Woolf: *Nurse Lugton's Curtain*[14] and *The Widow and the Parrot*. In *Nurse Lugton's Curtain*, we discover the eponymous nurse dozing in her rocking chair with a width of blue patterned material draped over her knees. Intended to be a curtain for the drawing room of her employer, Mrs. Gingham, the animals depicted on the material come to life as Nurse Lugton sleeps, only to be frozen back in place on the curtain when she wakes. Woolf's other children's tale, *The Widow and the Parrot*, is a story of an old lady, Mrs. Gage, who loves animals and who inherits her late brother's estate. Arriving to claim her inheritance, Mrs. Gage discovers nothing but a dilapidated house and a parrot named James. My readings of *The Widow and the Parrot* and *Nurse Lugton's Curtain* reveal the intense movement of becoming, and specifically becoming-animal, in these texts, and show how becomings-animal may, in turn, disrupt our preconceived notions of what 'a child' and 'an animal' may be.

To progress from becoming-animal to becoming-plant, I then discuss J.-M. Gustave Le Clézio, one of France's most renowned contemporary authors. His first novel *Le Procès-Verbal* [The Interrogation] (1963), to which Deleuze alludes in *Critique et Clinique* [*Essays Critical and Clinical*] (1993), received the Prix Renaudot in 1963, and in 2008 he received the Nobel Prize for literature for his complete work. In an interview with children's literature scholar Sandra Beckett given in 1993, Le Clézio, evoking to some degree the position of Jacqueline Rose, states that 'there is no literature for children' (Beckett 1997: 197). It is perhaps not surprising then to learn that 'all Le Clézio's texts published in children's collections are extracts from two collections of short stories intended for an adult readership' (Beckett 1997: 198). *Voyage au pays des arbres* [Journey to the Country of Trees] is his only text written intentionally for young readers, and is described by Le Clézio as 'rather a story which ought to be read aloud, to children who are not yet able to read' (Beckett 1997: 198). Le Clézio's only intentional children's story is one which he sees as a communal experience, bringing adult and child together in the shared experience of a text read out loud. In *Voyage au pays des arbres* (written earlier but only published in 1978 by Gallimard Jeunesse, and illustrated by Henri Galeron), a little boy, named Hihuit,[15] who longs to travel, finds his way into a forest at night and discovers a universe where the trees come alive and dance all night. Given Deleuze's disdain for trees, this text may appear un-Deleuzian. A similar critique could be made of Woolf's *The Widow and the Parrot*, due to Deleuze's loathing of domesticated animals. Woolf's and Le Clézio's texts nonetheless reveal possibilities for many becomings, in particular becoming-molecular and becoming-plant.

To consider becoming-imperceptible, I turn to the Guatemalan Nobel laureate Miguel Angel Asturias and his philosophical fairy tale published a year before his death in 1974, entitled *El Hombre que lo tenia todo, todo, todo*, translated into French and published by Éditions G.P. (Générale de Publicité) as *L'Homme qui avait tout, tout, tout* [The Man Who Had Everything, Everything, Everything] (1973). Asturias is one of the authors to whom Deleuze refers, albeit briefly, in *L'île déserte et autres textes: Textes et entretiens 1953–1974* [*Desert Islands and other texts 1953–1974*] (2002), but they share another important link: Asturias turned to Jacqueline Duhême, children's literature illustrator and long-time friend of Deleuze, to illustrate his work. Deleuze says of Asturias's writing that it reveals a 'power of metamorphosis [...] and it emanates from other landscapes: the Savannah, the pampas, a fruit company, a field of corn or rice' (DI 290E/402F): a notion that he evokes in his correspondence with Duhême on the publication of *L'Homme qui avait tout, tout, tout*. Deleuze wrote to Duhême: 'Jacqueline, I was happy to read the book. It's a beautiful text. I find your drawings complement it particularly well: they convey the image of such thick vegetation that the slightest movement would require magical forces' (Duhême 1998: 100). Duhême's illustration for the cover of the tale depicts a jungle-like scene, evoking the rich landscape of Asturias's Guatemalan heritage, with the youthful man who has everything perched in the trees, arms outstretched as if flying. It is not this vegetation that leads to becoming-imperceptible in this text, however. Apart from possessing everything, this man has one curious particularity: at night, his lungs become magnetic and attract metal from all around. This malediction reminiscent of the inherited *fêlure* or crack Deleuze sees in Émile Zola's Rougon-Macquart series can only be relieved if Asturias's nameless protagonist lies on a bed of salt at night. Asturias's text explores the limits of the human body through a merging of the artificial and the natural and reveals how the physical can give way to becoming-imperceptible.

Chapter 3 concludes by considering Lewis Carroll's Alice, who for Deleuze epitomises pure becoming. Bemused by her paradoxical movements of growing up and down, of getting bigger and smaller, during her stay in Wonderland, Alice clutches at a sense of self through the act of recitation, of multiplication tables, geographical facts and poetry. These failed recitals give rise to humorous parodies, but more importantly allow for the dissolution of Alice's self which allows for her pure becoming, divested from uni-directional time. In her pure becoming, Alice ages incorporeally, bringing her childhood and adulthood into contact with each other, permitting the emergence of a molecular child in a childhood-block that endures across all time.

In order to grow up, child protagonists often have to journey, and journeying is therefore a common trope in children's fiction, taking a character away from and then returning him or her, newly initiated and matured, home. Deleuze, with Guattari, asks us not to journey to and from somewhere, but to move rhizomatically from the middle, creating maps and tracing dynamic lines as we proceed. Chapter 4 focuses on the cartographies of children's literature and the maps and lines composed by journeying child characters. To explore such Deleuzian journeys I draw predominantly on Pierrette Fleutiaux's *Trini à l'île de Pâques*, Michel Tournier's *Vendredi ou la vie sauvage* and André Dhôtel's *Le Pays où l'on n'arrive jamais*.

Despite his vast *œuvre*, French novelist, storyteller and poet, André Dhôtel (1900–91), is best known for his text *Le Pays où l'on n'arrive jamais* [The Country Always Beyond Reach] (1955) thanks to the Prix Fémina it received. For many critics, though, *Le Pays où l'on n'arrive jamais* 'is not, aggravatingly, what one could call his masterpiece' (Frankart 2012: 39). It follows in the tradition of Alain-Fournier's (1886–1914) *Le Grand Meaulnes* [The Wanderer] (1913) and Henri Bosco's (1888–1976) *L'enfant et la rivière* [The Child and the River] (1945) in that its protagonists are driven by a desire to roam, attempting to find something lost to them. *Le Pays où l'on n'arrive jamais* is, like its predecessors, an example of *l'école buissonnière*, where children play truant, to partake of a more natural schooling in the countryside away from the constraints and regulations of the academy. The expression *faire l'école buissonnière* is therefore synonymous with actions such as walking, wandering, meandering and roaming. Dhôtel's protagonist, Gaspard, is an otherworldly boy (rather in the vein of Antoine de Saint-Exupéry's *Le Petit Prince* or Maurice Druon's Tistou). Left in his aunt's care as a baby by his itinerant parents, Gaspard's innate curiosity frequently sparks incidents which would endanger other children but leave him relatively unscathed. The accumulation of these incidents lead villagers to believe that Gaspard is visited by a hidden curse and, as a result, he has a lonely and somewhat mundane existence working at his strict aunt's auberge. This humdrum life is disrupted when, during one of his many walks in the countryside surrounding his aunt's guesthouse, Gaspard encounters a runaway child. They connect and Gaspard learns that the child is fleeing the Belgian city of Antwerp in search of family and homeland. On his travels to help the fugitive child, Gaspard befriends and is aided by other colourful characters: a barber, a travelling musician and his sons, and an entrepreneurial boy. Gaspard has an innate longing to be in the verdant Ardennes countryside surrounding his aunt's auberge in the fictitious village of Lominval,[16] and Dhôtel's descriptions focus on the familiar countrysides of his birthplace, the Meuse and the Ardennes. Danielle Henky considers that 'for Dhôtel as for Alain-Fournier or Bosco for example, the staging of the moment when the child becomes aware of its life in childhood (*sa vie en enfance*) [. . .] is crucial' (Henky 2012: 73). This, for Gaspard, comes as his nomadism surfaces as he learns to understand the maps immanent within him.

The acclaimed French novelist Michel Tournier (1924–2016) received the Grand Prix du Roman de l'Académie Française for his first text, *Vendredi ou les limbes du Pacifique* [Friday, or the Other Island] in 1967, and 'almost immediately after the publication of his first novel, Tournier felt the need to rewrite his Robinsonnade "in a leaner, tauter form"' (Beckett 2009: 74). His *Vendredi ou la vie sauvage* [Friday and Robinson] appeared in 1971, 'reluctantly published' by Flammarion, who 'pessimistically predict[ed] that it would not be a success' (Beckett 2009: 74).[17] In these retellings of Daniel Defoe's *Robinson Crusoe* (1719), Tournier's Robinson is shipwrecked on a desert island, which he names Speranza, or hope in Italian. In the initial part of the novel, Robinson spends his time taming the island's flora and fauna, cultivating crops, and creating structures and laws; in short, organising and civilising the island. His only companion is Tenn, the ship's dog, until the arrival of Vendredi (Friday), who flees a sacrificial party of native Araucanians who have previously come to the island to carry out such acts. After a period of subservience, where Robinson civilises Friday, teaching him English and educating him in his strict and regimented ways of the island, an explosion of gunpowder left over from the shipwreck destroys everything that Robinson has worked to establish. After the explosion, in the second part of the novel, it is Friday who guides Robinson, 'the end result is Robinson becoming elemental on his isle' (LOS 342E/351F). Tournier's novels differ from Defoe's in that Tournier's Robinson chooses to remain on Speranza after the appearance of the *Whitebird*, a British vessel. Friday, mesmerised by the ship with its lofty rigging, secretly leaves the island as the *Whitebird* departs.

After an exploration of the endpaper maps in children's literature, typified by Arthur Ransome's *Swallows and Amazons* and taken up in *Trini à l'île de Pâques*, Chapter 4 moves on to consider the paradoxical endpaper map of *Through the Looking-Glass, and What Alice Found There*. The chapter then pursues the cartographic activity of child protagonists and the characters who have access to maps emanating from within, which in turn encourages their innate nomadism. Chapter 4 concludes by considering the nature of the desert island which exists in a time apart, a paradoxical time of molecular childhood which does not exist in opposition to adulthood.

Chapter 5 returns to the sense and more specifically the nonsense of children's literature and the voices that create this interplay of (non)sense within children's literature. Whilst I refer to Lewis Carroll's Alice, either from *Alice's Adventures in Wonderland* or *Through the Looking-Glass*, in each of my chapters, it is in this chapter that my extended discussion of Alice occurs. Bored by sitting next to her grown-up sister on the riverbank, Alice follows a White Rabbit down a rabbit hole where she meets all manner of odd creatures who provoke and destabilise the ways in which she views and comprehends the curious Wonderland around her. They replace her learnt, established rules and codes by ones which appear to defy common sense. Scholars of children's literature consider that the publication of *Alice's Adventures in Wonderland* 'marked the liberation of children's literature from the hands of the moralists and didacts. With its fantastic plot, extravagant characters, parodies of poems and songs, and use of nonsense, it revolutionized children's literature' (O'Sullivan 2010: 61). Moreover, presaging somewhat Deleuze's own radical shift in literary approach, Carroll was oblique 'when asked about the meaning of the Alice books, [replying] serenely that he was content for the meaning to be decided by the reader'; as Juliet Dusinberre goes on to note, 'in 1865 such abrogation of authorial mastery was unprecedented in the children's book' (Dusinberre 1999: 42). Other scholars of children's literature consider Carroll's suppression of common sense as more sinister: Maria Nikolajeva reads *Alice's Adventures in Wonderland* as a text 'in which the child is threatened and humiliated' (Nikolajeva 2010: 57) by Wonderland's authoritarian inhabitants who manipulate and distort sense and meaning to suit their own ends and purposely, to disempower Alice. For Deleuze, however, it is precisely this interplay of sense and nonsense that is of interest in Carroll's text. In his preface to *The Logic of Sense*, he writes:

> the work of Lewis Carroll has everything required to please the modern reader: children's books, or rather, books for little girls; splendidly bizarre and esoteric words; grids; codes and decodings; drawings and photographs; a profound psychoanalytic content; and an exemplary logical and linguistic formalism. Over and above the immediate pleasure, though, there is something else, a play of sense and nonsense [. . .] The privileged place assigned to Lewis Carroll is due to his having provided the first great account, the first great mise en scène of the paradoxes of sense. (LOS xiiiE/7F)

Through Carroll's play on sense and nonsense, I consider how Alice tries in vain to recreate a majoritarian, adult language, but through stuttering and recourse to persiflage manages to make language vibrate and create her own unique style. I go on to consider the strange words invented by Humpty Dumpty. This self-proclaimed master of meaning invents esoteric and portmanteau words, and in doing so succeeds in pushing language through its fragile surface of sense to its outside. I end this chapter by advocating for what I term the zeroth voice: a voice of the molecular child called out of the reading of texts which forms at the zero point of thought, as (non)sense is created.

To augment my readings in this chapter, I also draw on James Joyce's *The Cat and the Devil*, whose eponymous Devil has recourse to *mots-cris* or howl-words to escape the constraints of majoritarian linguistic codes. Joyce's tale has a simple premise: the people of the French town of Beaugency require a bridge to help them cross the wide Loire river, but do not have the financial means to pay for the bridge themselves. The Devil, whose penchant for his daily newspapers allows him to learn of this predicament, offers to build the bridge on condition that he will receive as payment the soul of the first person to cross it. The Devil creates a beautiful bridge in just one night, but the cunning major of Beaugency, Monsieur Alfred Byrne,[18] tricks the Devil by forcing a white cat to cross the bridge first, thus releasing the people of Beaugency from the pact and freeing them to enjoy the bridge.

Joyce wrote this tale in a letter, dated 1936, to his polyglot grandson, Stephen Joyce. His tale, signed Nonno, is followed by a postscript, which explains that the Devil 'mostly speaks a language of his own called Bellsybabble'[19] (Joyce 1975: 384). Joyce's tale, published only posthumously as a children's book, has been translated into many languages, and many editions of the text exist. Here, I focus on the following four editions: the 1964 edition, illustrated by Richard Erdoes; the 1965 edition, illustrated by Gerald Rose; the 1966 edition, illustrated by Jean-Jacques Corre; and the 1990 edition illustrated by Roger Blachon.[20] This latter edition includes a letter written by Joyce's grandson addressed to the readers of the text, dated 1989. In this letter, which mirrors his grandfather's own letter, 'Stephen Joyce, originally the four-year-old recipient and reader of the story, becomes the writer who pens a letter to a child audience. [...] Casting himself as both grandfather and grandson and oscillating between these two roles throughout the letter' (Sigler 2008: 540). Stephen Joyce thus accentuates the double pull of children's literature to both child and adult. His letter creates a doubling of the tale's bridge motif, encouraging young readers not simply to cross Joyce's bridge in reading the text ('the reading of the letter itself amount[s] to a crossing process' (Garnier 2003: 101), poised as it is between the letter and its postscript), but also to remember Joyce as they cross into adulthood and pursue their reading of Joyce in their adult years.

In my final chapter, I turn to a small children's picture book, *L'Oiseau philosophie*. Published shortly after Deleuze's death, this unassuming book is at first glance an enchanting testimony to a three-way friendship between Gilles Deleuze and his long-time friends, Jean-Pierre Bamberger and Jacqueline Duhême. Yet, *L'Oiseau philosophie* is much more than that. It epitomises the very paradoxes of children's literature discussed above, the curious pull to both child and adult. On the one hand, it is a colourful, vibrant picture book replete with exquisite illustrations by Jacqueline Duhême. Its small, square presentation makes it perfectly sized for the tiny hands of the young reader who might delight in the images of animals and children within its covers. On the other hand, *L'Oiseau philosophie* is a philosophical text, composed of excerpts from Deleuze's *Dialogues*, written with Claire Parnet, and published in 1977, and *Qu'est-ce que la philosophie?*, written in collaboration with Félix Guattari in 1991 – texts more typically found in the hands of adult philosophers than young readers of picture books. *L'Oiseau philosophie* then draws us in two directions at once: to image and to word; to child and to adult; to the very youngest and, by their very nature, the most inexperienced of readers and to the most erudite of scholarly readers. In this chapter, I consider the images of a bird and a witch that recur throughout *L'Oiseau philosophie* and how each of these lead us beyond ourselves on liberating lines of flight. Duhême's unusual portrayals of indefinite child figures give us an image of Deleuze's child: a joyous molecular child, accessible to us through all moments in life, even death, and which escapes the limitations of Chronos and plays in the connectable time of Aiôn.

After the initial excerpt presented in *L'Oiseau philosophie*, which reminds us how to read a book ('as you would treat a record you listen to, a film or a TV programme you watch' (D 3–4E/10F)) and advocates for the intense encounter that is reading, the following double-page spread presents a line drawn from *What is Philosophy?*: 'to think is always to follow a witch's flight' (WP 41E/44F). This whimsical statement seems more at home in a child's picture book than in the final instalment of Deleuze and Guattari's unprecedented collaboration. The image of the witch's broom or flight nevertheless bookends Deleuze's *œuvre*. It stems from Deleuze's early career when he found himself on his own witch's broom through his readings of Spinoza, and it is an image to which he returns in his final book *Essays Critical and Clinical* to describe how great authors 'make the language take flight, they send it racing along a witch's line' (CC

The Paradoxes of Children's Literature

109E/138F). Of Spinoza, Deleuze says: 'but he more than any other gave me the feeling of a gust of air from behind each time you read him, of a witch's broom which he makes you mount' (D 15E/22F). Indeed, as Ian Buchanan suggests, Deleuze's 'monographs on Hume, Bergson, Nietzsche and Spinoza written in the early part of his career [. . .] enabled Deleuze to think differently; they were his lines of flight or "witch's brooms" that took him outside and beyond the confines of his situation' (Buchanan 2009: 208), allowing him to break with convention and move on to do philosophy in his own way. 'The witch's flight[21] [is] not a secure thought operation' (Stengers 2009: 32), but an exhilarating one. A racing, mad vector that breaks with the ordinary. *Deleuze in Children's Literature* allows us to mount our own witch's broom and gives us the perhaps childlike feeling of being blown along by an invisible wind, 'a witch's wind' (D 75–6E/91F), by an unseen force which allows us to move wildly and to explore unusual lines and directions. It is 'a witch's line that escapes the dominant system' (CC 5F/15F) of representation and interpretation, of rigidly fixed childhoods, of sequential periods of life. It is the witch's line that helps us make *sense* of the paradoxes of children's literature with its molecular child. It is the witch's line that we now seek in this exploration of children's literature.

Finally, a word about what this study is not. Despite the centrality of psychoanalysis to the discussion of children's literature and despite Deleuze's investment in the discourse of psychoanalysis, I do not engage significantly with psychoanalysis in this text. In Chapter 2, I touch on the differences between Deleuze's conceptualisation of repetition and the reactionary repetition of Freud's *Beyond the Pleasure Principle*. Chapter 3 shows how psychoanalysis impedes becoming with its penchant for Oedipalised animals and the possessive and the personal. In Chapter 3, I also explore childhood blocks which allow us to reconsider the sequential periods of life – childhood, adolescence, adulthood – as malleable and contiguous, moving us away from the repeated childhood traumas of psychoanalysis. Lastly, in Chapter 6, I discuss the BwO (Body without Organs) as Deleuze's antidote to psychoanalysis. A more in-depth engagement with Deleuze, psychoanalysis and children's literature is a larger undertaking, worthy of a book-length study in and of itself.

Notes

1. *Deleuze et les écrivains: Littérature et Philosophie* (Gelas and Micolet 2007) provides an exhaustive index of the literary references that permeate Deleuze's *œuvre*.
2. I am not referring here to juvenilia, or the writings of well-established authors produced during their childhood.
3. Children's literature scholar, Jack Zipes, adopts a similar position in *Sticks and Stones: The Troublesome Success of Children's Literature from Slovenly Peter to Harry Potter* (2001). He acknowledges that children are actively involved in the creation of 'their own literary products, journals, newspapers, cartoons, comics, plays and videos. But the institution of children's literature is not of their making' (Zipes 2001: 40).
4. Lesnik-Oberstein extends Rose's thesis of the impossibility of children's fiction to the criticism of children's literature itself.
5. For accounts of the child in Deleuze's work see: Hickey-Moody 2013; Ord 2014; Bohlmann and Hickey-Moody 2019.
6. I discuss the indefinite article in more depth in Chapter 3.
7. Many terms appear somewhat interchangeable in Deleuze's work. An encounter is also a becoming, a concept which I explore in greater depth in Chapter 3.
8. For readers less familiar with Deleuzian terminology, assemblage is the standard translation of the French *agencement* used by Deleuze and Guattari to capture the ways in which heterogeneous terms come together and create relations between them. A helpful analogy is the bicycle. A bicycle, for example, is a collection of metal parts (gears, chains, handlebars, a saddle, pedals, wheels, etc.) put together in a certain way, but this assembled collection of parts, like the packets of flat-packed furniture, which have numbered pieces which must fit together to form a preconceived object, is not the Deleuzian assemblage. A bicycle, on its own, it is nothing more than the parts that compose it. It is only in coming-together with a person that this collection of parts is transformed: the bicycle 'only works when it is connected with another "machine" such as the human body; and the production of these two machines can only be achieved through connection. The human body becomes a cyclist in connecting with the machine; the cycle becomes a vehicle' (Colebrook 2002: 56). Merely placing any object on a bicycle will not create such an assemblage, a bicycle needs a human being to connect to it; with feet placed on its pedals and hands on its handlebars. When balance is achieved, the bicycle assemblage functions. It does not express unity but transformation, and transformation of both parts of the assemblage. The person riding the bike has new freedom and is able to travel greater

distances. The immobile collection of parts is now machining with its rider, gaining movement from the energy of its rider. The assemblage comes about through desire: the rider desires to move more quickly, to be energised from a bicycle ride. The human body and the bicycle come together and are transformed. Machining with the bicycle, the human body is liberated and deterritorialised, as a child free-wheels down a hill, legs outstretched for example. Reterritorialisations are never far away, however: the wobbly child learning to assemble with the bicycle understands the inevitability of reterritorialisation as the child loses balance and falls off the bike, causing the fragile assemblage to break apart. Implications of safety and traffic laws keep cyclists in check, obliging us use our bicycles in molar, stratifying ways: they make us resist weaving all over the road, doing wheelies and so on. Moreover, the assemblage 'produces utterances' (D 51E/65F), to which the many online glossaries of cycling terms and jargon attest, giving us specific expressions for such de- and reterritorialisations, such as the 'endo', where the bicycle flips over its front wheel, or the 'wipe-out', where the cyclist completely loses balance and crashes. In short, the assemblage is a 'complex constellations of objects, bodies, expressions, qualities, and territories that come together for varying periods of time to ideally create new ways of functioning' (Livesey 2010: 18). See also Wise 2007 for further discussion of the assemblage.
9. See Nodelman 1985 and 2008.
10. Unillustrated versions of these *contes* can also be found in Ionesco's autobiographical *Présent Passé, passé Présent* (1968).
11. In *Deux Régimes de Fous: Textes et entretiens 1975–1995* [*Two Regimes of Madness: Texts and Interviews 1975–1995*] (2003), Deleuze refers to Henri Gobard, a linguist teaching at Vincennes, as capable of producing 'theatre worthy of Ionesco' (TRM 69E/63F). Deleuze wrote the preface for Gobard's *L'Aliénation linguistique: Analyse tétraglossique* (1976).
12. In the original French, Deleuze uses the term *ritournelle*, translated from the Italian *ritornello*, which literally means 'little return' and is used to describe a recurring passage in Baroque music. The standard translation of Deleuze's *ritournelle* is refrain. I use both terms interchangeably in this text.
13. Fleutiaux's work *Histoire du gouffre et de la lunette* [*The Story of the Abyss and the Spyglass*] (1976) is subject to a lengthy discussion in *A Thousand Plateaus*. Deleuze and Guattari draw on this text to discuss the lines which compose us. They identify three types of lines: lines of molar or rigid segmentarity; lines of molecular or supple segmentation; and lines of flight (ATP 195–7E/239–241F). Molar lines are 'conventional trajectories regulated by codes that impose broad social categories, fixed identities and pathways discretely divided into

clear segments' (Bogue 2003: 159). Molecular lines are more fluid and supple. They create fissures, ruptures, cracks and minute disturbances in the molar regimes that contain us. Lines of flight 'no longer tolerate[] segments; rather [they are] like an exploding of the two segmentary series' (ATP 197E/241F). Deleuze likens lines of flight to 'children leaving school at a run' (ATP 202E/248F). Lines of flight have the potential for change and transformation, for the creation of the new, but they risk going nowhere and returning to more rigid, molar lines. Lines of flight is the standard translation for *lignes de fuite*. The French verb *fuir* means to flee, to escape, to leak (*une fuite d'eau* – a water leak). Its translation as lines of flight should not be confused with the action of flying. I discuss these lines in greater depth in Chapter 4.

14. Kristin Czarnecki details the discovery of Woolf's short children's text as follows: 'It was in the second of the three large Dalloway manuscript notebooks amid pages depicting Septimus Warren Smith's final scene, when he hurls himself out the window at the approach of Dr. Holmes, intent on separating him from his wife, Rezia. Just moments before, Septimus had been helping Rezia sew a hat, adding felt and flowers and laughing with his wife in a lovely and all too rare moment of lucidity' (Czarnecki 2011: 222). In the *Times Literary Supplement*, Wallace Hildick discusses the provenance of the text, wondering 'about the therapeutic motive' (Hildick 1965) behind the story and if 'it provided a respite for Woolf from working out the scenes of madness and suicide in Mrs. Dalloway' (Czarnecki 2011: 222). Or speculating if it is a 'simpler, more childlike dream' (Hildick 1965) serving as an alternative to Peter Walsh's dream having fallen asleep in Regent's Park next to an old woman knitting. Woolf's diary entry of 7 September 1924, however, mentions 'a delightful afternoon spent with her young niece, Ann' (Czarnecki 2011: 222), and Leonard Woolf's subsequent corroboration of this allows Hildick to surmise that 'one of the stories the girl heard [. . .] was this one about Nurse Lugton' (Hildick 1965). Whilst Woolf's text may not have been intended for publication, the discovery of the draft shows that the author had spent time revising and improving her text. Its classification as a children's text remains improbable for some. In an article on the children's texts of high modern authors, Hope Howell Hodgkins points out that in the edition illustrated by Julie Vivas Woolf's prose is 'typically graceful, with far more subordinated clauses than the usual children's book, let alone the usual picture book (an opening sentence employs no fewer than five semicolons)' (Hodgkins 2007: 361). She continues 'Julie Vivas's paintings in a recent edition employ color and whimsy appropriately. Yet the illustrations add no extra information or emotional content. In fact, the tale contains little excitement; we have no fascinating narrative, no causality to illustrate. The bland effect may not be the illustrator's

fault but a condition of the text, which, of course, was not originally conceived as a picture book. High modernism's antinarrative bias is all too evident here and deadly for readers who want an engaging story' (361). Picture books are intended for the youngest of readers, or children who are not yet able to read, but who listen to a story being read and observe the pictures in the book as the pages are turned. It is clear through Hodgkins' reading of *Nurse Lugton's Curtain* that she cannot conceive that such readers could ever be 'plugged in' to such a text because of its literariness.

15. Sandra Beckett (1997) points to the influence of Native American culture on Le Clézio, evident in the little boy's name and the names of the trees.
16. According to Dhôtel, the fictitious Lominval is located where the actual village of Sécheval is found. See Frankart 2012.
17. See Beckett 2009 for an extended discussion of Tournier's crossover writing and specifically the creation of *Vendredi ou la vie sauvage*.
18. Joyce's mayor 'wore a scarlet robe and always had a great golden chain round his neck even when he was fast asleep with his knees in his mouth' (Joyce 1975: 382).
19. Readers of *The Cat and the Devil* (Hodgkins 2007; Reynolds 2007; Sigler 2008) agree that Joyce casts himself as the eponymous Devil. In naming the Devil's invented language Bellsybabble 'Joyce, still in the throes of writing the polyglot *Finnegans Wake*, jests about his own devilish creation of a literary "Tower of Babble"' (Hodgkins 2007: 363). His humorous and slightly mocking description of the Major of Beaugency in his mayoral attire and who arrives to the inauguration of the new bridge to 'the sound of bugles' (Joyce 1975: 383) reflects Joyce's view of his contemporary, Alfred Byrne, the Lord Major of Dublin, and in particular his penchant for pomp and fanfare. The illustrations by Gerald Rose, Jean-Jacques Corre and to a lesser extent, Roger Blachon reinforce the image of Joyce in the Devil's role, depicting the Devil with dark hair, small round spectacles and a moustache. I explore the relationship of the Devil's Bellsybabble to childhood voice in more detail in Chapter 5.
20. For ease of reference, I take all quotations of Joyce from the *Selected Letters of James Joyce*, edited by Richard Ellmann (Joyce 1975).
21. Kara Keeling (2007) uses the concept of the witch's flight in her excellent text: *The Witch's Flight: The Cinematic, the Black Femme, and the Image of Common Sense*.

2

Pure Repetition and Aiôn

a desire for the same story to be repeated along with the knowledge that it cannot ever be exactly the same, an impossible longing for a simultaneous sameness and difference. (Watson 2000: 8)

making repetition the category of the future: making use of the repetition of habit and that of memory, but making use of them as stages and leaving them in its wake [...] making it so that repetition is, for itself, difference in itself. (*Difference and Repetition* 94E/125F)

In 1987 Susan Gannon began her editorial to the *Children's Literature Association Quarterly* with the following words: 'repetition is one of the most familiar features of children's fiction' (Gannon 1987: 2), and across the spectrum of texts for children there are many repetitions at play. These may be internal to the text whether oral or written, such as the repeated patterns of poetry and playground rhyme. They may be repetitions of picture books where image and text simultaneously reiterate each other, or the repetitions of generic conventions in form and content, of family life or school-based scenarios for example. The repetitions of series fiction, where familiar characters recur in familiar situations over a number of sequenced volumes may also be compared to the indulgent repetitions of re-reading a favourite book time and time again. At a time when the study of children's literature was making forays into the academy, and children's literature was establishing itself as genre in its own right, Gannon points not simply to a key feature of this literature, but to one that equally creates paradox and causes concern. Adults in general and adult scholars in particular are often baffled as to why young readers are attracted to repetitive texts. To the outside observer, such texts may appear two-dimensional and stereotyped. The young reader, in contrast, is drawn into this repetition and apparently finds pleasure in repeatedly encountering the same characters, situations and themes.

In *Becoming a Reader: The Experience of Fiction from Childhood to Adulthood*, J. A. Appleyard acknowledges this paradox of repetition and the difference in adult and child understandings and conceptions of repetition. He comments on series[1] such as Nancy Drew and The Hardy Boys, writing that, 'what to adults seems repetitive in these stories must to the child appear as confirmation that in diverse new areas of experience, what counts is still recognizable and familiar' (Appleyard 1994: 63). Not only are plots, characters and scenarios formulaic and repetitive but, Appleyard continues, young readers also read specific volumes repeatedly: 'repetitive reading of these stories is a clue to their attraction [. . .] the true fan may reread the same book "at least a dozen times"' (85). Victor Nell, whilst not discussing young readers in particular, describes such a process as 'reading gluttony' and discusses a 'gluttonous reader, a text gobbler who swallows books whole, achieving that pinnacle of gluttonous security, the ability to eat the same dish endlessly, passing it through his system whole and miraculously wholesome, ready to be re-eaten again and again' (1988: 239). This dichotomy between the judgements of adult critics and young people exists because of the nature of traditional approaches to literature which focus on the concept of comparative difference. When such difference cannot be demonstrated, the literature concerned is typically rejected as inferior. For Perry Nodelman this is one reason for the unhappy position of children's literature in the field of critical theory. Traditional approaches look for distinctiveness and uniqueness amongst and within texts and this 'thwarts would-be interpreters simply because so *few* children's novels move much beyond the formulaic or the stereotypical' (Nodelman 1985: 5, original emphasis).

Anyone who has observed children at play will understand how they thrive on repetition and see it as a source of fun. In J. D. Salinger's short story *For Esmé – with Love and Squalor*, Esmé's brother, Charles, when meeting someone for the first time, always asks them the same riddle: 'what did one wall say to the other wall?' (Salinger 1994: 73). When Charles repeats the riddle to Esmé's interlocutor (X), he answers it (meet you at the corner) and the fun disappears. Bruce Butts comments that 'it is quite apparent to both reader and X that what had delighted Charles had been the opportunity to revisit his joke. Over and over. It is evidently a tireless source of amusement to him' (Butts 2003: 278). Where children appear to revel in repetition, adults, it would appear, do not conceive such repetition in the same way, remaining distanced from the very mechanisms creating this appealing repetition. Indeed, Sigmund Freud makes this very observation in his *Beyond the Pleasure Principle* (1920), writing:

nor can children have their pleasurable experiences repeated enough [...] it is hardly possible to persuade an adult who has very much enjoyed reading a book to re-read it immediately. Novelty is always the condition of enjoyment. But children will never tire of asking an adult to repeat a game that he has shown them or played with them, till he is too exhausted to go on. And if a child has been told a nice story, he will insist on hearing it over and over again rather than a new one; and he will remorselessly stipulate that the repetition be an identical one [...] None of this contradicts the pleasure principle; repetition, the re-experiencing of something identical, is clearly in itself a source of pleasure. (Freud 2015: 29)

Repetition yielding pleasure is, then, the foundation of psychoanalytic theory: we seek pleasure and attempt to avoid pain in order to satisfy our basic needs. Yet, seemingly contrary to this pleasure principle, we may also repeat behaviours that bring us discomfort.

In *Beyond the Pleasure Principle* Freud considers this compulsion to repeat unpleasant situations.[2] By observing his grandson repeatedly discarding and recuperating a wooden reel on a string (the *fort-da* game[3]), Freud remarks how this repetition of pulling the string back and returning the reel allows the child to conquer an unpleasant situation. The child's gesture is a reaction to and a compensation for his mother's absence over which he had no control. Ian Buchanan formulates it thus: 'repetition is the unconscious's means of obtaining mastery over discomforting stimuli; as such, it is both a mechanism of defence and an attempt at self-cure' (Buchanan 2015: 32). Buchanan continues: 'the crucial point to note here is that the compulsion to repeat occurs at a level below the conscious or even preconscious thought – it belongs to the order of the drives and is therefore experienced by the subject as an inexorable pressure, something that they are helpless to avoid' (32). This is Freud's death drive:[4] '*an urge inherent in all organic life to restore an earlier state of things*' (Freud 2015: 30, original emphasis) not governed by the pleasure principle.

The job of psychoanalysis is, then, to root out the cause of our repetitions. For Freud, we are always repeating something, or as Deleuze puts it, 'something always has to recall something else – metaphor or metonymy' (D 77–8E/96F). The question is what? – an event, a trauma that our unconscious has carefully repressed and that we repeat at a later stage in life. As Deleuze remarks, psychoanalysis 'taught us that we are ill from repetition, but it also taught us that we are healed through repetition' (LOS 327E/333F). This is where Deleuze departs from Freud and psychoanalysis: whereas psychoanalysis attempts 'to discipline the forces of the unconscious, to enfeeble them, and to put them out of action, Deleuze, on the contrary, stresses the rich, creative, and even artistic forces of a productive unconscious' (De Bolle 2010: 9). Deleuze is not fully opposed to Freud's conceptualisation of the death drive, taking 'from Freud the idea that death is the source of symptomatic repetitions, but argu[ing] that the death instinct can be viewed as a positive, productive principle and not simply a destructive or entropic one' (Tynan 2012: 7).[5] Deleuze's repetition is no longer the representational and reactionary repetition of psychoanalysis, rather it 'has a fully positive meaning. It is an original force that coincides with life itself and that acts independently of any representational thinking. It is not a response to a failure of remembrance or a desperate way to deal with it, or a way to get cured' (De Bolle 2010: 11).

This chapter confronts the paradox of repetition in children's literature by drawing on Deleuze's concept of repetition developed in his ground-breaking *Différence et Répétition* (1968). Deleuze's concepts of pure repetition and pure difference or repetition for itself and difference in itself enhance our understanding of what might make young readers return to the same book time and time again or read something which is quite near to the original apart from minor variations. Deleuze can help us explain why young readers appear to enjoy and to revel in such predictability and minute variations on a theme, when critics and pedagogues only appear to see the 'same' ad infinitum. The first part of this chapter considers Eugène Ionesco's *Contes 1, 2, 3, 4*, an absurdly repetitive picture book, illustrated by Étienne Delessert, whose narratives are composed of nothing but repetitions and appear to go nowhere but in circles. Reading such a text from a Deleuzian perspective allows us to move away from a conventional analysis of comparative difference which from the outset is bound to fail, to an experience of repetition lying beyond analogy. In the second part of this chapter, I consider Pierrette Fleutiaux's Trini novels, *Trini fait des vagues* and its sequel *Trini à l'île de Pâques*, coupled with Deleuze and Guattari's notion of the ritournelle, which shows us how repetition, like a musical refrain, can resonate through time and space, connecting authors' writing for children and adults and allowing for the emergence of a molecular child. The final part of the chapter turns to Miguel Angel Asturias's text *L'Homme qui avait tout, tout, tout* and Lewis Carroll's Alice, both her experience at the Mad Hatter's tea party and her encounter with the White Queen, to consider how Deleuzian pure repetition opens up its own unique temporal space in which all times coexist: the time of Aiôn.

Pure Repetition

When editors Harlin Quist and François Ruy-Vidal asked Étienne Delessert to name an author for whom he would like to illustrate, the Swiss-born illustrator suggested 'somewhat out of bravado' (Noiville 2009) the names of two absurdist dramatists, Samuel Beckett and Eugène Ionesco: 'two authors who he had discovered in Lausanne around the age of seventeen and who had completely changed his view of the world' (Noiville 2009). Quist returned with four tales by Ionesco that Ionesco would tell his daughter, Marie-France, and that were 'originally written to form part of his memoires' (Reynolds 2007: 57). Delessert was surprised by the texts, expecting 'a long text, which would have been a contemporary *Alice in Wonderland*' (Delessert 2015: 83). Ionesco was surprised too, 'he had envisaged a little Josette – his daughter Marie-France – better behaved, blond, and he found a boisterous little girl, skilled in repartee, like in his text' (Neeman 2009).

In Eugène Ionesco's *Conte 1* we meet Josette, aged 33 months, who, with her father, 'an alter-ego for Ionesco' as Kimberley Reynolds suggests (2007: 57), gets caught up in myriad pure repetitions. 'One morning, as she would do every morning' (Ionesco 2009: 7), Josette creeps quietly up to her parents' bedroom door, attempts to open it, loses patience and then wakes her parents who are sleeping off the revelry of the previous night.[6] This is a repeated behaviour for Josette: as is her parents' carousing: 'that day, the daddy and the mummy were tired. The day before, they had been to the theatre, to the restaurant, then after the restaurant to the puppet theatre' (7). The list of their activities is reiterated later in the tale as Josette's parents fall asleep once again: 'the daddy and the mummy fall asleep again because they were very tired, they had been to the restaurant the day before, to the theatre, again to the restaurant, to the puppet theatre, then again to the restaurant' (22). This second iteration includes extra occurrences of their time spent at the restaurant, however. The expectation of this behaviour, both parental and filial, is projected into the second tale, but broken by a simple negation. Her father has risen early: 'that morning Josette's daddy had got up early. He had slept well because the previous evening he hadn't been to the restaurant to eat sauerkraut' and her mother has already gone out as 'she hadn't been to the restaurant, she hadn't been to the puppet theatre, she hadn't been to the theatre, she hadn't eaten sauerkraut' (35). The spiralling repetition continues when Jacqueline, the housekeeper, brings breakfast in to the slumbering parents. The housekeeper announces the contents of her tray thus: 'here is your morning paper, here are the postcards you have received, here is your milky coffee with sugar, here is your fruit juice, your croissants, your toast, your butter, your orange marmalade, your strawberry jam, your fried eggs, your ham' (8). The lengthy list of breakfast items is mirrored in Étienne Delessert's image showing a pictorial repetition of the items (two plates of eggs and ham, two glasses of orange juice, two coffee cups, two spoons, their morning newspaper and their postcards which portray the image of a rhinoceros, etc.). Josette's parents, suffering from their multiple trips to the restaurant, refuse breakfast, causing the list of items to be repeated again in the negative: 'they don't want the toast, they don't want the croissants, they don't want the ham...' (10). The negation of the phrases creates a subtle variation as does the fact that the announced strawberry jam turns out to be an orange marmalade ('it wasn't even strawberry jam, it was orange marmalade' (10)). The list is repeated once again as Josette consoles herself by eating her parents' breakfast, which she shares with Jacqueline. These subtle changes to Josette's parents' routine or to the list of breakfast items are not an attempt to disguise repetition and to create sameness. Variation, for Deleuze, is 'not added to repetition in order to hide it, but is rather its condition or constitutive element, the interiority of repetition par excellence' (DR xviE). The minute variations noted in the scenes above thus reveal the essential quality of Deleuze's repetition: the difference in repetition.

Deleuze's thought departs from the concept of comparative difference that has always dominated Western thought; indeed, Michel Foucault remarks in *Theatrum philosophicum* (his critique of Deleuze's *Difference and Repetition* and *The Logic of Sense*), that 'it [difference] is generally assumed to be a difference *from* or *within* something' (Foucault 1980: 181). Deleuze, however, moves away from thinking of difference in relation to uniqueness, equivalence and representation, and requires difference to be conceived of differentially, as Foucault's text further shows:

> what if [thought] conceived of difference differentially, instead of searching out the common elements underlying difference? Then difference would disappear as a general feature that leads to the generality of the

concept, and it would become – a different thought, the thought of difference – a pure event. As for repetition, it would cease to function as the dreary succession of the identical, and would become displaced difference. (Foucault 1980: 182)

Deleuze turns to 'Warhol's remarkable "serial" series' (DR 294E/375F) to elaborate on the difference in repetition. We should not be concerned about recognising differences between Warhol's serial images, that one Marilyn silkscreen painting is different from any of the twenty others in *x* or *y* respect, rather Warhol's 'Pop Art pushe[s] the copy of the copy, copy of the copy, etc., to that extreme point at which it reverses and becomes a simulacrum' (DR 293–4E/375F). Unlike Baudrillard, whose 'precession of the simulacrum' (Baudrillard 1994: 1) has resemblance lead to the destruction of the original, by the model first resembling then replacing the source, the Deleuzian simulacrum resembles nothing. It consists in 'denying the primacy of original over copy, of model over image' (DR 66E/92F). Deleuze pushes the notion of a copy of a copy to the point 'at which everything changes nature, at which copies themselves flip over into simulacra and at which, finally, resemblance [. . .] gives way to repetition' (DR 128E/168F). By turning away from resemblance, the simulacrum internalises pure difference, not by forcing all copies onto a model, 'but overturn[ing] all copies by *also* overturning the models' (DR xxE/3F). It does not destroy the original but becomes an entity distinct from it. Stephen Zepke writes that 'Warhol succeeds in producing simulacrum by foregrounding the way an image's repetition introduces necessary differences. Each work in the series differs from others, but this difference is not a consistent object that structures the work [. . .] but is the genetic element immanent to their production, the differing difference which does not stay the same' (Zepke 2005: 33). In a similar vein, Delessert's illustrations for Ionesco's enumerated tales – which, for Kümmerling-Meibauer and Meibauer (2011: 103), are an example of the 'Pop art picturebooks [. . .] that emerged around 1970' – are simulacral. Annemie Leysen considers that Delessert's pictorial

> universe [. . .] is fantastic and overwhelming: magic and realism, grotesque and recognizable, close-ups and wide sceneries, all in striking colors. His world is unnerving, funny, and always surprising. As the famous American artist and illustrator David Macaulay once said: 'I am repeatedly struck by Delessert's extraordinary ability to weave together confusion and order, the bizarre and the familiar, the grotesque and the

charming into a highly personal yet universally accessible world.' (Leysen 2010: 17–18)

Delessert himself comments on the synergy between author and illustrator, between text and image: 'Ionesco's way of thinking completely corresponds to my way of drawing ... The same flights of imagination. The same way of starting from realistic situations and injecting folly and quirkiness into them' (Noiville 2009). In *Conte 1*, repetition reaches its apogee when Josette finally wakes her father and requests he tell her a story. The story is told in a transient state somewhere between sleep and waking and concerns a little girl called Jacqueline:

> little Jacqueline's daddy was called Mr. Jacqueline. Little Jacqueline had two sisters who were both called Jacqueline and two small male cousins who were called Jacqueline, and small female cousins who were called Jacqueline and an aunt and an uncle who were called Jacqueline. (Ionesco 2009: 15)

As the story continues, it transpires that the aunt and uncle's friends, their son and daughter, the daughter's three dolls, the son's friend and his wooden horses and tin soldiers are also all called Jacqueline. Delessert's image of the Jacqueline families over the double page captures the textual repetition. He portrays the families with identical hairstyles wearing identically striped suits and dresses. His comments on his decision to make 'all the Jacquelines, male and female, resemble each other [...taking] on a notion of social commentary on the masses of consumers who share the same habits' (Delessert 2015: 83–5) further align his work with the Pop Art movement. The position of his image across a double page also creates the illusion of being caught up in a mirrored image as the story continues to spiral into the abyss, as the two families meet up in the Parisian public park, the Bois de Boulogne. Delessert's image of the Jacqueline families is no longer a mere copy but has flipped over into a simulacrum and adds to the hallucinogenic effect of the story.

For children's literature scholar, Jean Perrot, 'the absurd stems from the repetition of the name Jacqueline' (Perrot 1999: 136). From a Deleuzian perspective, however, such repetition reveals more than absurdity. Deleuze and Guattari remark in their text, *Kafka: Toward a Minor Literature*: 'children are well skilled in the exercise of repeating a word, the sense of which is only vaguely felt, in order to make it vibrate around itself' (K 21E/38F). With their dizzying repetitions, Ionesco's tales, labelled 'for children less than three years old', reveal how words and the sounds that compose them can resonate around us. It is almost impossible to read this text aloud without faltering and stuttering. The extreme repetition of Jacqueline (thirty-three times in total in this section of the story) deterritorialises the mouth uttering it, as Delessert's simulacral imagery disturbs the eyes observing it and, in a similar vein to the tongue-twisting delight of Dr. Seuss's *Fox in Socks* (1965), results in a departure from sense.[7]

A double-page image without text allows both reader and storyteller to pause briefly from the swirling excess of Jacquelines. Although for Kümmerling-Meibauer and Meibauer, 'the pictures that cover a double spread without any accompanying text do not refer to the story, leaving their interpretation to the viewer' (2011: 108), they allow for repetition to move from verbal to visual. Pictorial motifs present on previous pages recur in these images: a butterfly, the tin soldiers and Jacqueline and her family in their striped clothes are to be found wandering among the fabulous creatures placed on pedestals in the Bois de Boulogne. For Barbara Novak, these creatures can 'trace their lineage back to Hieronymus Bosch' (Novak 1970: 224): some are identifiable animals (a lion and insects, one holding a pocket watch resembling the watch from the first illustration in the tale), others are strange metamorphoses of pigs with butterfly wings and antennae, a monkey with human ears, a fish with frog's legs. Even one of Maurice Sendak's monsters from *Where the Wild Things Are* is hopping around the pedestals.[8]

The Jacqueline story rebounds once more when Josette goes out shopping with the housekeeper, allowing her father to nod off again. Josette meets a little girl whose real name is Jacqueline and launches into a retelling of the story herself, creating a scene reminiscent of Mr. and Mrs. Smith's discussion of Bobby Watson's death in Ionesco's *La Cantatrice chauve*:

> I know, Josette says to the little girl, your daddy is called Jacqueline, your little brother is called Jacqueline, your dolly is called Jacqueline, your granddad is called Jacqueline, your rocking horse is called Jacqueline, your house is called Jacqueline, your potty is called Jacqueline ... (Ionesco 2009: 24)

To accompany Josette's retelling of her absurd story, Delessert portrays the child Jacqueline's characteristic curly hair and morphs it into a sheep, then into tree tops and a moustache before creating a cloud formation above mountain range on the next double-page spread. Jacqueline's monstrous head sits atop the highest peak and her family peer through the hollow opening of her pupils. Along the winding mountain road, myriad simulacral, miniature Jacqueline figures march waving eye-shaped banners. In the shop, all the adults present turn to stare at Josette 'with wide frightened eyes' (Ionesco 2009: 29). The housekeeper who has previously warned the father of such a mind-bending story – 'you will make the little one mad' (18) – attempts to appease the shocked customers thus: 'it's nothing, says the housekeeper calmly, don't worry, they are only the stupid stories her father tells her' (30). Her dismissal of Josette's story is the final phrase of *Conte 1* and is accompanied by an image of the housekeeper with finger to lips as if hushing the dissenting voices. In behaving in such a way, the housekeeper aligns herself with a conventional view of repetition which 'depends entirely upon the reflection of an observer' (DR 294E/377F) who is necessarily outside repetition, comparing all subsequent iterations to a first time also necessarily outside repetition. As Deleuze writes, in such a case 'the repetition remains external to something which is repeated and must be supposed primary; a frontier is established between a first time and repetition itself' (DR 294E/376F). Repetition is this case is reduced to mere analogy. In Ionesco's tales, both father and daughter are internal to the repetition the stories perpetuate. The father does not heed the housekeeper's warnings that he will make his daughter go mad. Instead both father and daughter, mirroring the parent and child who may share the story at home, revel in the pure repetition of their stories, immersing themselves in the myriad other repetitions that repetition for itself produces and enjoying the frisson of pure difference.

Ritournelle

In *A Thousand Plateaus* Deleuze and Guattari offer another way of understanding repetition: the ritournelle. For Deleuze and Guattari, it is possible to open the circular boundaries of the home and venture out into the world because of the ritournelle. The functions of this refrain are threefold: it is the song the lost child sings over and over, creating a stability reminiscent of the home; it is the music that accompanies the home, the wall of sound that delimits its boundaries, its circular organising space; and it is the opening in this circle through which others are allowed into the home and the music which accompanies journeys away from home. These functions also align closely with the 'home-away-home' (Reimer 2009; Nodelman

2008) motif so prevalent in children's literature, with roots in traditional fairy tales and folk-tale narratives (Bettelheim 1991; Propp 1994), and indeed, Deleuze and Guattari tell us that these three non-successive aspects of the ritournelle are 'found in tales (both horror and fairy tales)' (ATP 312E/383F). In Pierrette Fleutiaux's *Trini fait des vagues* and its sequel *Trini à l'île de Pâques,* a whistled sea shanty pervades. In the first volume, Trini is on holiday in Royan on the Atlantic coast, so that her sister, Séréna, can prepare for her *concours* (a competitive examination) to become a police inspector. Their tranquillity is disturbed when Séréna discovers that a young hairdresser, Mona, whose physical appearance resembles that of a Barbie doll, has mysteriously disappeared. Trini, along with her pet, Mousie, 'a special mouse' (Fleutiaux 1997: 14), attempts to solve the case so that her sister can concentrate on her exam preparation. During her stay in Royan, Trini is befriended by a young boy named William, and through him and her neighbour Madame Serlier she learns more about the history of the seaside town: how it was destroyed by Allied bombings in 1945 and although most residents had fled beforehand, some families remained. William accompanies Trini to Leclerc, a large supermarket on the outskirts of town, as Trini tries to unravel the link between the strange feeling she has in the Barbie doll section of the supermarket and the missing hairdresser. As William waits for Trini on the opposite pavement in her hesitant attempts to roller skate across the road, he whistles 'a sea shanty' (54). The last line of this tune becomes their code word and announces the drama to come:

> heave ho, this chorus would immediately become our password, the sign of our secret agreement, but at this moment when we exchanged it for the first time, with so much oblivious joyfulness; neither William nor I could imagine the terrifying adventure it was pulling us towards. (58)

Trini discovers that one of the residents whose family remained in Royan at the time of the Allied bombings, Belgrand-Duffard, yearns for the pre-war Royan where society and language were not influenced by the North American culture and the English language. His unstable mental health leads him to destroy the Barbie dolls in the local supermarket, which he deems inappropriate for children, and then to kidnap Mona, the young Barbie-like hairdresser. Belgrand-Duffard then drugs her and forces her to play the role of one of his ancestors. Trini stows away in his van, finds Mona, but becomes Belgrand-Duffard's prisoner herself. Through role-playing with him, persuading him she is his cousin, Adelaide, she is able to avoid being drugged as Mona is. After a conversation with Madame Serlier, William realises that the person responsible for Trini's disappearance must be one of the descendants of the families who remained in Royan during the bombings, and he sets off to find her. He whistles his favourite tune which Trini hears: 'it was a whistle. Clear, but very faint . . . The sailor's shanty!' (159). After signalling out the window with her torch, Mousie, who had previously escaped, reappears with a note from William tied to her tail and Trini realises she will be saved.

Fleutiaux's sequel, *Trini à l'île de Pâques*, continues the initial storyline in Royan before moving to Easter Island, where Trini and Séréna are sent on an undercover mission to resolve the mystery of disappearing artifacts. William's refrain offers hope again when Trini is captured and imprisoned underground by 'a millennial sect' (Fleutiaux 1999a: 152) which intends to blow up the island. Trini, in a semi-conscious state, 'dreams that she hears William's song, the sailor's shanty (158), and as a result sends Mousie through a hole with a shoe lace tied to her tail, in an inverse re-enactment of the denouement of the previous volume. In their journeys away from home, Trini and William are caught up in a continual movement of de- and re-territorialisation and their heave-ho chorus accompanies them in this. In the act of deterritorialisation, there is necessarily reterritorialisation: in moving away from home there is necessarily a return, but never a return of the same. As Deleuze and Guattari write: 'the great refrain arises as we distance ourselves from the house, even if this is in order to return, since no one will recognize us any more when we come back' (WP 191E/181F). The ritournelle is then both beginning and return as 'each beginning is already a return, but this beginning always implies a gap, a difference' (Zourabichvili 2003: 75). This is all the more significant when reading a series or a sequel, as each beginning (again) is a return, but only in the sense of pure difference.

Echoes of Trini and William's childhood refrain permeate more than just Fleutiaux's writing for young readers. Her 1999 novel for an adult readership entitled *L'Expédition* [The Expedition] takes her readers to Easter Island once more. Angèle Lapérierre, the protagonist of *L'Expédition*, is haunted by her memories of reading Pierre Loti's *Île de Pâques* [Easter Island] (1899) as a child, and notably this lengthy description of the island in Loti's dedication of his text to his friend Albert Vandal:

Pure Repetition and Aiôn

there is, in the middle of the Pacific Ocean, in an area where no one ever goes, a mysterious and isolated island; no other land lies in its vicinity and, at more than eight hundred leagues from everywhere, vast, moving waters surround it. Tall monstrous statues are planted there, works from an unknown race now disappeared, and its past remains a mystery. I landed there, in my prime, on a frigate, through days of high winds and dark clouds; the memory of a country, half fantastic, of a land of dream, has always stayed with me. (Loti 2013: 7)

The adult readers of *L'Expédition* may 'hear' echoes of their youthful readings of the Trini novels in this text. The description of Royan and its beauty before the Allied bombings resonates with those in the Trini texts, and Madame Lescure's neighbourly hospitality mirrors that of Madame Serlier. A child reader of Fleutiaux's Trini texts who grows up to discover Fleutiaux's writings for adults, in particular *L'Expédition*, or an adult reader who then comes across Fleutiaux's writings for children, may find as Angèle Lapérierre does herself, that 'the words had lost themselves in the mists of childhood, but they had never ceased to resonate, like a curl of far-off mist, the wave of this echo endlessly losing itself and finding itself in the tangle of my nerves, like a call that can never die' (Fleutiaux 1999b: 14). Trini and William's repeated refrain permeates the Trini sequels and emerges in *L'Expédition* mirrored in the ever-returning and deterriorialising ritournelle of the childhood reading of Loti's *Île de Pâques* which bewitches Lapérierre's adult life. A simple heave-ho refrain circulates through texts destined for separate readerships of child and adult. In its passage, however, the ritournelle gathers up the disparate timeframes of childhood and adulthood across Fleutiaux's *œuvre* and with it, readers in various ages of life. As the ritournelle circulates, it brings child and adult, childhood and adulthood into contact with one another, effacing codified boundaries between each. No longer contained by pre-described categories of child or adult, childhood or adulthood, but touched by and encompassing both, a supple molecular child emerges through the presence of the ritournelle.

In Ionesco's *Contes*, the ritournelle resonates in the rich imagery of the texts. Delessert creates a ritournelle of one of Ionesco's most well-known texts with his illustrations. A rhinoceros graces the cover of this compilation and then recurs on Josette's parents' postcards, before appearing again on a pedestal in the Bois de Boulogne and then in the jardin zoologique of the larger Parisian park, the Bois de Vincennes, in *Conte 3*. In *Conte 4* this visual ritournelle captures two other texts before returning to *Rhinocéros*. When Josette's father takes refuge in the bathroom as his daughter plays hide and seek, Delessert's images transport the father to a room of empty chairs (*Les Chaises*), then to a scene where giant feet sprout vibrantly coloured mushrooms (*Amédée ou comment s'en débarasser*), before he grows a rhinoceros horn himself and is chased across a double-page spread by two giant rhinoceros. The ritournelle may then resonate verbally or visually across time and space, linking past, present and future, childhood and adult readings, and merging child and adult into a new molecular child with its own unique temporality: 'a crystal of space-time' (ATP 348E/430F). For Deleuze and Guattari, 'time is not an a priori form; rather, the refrain is the a priori form of time, which in each case fabricates different times' (ATP 349E/431F). It is to the relationship between time and repetition that we turn now in the following section.

Aiôn

Ionesco's *Contes*, as we have seen, are acutely repetitive and simulacral in nature, and as such are expressions of pure difference. Time in these tales, although it is ever present, appears to go nowhere. In the foreground of the first image of *Conte 1*, a cat waits with Josette. In a scene reminiscent of the appearance of the White Rabbit in *Alice's Adventures in Wonderland*, the cat studies a pocket watch intently. The inscription on the watch tells us that it is 'made in dreamland' (Ionesco 2009: 6) and, as if following a dreamland logic, the pocket watch unusually has a mouse appearing from a slot where normally a cuckoo would pop out.[9] Delessert's image shows Josette waiting impatiently for her parents to rise, as the minutes slowly tick by until the impositions of adult time restrictions are lifted and she can enter her parents' bedroom. Ionesco's text implies that these actions are habitual and expected. For Deleuze, there is an undeniable relationship between expectation and repetition, which he develops in *Difference and Repetition* with his three passive syntheses of time on which his concepts of repetition for itself and difference in itself rest. Deleuze draws on the work of David Hume (1711–76) and Henri Bergson (1859–1941). Hume was influential for his work on causality and in his *Enquiry Concerning Human Understanding* he demonstrates that repeatedly experiencing two related events in the past provokes expectation of similar occurrences in the future: 'after a repetition of similar instances, the mind is carried by habit, upon the appearance of one event, to expect its usual attendant, and to

Pure Repetition and Aiôn

believe that it will exist' (Hume 2008: 71). Hume argues that causal relationships are not based on reasoning but on observation and experience: the clock repeatedly ticks and tocks, and the experience of this culminates in the expectation and belief that tock will continue to follow tick in the future. Or in Josette's case, her parents repeatedly spend nights out on the town, and have trouble getting up the following morning, causing Josette to expect such behaviour in the future. Deleuze takes the past ticking (A) and tocking (B) of the clock and contracts them into a single tick-tock (AB): a single habitually repeated event – the night-out-sleep-late-Josette-waiting event. Bergson provides a similar example of the clock striking four. Being distracted, Bergson is not able to simply count the number of strikes and so attempts to estimate; he notices that his 'feeling [. . .] had thus ascertained in its own way the succession of four strokes but quite otherwise than by a process of addition' (Bergson 2000: 127–8). When Bergson's clock strikes (A, A, A,) a fourth strike (A) is expected to follow the third because it has consistently done so previously and 'the number of strokes was perceived as a quality and not as a quantity' (128). Of significance in these two examples is that 'expectation is not only a matter of expecting a particular thing to follow another because they have done so in the past. It is also a matter of expecting a particular conjunction of independent things to make one. Furthermore, it is to expect a great number of perhaps unidentified unconscious things to come together to form a unit' (Williams 2003: 88). Deleuze insists that 'contraction also refers to the fusion of successive tick-tocks in a contemplative soul', adding that 'when we say that habit is a contraction we are speaking not of an instantaneous action which combines with another to form an element of repetition, but rather of the fusion of that repetition in the contemplating mind' (DR 74E/101F). For Deleuze, expectation is therefore only possible for two reasons: it can only exist in respect to the three syntheses of time, of the contraction of the past projected into the future through the present, and in the contemplating mind, in the person who experiences it. Deleuze writes of the former:

> in all three syntheses, present, past and future are revealed as Repetition, but in very different modes. The present is the repeater, the past is repetition itself, but the future is that which is repeated. Furthermore, the secret of repetition as a whole lies in that which is repeated, in that which is twice signified. The future, which subordinates the other two to itself and strips them of their autonomy, is the royal repetition. The first synthesis concerns only the content and the foundation of time; the second, its

> ground; but beyond these, the third ensures the order, the totality of the series and the final end of time. A philosophy of repetition must pass through all these 'stages', condemned to repeat repetition itself. However, by traversing these stages it ensures its programme of making repetition the category of the future: making use of the repetition of habit and that of memory, but making use of them as stages and leaving them in its wake [...] making it so that repetition is, for itself, difference in itself. (DR 94E/125F)

In Deleuze's first synthesis then, habitually recurring events are contracted in the past and projected through the present and onto the future. This living present is not static, however. It is rather one that passes away. These passing presents are, through the second synthesis, stored in memory and become past and are repeated when memory is recalled. To avoid the situation where 'history repeats itself' without moving on, or of 'coming full circle', a third synthesis of time has to be accepted 'since its absence would reduce the drive to the new to a repetition of the past' (Williams 2003: 102). This third synthesis prevents such futility and nihilism and instead allows time to be ruptured or unhinged. At the moment of this 'caesura' (DR 89E/120F), time is divided into a before and after, a past and future, destroying the repetitive circularity of time thus far. At this point, there is 'a feeling that nothing will be the same again [...] that the past, as a whole, will not return at any part of the future' (Williams 2003: 102). In leaving behind the whole of the past, there is the possibility for a new future: it is 'a belief of the future, a belief in the future' (DR 90E/122F).

When the waiting is over and Josette's father wakes, this unhinging of time occurs. The boredom of the slowing dragging minutes is erased and fantasy and storytelling take over. Time is now 'out of joint [...] liberated from its overly simple circular figure' (DR 88E/119–20F): the repetitious circle of habit and memory has been broken and replaced by an 'empty form of time' (DR 88E/119F). This empty form of time is also one of repetition, not of a Nietzschean eternal return, but rather repetition for itself: the pure repetition in which Josette and her father revel during their absurd storytelling. Deleuze writes:

> we rely upon the overly simple circle which has as its content the passing present and as its shape the past of reminiscence. However, the order of time, time as a pure and empty form, has precisely undone that circle. It has undone it in favour of a less simple and much more secret, much more tortuous, more nebulous circle, an eternally excentric circle, the decentred

Pure Repetition and Aiôn

circle of difference which is re-formed uniquely in the third time of the series. (DR 91E/112F)

Later in *Difference and Repetition*, Deleuze names this empty form of time Aiôn, and explores the relationship between Aiôn and Chronos in *The Logic of Sense*. Aiôn, he writes, in a passage mirroring that of *Difference and Repetition*,

> stretches out in a straight line, limitless in either direction. Always already passed and eternally yet to come. Aion is the eternal truth of time: pure empty form of time, which has freed itself of its present corporeal content and has thereby unwound its circle, stretching itself out in a straight line. It is perhaps all the more dangerous, more labyrinthine, and more tortuous for this reason. (LOS 189E/194F)

Deleuze's third order of time, Aiôn, is not a nihilistic, ever-returning circle, but a circle that has been ruptured and stretched out to form an infinite 'line' always encompassing both that which is past and that which is still to come at any point on that line. Aiôn is then 'the indefinite time of the event, the floating line that knows only speeds and continually divides that which transpires into an already-there that is at the same time not-yet-here, a simultaneous too-late and too-early, a something that is both going to happen and has just happened' (ATP 262E/320F). It is the time of the 'never jam *to-day*' scenario which Alice encounters through the White Queen as they meet in the fourth square of the looking-glass land. Helping the rather dishevelled White Queen to fix her shawl and her hair, Alice suggests a lady's maid would be of use to her and the following conversation ensues:

> 'I'm sure I'll take you with pleasure!' the Queen said. 'Twopence a week, and jam every other day.'
> Alice couldn't help laughing, as she said, 'I don't want you to hire *me* – and I don't care for jam.'
> 'It's very good jam,' said the Queen.
> 'Well, I don't want any *to-day*, at any rate.'
> 'You couldn't have it if you *did* want it,' the Queen said. 'The rule is, jam to-morrow and jam yesterday – but never jam *to-day*.'
> 'It *must* come sometimes to "jam to-day,"' Alice objected.
> 'No, it can't,' said the Queen. 'It's jam every *other* day: to-day isn't any *other* day, you know.'
> 'I don't understand you,' said Alice. 'It's dreadfully confusing!' (Carroll 2008: 172–3, original emphasis)

The White Queen's seemingly illogical attempts to confuse Alice and trick her out of her wage reveal the specificities of Aiôn: Aiôn is, to paraphrase Deleuze, the time in which 'no one ever *has* jam, but has always *just had* jam or is always *going to have* jam' (LOS 74E/80F my emphasis, quotation altered). The White Queen's untidy and somewhat unhinged appearance exposes this very unhinging of time. The White Queen has undone her circle of time and is functioning in the labyrinthine caesura, where she cries with pain in anticipation of pricking her finger and where she remembers the 'things that happened the week after next' (Carroll 2008: 173): a casual remark which captures the very essence of a past-future event.

It is not just the White Queen who moves 'in both directions at once and forever sidesteps the present' (LOS 89E/95F), the White King's Anglo-Saxon messengers, Haigha and Hatta, also represent the bi-directionality of Aiôn with 'one to come, and one to go [. . .] one to fetch, and one to carry' (Carroll 2008: 194), always pulling in two opposing directions. The Mad Hatter and the March Hare, as they are known in *Alice's Adventures in Wonderland*, appear to live in different directions, 'but the two directions are inseparable; each direction subdivides itself into the other, to that point that both are found in the other' (LOS 91E/97F). Having murdered time and 'destroyed [. . .] measure' (LOS 91E/97F), the Mad Hatter and the March Hare exist in their limitless tea-time, an unregulated, unmeasured, non-chronometric time apart governed by the infinitive. For Ronald Bogue,

> Aion is the time of a simultaneous past-future, with the flow erratically moving forward and backward. It is the time of the infinitive, in the sense that it is all the tenses of a verb wrapped up in a single generative unit. In the domain of Aion, 'to live' is the generative source of 'I will live', 'He has lived', 'They might have been living', and so on. (Bogue 2010: 28)

Aiôn is not what the villain, Belgrand-Duffard, from *Trini fait des vagues* wishes to capture. He desires 'that the present disappear, that the past return, that time slide over itself and cease to flow' (Fleutiaux 1997: 150), but such a freezing of time is not Aiôn. Aiôn does not provide a return of the past, but rather an interconnectivity of all times. It is the time of the latent potential of infinitives rather than the time of tenses restricted by aspect, mood and number.

For Josette, her Chronos, her 'ordinary, commonsense time' (Bogue 2010: 11), is ruptured when her father begins his repetitive storytelling and a new time and space open up for both father and daughter: Aiôn. Similarly, in Miguel Angel Asturias's text *L'Homme qui avait tout, tout, tout*, ordinary everyday time is suspended. In this

Pure Repetition and Aiôn

tale, alarm clocks dominate at the outset. The otherwise nameless man has every conceivable alarm clock to rouse him, necessitating the use of an umbrella to transform the noise of their ringing into a shower of raindrops rather than a cacophony of sound. An alarm clock, of course, is set to mark a particular moment in time at which point the person hearing it is supposed to wake up. The innumerable alarm clocks in Asturias's tale have an unusual effect on the verb they control. Each alarm is accompanied by a variation of the verb *se réveiller* [to wake up]. The verb behaves correctly in the singular forms – *je te réveille, tu me réveilles, il se réveille* [I wake you up, you wake me up, he wakes up]. In the plural forms, however, the verb absorbs the sound of the alarm into its structure – *ils se réveillent-dong* [they are wake-ding-donging]. Ending with an almost impertinent imperative – *réveillez-vous cou-cou* [wake up cuckoo] (Asturias 1999: 7–8) –and creating an irregular, but onomatopoeic verbal form. The man who has everything is able to escape these demanding time machines when, after breakfasting, he enters 'a long, tubular room, in the form of a tunnel with changing walls, floor and ceiling – a kaleidoscope room' (21). Just as Lewis Carroll's Alice descends into the rabbit hole or goes through the looking-glass and suspends her Chronos, so this tunnel of multiple reflections and mesmerising, symmetrical and simulacral images dissolves the man's highly chronometric time: 'time went by; not years but centuries. Generations and generations of kaleidoscopic stars, of man-stars, of woman-stars. On, off. On, off. Life. And there inside the man who had everything did not age, he was the same age he was entering the gallery – 33 years old' (22). Entering this tunnel of simulacral images allows everyday time to give way to the caesura in time, Aiôn, and, as we shall see in the following chapter, is what allows the man who has everything to become.

Whilst in some respects Aiôn is distinct from Chronos, it is nonetheless 'immanent within Chronos, and the two only appear in mixtures, as coexisting temporal realities' (Bogue 2010: 96). Aiôn disconnects Josette and her father from their Chronos and yet stems from within it too. As James Williams writes:

> it is never that we have only the present, or only the past, or only the future, with other times as lesser dimensions. It is never that we have only Chronos or only Aiôn. Instead, all of these times coexist and together provide a complete view of time irreducible to any one of its elements or to an overall rule for their articulation. (Williams 2011a: 140)

What matters is not how many times father and child have reproduced these stories, whether this is the first, second or third iteration of the storytelling. Of import is the oscillation between past and future along the labyrinthine, rhizomatic time line of Aiôn. Such interconnectivity permits the bizarre scenes as Josette's father is doing his ablutions in the bathroom during *Conte 4* where he is transported to Ionesco's other plays. It allows the presence of past plays to infuse the present narrative. It allows echoes of childhood readings to recur in adulthood. The flux of Aiôn contains all possible times in one moment of time and all possible iterations of the stories in one moment in time: the pure potential of the infinitive 'to tell a story'. This time cannot be conceived of from the outside, but only from within. The housekeeper who remains external to the stories told can have no feeling for this new time and space. Just as Josette and her father are caught up in the pure repetition of their storytelling, so the parent and child who share the story at home become disconnected from their Chronos to exist molecularly in their own unique crystal of time and space in which childhood and adulthood, and indeed all times, coexist: Aiôn.

Conclusion: Aiôn, a Time of Molecular Childhood

In their reading preferences children often demonstrate what would appear to be, as Victor Watson points out, 'an impossible longing for sameness and difference' (Watson 2000: 8). From conventional, hermeneutic standpoints, texts which come close to providing this experience are considered formulaic and inferior, at best 'variational' (Nodelman 2008: 236). Turning to Deleuze's concept of repetition for itself can, however, transform our readings of such highly formulaic or acutely repetitive texts. With Deleuze, such texts are no longer caught up in the seemingly impossible paradoxical bind of repetition, but reveal instead the liberating and transformative nature of repetition for itself. Subtle variations in these texts expose the difference in repetition and should not be observed and compared but experienced intensively. Readers of the text should allow themselves to be caught up in the frisson of repetition which arises from imagery or wordplay and the ensuing unhinging of time this provokes.

Deleuze and Guattari provide the concept of the ritournelle as another way of conceiving pure repetition, which aligns itself closely with the traditional home-away-home structures of children's literature. The ritournelle accompanies us in the deterritorialisation we undergo leaving the home and in the difference encountered when we return. This concept is useful in thinking the interconnectivity of authors' writing, especially those authors who write for both adult and child readerships. The subtle reference to an adult text in the children's book, or the childhood reading that returns in our adult reading experiences, is the ritournelle spanning time and space and connecting our past to our present and pre-empting our future readings. This returning ritournelle is never a return of the same, however, but always an expression of pure difference, creating its own time-space which resonates across all times.

Aiôn, this unique temporality of pure repetition, is a liberation from the constraints of everyday time. In this unhinging of time, the circle of the eternal return is undone and the rhizomatic time of Aiôn opens up, simultaneously linking all times: past, present and future. Readers who enjoy highly repetitive texts gain access to this time of Aiôn, in which normal time is suspended. The labyrinthine nature of Aiôn means that time is no longer uni-directional: adulthood no longer succeeds childhood in a linear fashion, but may be bent backwards and forwards and around itself so that these two periods coexist. In Aiôn, or through the ritournelle, a supple, molecular child then emerges, surpassing traditional, rigid categorisations of child and adult and bringing each into the other. Aiôn is then a time of molecular childhood – an unformed, fluid childhood sweeping up and accessible to adult and child alike, ripe for further molecular transformations and becomings. It is to this concept of becoming that we now turn in the following chapter.

Notes

1. For extensive treatment of series fiction in children's literature see Watson 2000; Newland 2013; and Reimer 2014.
2. For Perry Nodelman, 'what Freud calls "the compulsion to repeat" is a central characteristic of children's literature, one that makes it doubly (i.e., repetitively) ambivalent. It repeats both to teach child readers and to please them; in each case, the repetitions ambivalently reinscribe repetitively opposite ideas of what children are and what adults want them to be' (Nodelman 2008: 235). Furthering his earlier argument presented above on the distinctiveness of children's literature, Nodelman goes on to argue that children's literature should rather be considered as 'variational', as he considers, although not drawing on Deleuze, that 'no repeated occurrence of the same event can ever possibly be merely a repetition of it' (235).

3. Deleuze considers that psychoanalysis failed to recognise the fort-da incantation of Freud's grandson as a ritournelle (D 99E/118F).
4. For further accounts of Deleuze's engagement with Freud, and the death drive in particular, see Williams 2003; Tynan 2012; Somers-Hall 2013; and Buchanan 2015 specifically for what the BwO (Body without Organs) owes to Freud's conceptualisation of the death drive.
5. See Chapter 6 for a discussion of Deleuze's conceptualisation of death and the BwO, and Chapter 3 for a discussion of Freud's deferred action.
6. Josette's father's behaviour and tardiness coupled with his reliance on alcohol is not unlike that of Berenger in Ionesco's *Rhinocéros* (1959).
7. I explore the notion of childhood voice and stuttering in more detail in Chapter 5.
8. The presence of the Sendak monster in Delessert's image would appear to be anachronistic, as *Where the Wild Things Are* (*Max et les maximonstres*) was only published in France in 1969. Delessert was, however, resident in the USA at this time, and Sendak's text had been published there some years earlier in 1963.
9. The cat recurs at the start of *Conte 2*, greedily clutching the mouse in its paw with clock reflections gleaming in its eyes. Josette and her father appear in the background. The father points at the clock on the wall which reads a little after seven, as opposed to quarter past eight in *Conte 1*, also revealing the variation in the second tale: Josette's father did not go out carousing and has therefore woken early.

3
Becoming-animal, Becoming-molecular, Becoming-imperceptible

All children, except one, grow up. (Barrie 1995: 1)

for all children [...] it is as though, independent of the evolution carrying them toward adulthood, there were room in the child for other becomings. (*A Thousand Plateaus* 273E/355F)

The notion of growing up with its directional preposition pervades all children's literature. As Roberta Seelinger Trites confirms in *Disturbing the Universe: Power and Repression in Adolescent Literature*, 'the idea of growth – the investigation of which characters have developed and which have not – is one of the most common principles in the study of children's and adolescent literature' (Trites 2000: 10). Inherent in the notion of growing up is a linear, uni-directional movement through time, towards a greater maturity, towards adulthood. Growing up implies evolving and changing, becoming different in some way from the child one used to be. Should this not occur, there is the danger that the child will be trapped in an eternal childhood like J. M. Barrie's eponymous Peter Pan. Deleuze and Guattari do not deny this movement towards adulthood but create room for other changes or becomings during the progression from child to adult. They conceive of the becomings of childhood as *in*volutionary rather than *e*volutionary.

Becomings break out of the molarity of growing up. For Deleuze and Guattari, they imply a desire to be drawn closer to a heterogeneous other, entering into a zone of proximity with that other and allowing oneself to have a molecular exchange with that other. Having 'no end outside itself' (Colebrook 2002: 145), becoming

start[s] from the forms one has, the subject one is, the organs one has, or the functions one fulfills, becoming is to extract particles between which one establishes the relations of movement and rest, speed and slowness that are *closest* to what one is becoming, and through which one becomes. This is the sense in which becoming is the process of desire. (ATP 272E/334F)

Becoming breaks down the preconceived binaries and molar categories that arrange us (adult-child, male-female, etc.). Individual subjectivities dissolve and boundaries between the two terms are effaced in this movement of becoming. As Patty Sotirin succinctly explains:

> becoming explodes the ideas about what we are and what we can be beyond the categories that seem to contain us: beyond the boundaries separating human being from animal, man from woman, child from adult, micro from macro, and even perceptible and understandable from imperceptible and incomprehensible. (Sotirin 2007: 99)

Deleuze and Guattari refer to the example of the wasp-orchid to illustrate their concept. In order to reproduce successfully, the orchid relies on the wasp for pollination and, conversely, the pollinator wasp depends on the orchid's nectar for its own survival. When both parts come together, they *become*, fusing to form a new *agencement*: the wasp-orchid, in this case. Bruce Baugh notes that '*agencement*, for which the standard translation is "assemblage," carries the connotation of "agency," not in the sense of individuals having intentions, but in the sense of "a cleaning agent", i.e. something capable of doing something, of producing an effect' (Baugh 2000: 54). Becoming is creative and generative and encompasses, then, a dual dynamic: as Deleuze states, 'as someone becomes, what he is becoming changes as much as he does himself. Becomings are not phenomena of imitation or assimilation, but of a double capture, of non-parallel evolution, of nuptials between two reigns' (D 2E/8F). This new assemblage has no distinct subject position of its own, and Deleuze and Guattari insist that 'becoming produces nothing other than itself. [...] What is real is the becoming itself, the block of becoming, not the supposedly fixed terms through which that which becomes passes' (ATP 238E/291F). Instead, both parts are caught up and deterritorialised in this a-parallel evolution to produce a block of becoming that is new and transformative and that may result in a new configuration: the wasp-orchid.

There are many types of becoming, including 'becoming-woman; becoming-child; becoming-animal, -vegetable, or -mineral; becomings-molecular of all kinds, becomings-particles'; and 'singing or composing, painting, writing have no other aim: to unleash these becomings' (ATP 272E/333F). As we saw in Chapter 1, the encounter that is reading – the coming-together of reader and book, and, in the case of children's literature, the coming-together of adult and child – is already a becoming which may give rise to the molecular child: a child not confined by molar categorisations but that exists in the blurring of boundaries between our pre-defined notions of 'adult' and 'child'. In this chapter, I consider other becomings unleashed by texts written for children by Virginia Woolf, Jean-Marie Gustave Le Clézio and Miguel Angel Asturias. These becomings may involve the whole text, just as '*Moby-Dick* in its entirety is one of the greatest masterpieces of becoming; Captain Ahab has an irresistible becoming-whale' (ATP 243E/298F), or the characters' becoming and how the reader or observer of the text may be swept up in this movement of becoming. This chapter will not then analyse how the child in the text or the child reader of the text changes or evolves but rather how they involve. Drawing on Woolf's *Nurse Lugton's Curtain* and *The Widow and the Parrot*, Le Clézio's *Voyage au pays des arbres* and Asturias's *L'Homme qui avait tout, tout, tout*, I will focus in turn on becoming-animal, becoming-plant, becoming-molecular and the progression to the cosmic formula of becoming, becoming-imperceptible. I conclude by considering Lewis Carroll's *Alice's Adventures in Wonderland*, which, for Deleuze, represents pure becoming, and how this helps us re-evaluate the idea at the very heart of children's literature: that is, growth.

Becoming-animal

In their discussion of becoming-animal, Deleuze and Guattari turn their attention to children, writing: 'note how they talk about animals, and are moved by them. They make a list of affects. Little Hans's horse is not representative but affective' (ATP 257E/314F). For them, children are particularly attuned to such becomings. Although children 'continually undergo becomings of this kind' (ATP 259E/317F), for Deleuze and Guattari psychoanalysis effectively sounds the death knell for becoming-animal as it 'has no feeling for unnatural participations, nor for the assemblages a child can mount in order to solve a problem' (ATP 259–60E/317F). They are very clear as to what becoming-animal is not: it is not 'phantasies or subjective reveries: it is not a question of imitating a horse, "playing" horse, identifying with one, or even experiencing feelings of pity or sympathy. Neither does it have to do with an objective analogy between assemblages' (ATP 258E/315F). Rather, it is a movement in which two heterogeneous entities are swept up, brought together through desire, through a longing for closeness on a molecular level. They state:

you become-animal only if, by whatever means or elements, you emit corpuscles that enter the relation of movement and rest of the animal particles, or what amounts to the same thing, that enter the zone of proximity of the animal molecule. You become animal only molecularly. You do not become a barking molar dog, but by barking, if it is done with enough feeling, with enough necessity and composition, you emit a molecular dog. (ATP 274–75E/336–37F)

Jacqueline Duhême, Deleuze's long-time friend and children's illustrator, provides an example of what becoming-animal both is and is not in her first children's book, which renowned French poet Paul Éluard wrote for her to illustrate, entitled *Grain-d'Aile*. *Grain-d'Aile*, a play on words of Paul Éluard's true name Eugène Grindel (Duhême 1986: 161), tells the story of a young, somewhat out of the ordinary girl, rather in the vein of Antoine de Saint-Exupéry's *Le Petit Prince*, who dreams of having wings, in fact 'growing up, for her, meant having wings' (Éluard 1997: np). Her favourite place is sitting on top of a pine tree surrounded by all the birds whose habits she knows so well and where a squirrel grants her wish and turns her arms into wings. Although Grain-d'Aile's wish is indeed fulfilled, she soon realises that arms and hands are much more practical for a little girl and she returns to the tree to be transformed back to normal by the squirrel. Grain-d'Aile is transformed into an angelic flying creature, but this is not her becoming in a Deleuzian sense. Grain-d'Aile does not simply imitate the bird, nor does she have any need to magically acquire a set of wings. As Deleuze tells us:

> to become is not to attain a form (identification, imitation, Mimesis) but to find the zone of proximity, indiscernibility, or indifferentiation where one can no longer be distinguished from *a* woman, *an* animal, or *a* molecule – neither imprecise nor general, but unforeseen and nonpreexistent, singularized out of a population rather than determined in a form. (CC 1E/11F)

From the outset, Grain-d'Aile already has 'zone of proximity' with birds, understanding their habits, songs, manners. She does not have a typical animal-child relationship but rather an animal relationship with animals. In growing wings, she gains the ability to fly but loses her becoming-bird and is reterritorialised through her anthropomorphism, only to be able to become-bird once more when the squirrel transforms her back to a little girl. Her becoming-bird comes from her desire, her yearning for proximity with birds, and not when given the gift of wings. In her becoming, neither a child nor a bird can be distinguished from each other.

Becoming-animal, Becoming-molecular...

In reading, or being read to, in perusing the pages of a picture book, or simply looking at its cover, the possibility of becoming-animal is opened up for the reader. Danger, however, is never far away and is inherent in becoming: 'the danger of finding yourself "playing" the animal, the domestic Oedipal animal' (ATP 260E/318F). In children's literature, both children and animals dress up in costumes to imitate each other, from the frilly petticoats of Beatrix Potter's Tabitha Twitchitt and her kittens to the elephant Babar's formal green suit, or Max in *Where the Wild Things Are* 'making mischief of one kind or the other' (Sendak 1963: np) in his wolf suit. As Keith Barker notes, 'in recent centuries animals and children have been linked together in terms of their privileged and protected position in the culture so inextricably that since the nineteenth century children's books have strongly featured animal characters either exhibiting strong human characteristics or showing empathy for such traits' (Barker 1998: 282). Such exchanges between human and animal, the anthropomorphisation of the animal and the animalisation of the human in the pretend play of the child, are ubiquitous in children's literature, but they block becoming in a Deleuzian sense. As Perry Nodelman comments:

> Max's problem is that he has given in to wild animal instinct and must learn a way to enjoy being 'human' again; he is a boy in a wolf suit, just as ambivalent as Peter Rabbit, an animal in a boy's suit. The depiction of animal children acting like humans or of human children acting like animals is so centrally characteristic of picture-book imagery that it tends to disappear; we so take it for granted that we do not often consider its significance [...] One has to conclude that such depictions express not just our relatively unimportant assumptions about the attributes of animals but also our deepest convictions about children and the nature of childhood. (Nodelman 1988: 117)

Nodelman's observation expresses the danger that becomings can find themselves reterritorialised in Oedipal desires, and, indeed, Deleuze and Guattari are aware of the inherent difficulty of their concept, questioning: 'isn't it rather that the acts of becoming-animal cannot follow their principle all the way through – that they maintain a certain ambiguity that leads to their insufficiency and condemns them to defeat?' (K 15E/27–8F). Although an Oedipal impasse may put becoming-animal at risk, in some cases it may remain possible. When, for example, Max reaches 'the place where the wild things are' (Sendak 1963: np), he no longer needs to mimic wolf-like behaviours; rather, he and the reader of *Where the Wild Things Are*

are contaminated by the closeness of the 'wild rumpus'. Becoming-animal, then, is 'to participate in movement, to stake out the path of escape in all its positivity' (K 13E/24F), and it is this trajectory which allows an escape from the Oedipal dilemma in a block of becoming. As Ronald Bogue puts it, 'the essence of becoming-animal and the line of flight [is] not absolute freedom, only a way out' (Bogue 2003: 77). In such a becoming, both wild thing and child are swept up together by the block of becoming that passes between them and are effaced to create 'a new singularity, irreducible to either of the two parts' (Neimanis 2007: 282): a child-wild-thing assemblage endowed with new potential and in turn with new possibilities for lines of flight and new directionalities for the process of growing up.

In *Nurse Lugton's Curtain* by Virginia Woolf, the reader is presented with 'an almost Biblical parade of animals (reminiscent of the Ark story)' (Rohman 2013: 525) on the blue material draped across Nurse Lugton's knee. As Nurse Lugton snores, the animals gradually come to life, pictorially at first in Julie Vivas's version of the text, before being enumerated in the text itself: 'First went the elephant and the zebra; next the giraffe and the tiger; the ostrich, the mandrill, twelve marmots and a pack of mongeese followed; the penguins and the pelicans waddled and waded, often pecking at each other, alongside' (Woolf 2004: np). These are not the Oedipal animals that Deleuze dislikes, the animals of the nursery, nor are they the animals of the English countryside; they are the exotic, wild animals of the British Empire, more typically seen caged in the zoo.[1] Such wild beasts would have frightened the sleeping nurse, who was 'afraid even of poking through the bars with her umbrella at the Zoo!' The animals are static at first, a repeated motif on the fabric that rests on Nurse Lugton's knee, and illustrated in hues of blue to match the colour of the curtain. Only after they have tumbled off the curtain and have become animate do they gain in colour, moving past the reader from left to right, before processing off the page. Of all the animals presented, the most vibrant is the mandrill. Rohman writes in her reading of *Nurse Lugton's Curtain* that 'most descriptions of mandrills emphasise the male's brilliant colouration, with a red stripe down the middle of the face and ridged blue muzzle. The "rump" is strikingly saturated with bright pinks, blues, reds and purples. Indeed, the mandrill seems almost alien in its pigmentation' (Rohman 2013: 526). This vibrant monkey stands out not simply because of his colouring but also as he 'is the only creature who stares directly out at the reader' (527). The mandrill is not alone, but is part of a horde, which appears for the first time as a repeated pattern on the cloth, before the monkeys begin to clamber off the curtain to be fed 'beautiful golden rolls stuffed with quinces and rose leaves' (Woolf 2004) by the people of Millamarchmantopolis. This vibrant monkey is telling. For Deleuze and Guattari, 'wherever there is multiplicity, you will also find an exceptional individual, and it is with that individual that an alliance must be made in order to become-animal' (ATP 243E/297F). The mandrill represents this exceptional, anomalous individual within the pack whose gaze extends beyond the pages of the book to penetrate the reader's world and to draw the reader into the textual world, creating a zone of proximity between them, an exchange that opens up possibilities for becoming.[2]

Ronald Bogue reminds us that 'human interactions are structured by categories that enforce asymmetrical power relations: male-female, white-black (or brown, red, yellow), adult-child, human-animal and so on' (Bogue 2010: 20). Those who are in the position of power and domination are termed *majoritarian* by Deleuze and Guattari, and those who are not, *minoritarian*. Those on the receiving end of children's fiction, those who are invited to partake of it, are thus minoritarian, not necessarily quantitively as a group of children, but in their 'deviance from the norm' (Bogue 2003: 112) of the dominant adult world in which they find themselves. Most majoritarian adults, and parents in particular, would rather children behave as civilised human beings and not in an animalistic manner. This desire to civilise our young and thus make our children distinct from the young of the animal kingdom, coupled with the popularity and longevity of, for example, the fables of Aesop and La Fontaine, has meant that 'animals are also living metaphors, highly iconic emblems within our language and culture' (Braidotti 2008: 125). Monkeys are reputed for their imitative traits and mischievous behaviour, and, as a result, various idiomatic expressions related to them pervade language, especially in regard to children's behaviour (a naughty child may be a little monkey, children may monkey around or get up to monkey business and so on). Such sentiments also pervade children's literature. As Nodelman notes: 'the story of Peter Rabbit sums up a central dilemma of childhood – whether one should act naturally in accordance with one's basic animal instincts or whether one should do as one's parents wish and learn to act in obedience to their more civilized codes of behaviour' (Nodelman 1988: 116). One of the most popular monkey stories for children, *Curious George*, by H. A. and Margaret Rey, conforms to such a majoritarian reading of both monkey and child, and the child's progression towards maturity. June Cummins, in her postcolonial reading of the Curious George series, states:

> on one hand, the narrative works to convince children to identify with George, who is curious and mischievous like them, and thus learn lessons of obedience and compliance with him when he does. On the other hand, the books also instruct certain segments of their audience, specifically, young white boys, that while they may be like George now, they will grow up to be more like that Man in the Yellow Hat, that is, an adult. (Cummins 1997: 69)

A child, then, who monkeys around, like Curious George, and who imitates monkey behaviours, simply reproduces a prescribed majoritarian representation of a monkey. A child reader of *Curious George* may imitate monkey behaviours but can thus never achieve becoming-monkey with such a text. In reading *Nurse Lugton's Curtain*, however, the anomalous mandrill offers a child reader a way to disrupt the majoritarian classifications by becoming-monkey and by not merely imitating it. In becoming-monkey, the child reader is 'no longer burdened with the symbolic meanings' (Yin 2013: 335) of 'being a monkey' but is *in*volving creatively. A line of flight undoes the binaries of monkey and child, of human and animal, sweeping both parts up together, changing one as much as the other and carrying both off to something new.

This movement also undoes the subjectivity of *the child* and *the monkey*. It is worth quoting Deleuze at length here on the transition between definite and indefinite article in becoming:

> children express themselves in this manner – a father, a body, a horse. These indefinites often seem to result from a lack of determination due to the defenses of the consciousness. For psychoanalysis, it is always a question of *my* father, *me*, *my* body. It has a mania for the possessive and the personal, and interpretation consists in recovering persons and possessions. [...] Yet the indefinite lacks nothing; above all, it does not lack determination. It is the determination of a becoming, its characteristic power, the power of an impersonal that is not a generality but a singularity at its highest point. For example, I do not play *the* horse, any more than I imitate *this* or *that* horse, but I become *a* horse, by reaching a zone of proximity where I can no longer be distinguished from what I am becoming. (CC 65E/86F)

Becoming is always in constant flux, caught in the dual movement of deterritorialisation and reterritorialisation. Deterritorialisation occurs as becoming-monkey takes place, taking the child away from prescribed categorisations to a zone of proximity with the monkey through desire so that it no longer is identifiable as *the* child, a specific, definite, discrete object with its own distinct subjectivity as flagged by the definite article, but rather as an indefinite, non-specific child, stripped of subjectivity, who becomes.[3] If the Oedipal urge takes over, becoming-monkey fails: the child begins to mimic the animal and becomes burdened again with majoritarian, restrictive semantic coding of what 'monkey' should be. The movement of becoming may start up again, once the child stops mimicking and is once again drawn closer to a monkey.

Virginia Woolf's other children's tale, *The Widow and the Parrot* first appeared in *The Charleston Bulletin*, a daily family newspaper produced by Woolf's nephews, her sister Vanessa Bell's children. At first glance, *The Widow and the Parrot* appears a heavily moralistic and overtly didactic tale, dominated by domesticated, Oedipal animals. Mrs. Gage, the elderly, impoverished widow in question, 'was devoted to animals, and often went short herself rather than stint her dog of his bone' (Woolf 1988: np). Deleuze and Guattari warn us of these sentimental, domestic relationships with animals, writing that 'it is clear that the anomalous is not simply an exceptional individual; that would be to equate it with the family animal or pet, the Oedipalized animal as psychoanalysis sees it, as the image of the father, etc. Ahab's Moby-Dick is not like the little cat or dog owned by an elderly woman who honors and cherishes it' (ATP 244E/299F). In stark contrast to Nurse Lugton, who harms flies and worries the animals in the zoo with her umbrella, Mrs. Gage is caring and kind to animals and on meeting the eponymous parrot, James, 'Mrs. Gage at once went to her box and fetched some sugar which she had with her and offered it to the parrot, saying in a very kind tone that she meant him no harm, but was his old master's sister, come to take possession of the house, and she would see to it that he was as happy as a bird could be.' James, the parrot, stands out in the text as the mandrill does in *Nurse Lugton's Curtain*, but as a domesticated animal, a wild bird that has been trained and tamed. The parrot in this text has a human name and a human ability: speech, having 'learnt his language in the east'. In his attempts to lead Mrs. Gage to her late brother's fortune, Mrs. Gage even begins 'talking to him as though he were a human being'. The parrot guides her gestures and movements, and 'as the three thousandth coin was placed on the top of the pile, the parrot [flies] up into the air in triumph and alight[s] very gently on the top of Mrs. Gage's head'. Their relationship endures until her last breath when 'James the parrot shrieked out, "Not at home! Not at home!" and fell off his perch stone dead.'

'Such, she said, is the reward of kindness to animals': the moral of the tale is clearly spelled out, when Mrs. Gage, on her deathbed, tells the clergyman in attendance the whole story. Woolf's nephews recall being disappointed by her contribution to their daily family newspaper, recalling that her text was 'a tease. We had hoped vaguely for something as funny, as subversive, and as frivolous as Virginia's conversation. Knowing this, she sent us an "improving story" with a moral, based on the very worst Victorian examples' (Woolf 1988: Afterword). This text is indeed disappointing if taken at face value, especially if we consider that Deleuze thought that 'the only way to get outside the dualisms is to be-between, to pass between, the intermezzo – that is what Virginia Woolf lived with all her energies, in all of her work, never ceasing to become' (ATP 277E/339F). Ann Martin, however, reads *The Widow and the Parrot* as imbued with irony, writing that the text 'takes its ironic impetus from the Victorian sentimentality and pedantry that offended Woolf's modernist sensibilities' (Martin 2006: 97–8). If the tale is read in this way, as poking fun at the genre – and indeed humour is evident as, for example, Woolf's heroine 'seems to see no tension at all between her devotion to animals and her friendship with Mr. Stacey the pig farmer' (Preece 2011: 209) – then becoming-animal remains possible. The text is teeming with other animal bodies more attune to Deleuze's preferences. A letter from solicitors, 'Messrs. Stagg and Beetle', brings Mrs. Gage the news of her inheritance, and entering into the dilapidated home of her late brother, she notices an infestation of vermin as 'rats r[u]n along the mantelpiece'. Her brother, 'a miserly varmint', did not care for animals and 'liked worrying the poor insects [. . .] trim[ming] a hairy caterpillar with a pair of scissors'. In such a reading, Woolf is not then promoting domesticated and sentimental relationships with animals, there is no becoming-dog or becoming-talking parrot – the closest Mrs. Gage comes to becoming-bird is dropping on her knees and scrabbling in the ruins of her brother's cottage in search of his missing fortune, copying James 'scratching about in the sandy foundations [. . .] as you may have seen a hen scratch with her claws'. Reading this text as an ironic critique on moralistic animal tales of the Victorian era allows other becomings to surface: becoming-insect, becoming-rat with the vermin and insects that subtly infest the tale.

Becoming-plant

Aside from becoming-animal, children's literature endorses becoming-plant. In Jean-Marie Gustave Le Clézio's *Voyage au pays des arbres*, a little boy, named Hihuit, undergoes not a becoming-animal but a becoming-plant, and in particular a becoming-tree. Whilst the tree is inherently at odds with Deleuze and Guattari's rhizomatic thinking, they do admit that 'knots of arborescence' may persist even in rhizomatic structures. Indeed, the trees Hihuit encounters have many rhizomatic qualities. The trees give the impression that they are 'firmly rooted in the dark earth' (Le Clézio 1978: 6), but this is only a ruse to disguise their ability to uproot themselves and spread and move about in lateral ways. Trees also tell rhizomatic stories: 'they tell each other tree stories, stories without end or beginning which are not for men' (22). What brings Hihuit to his becoming-plant is his desire to travel. This is initially thwarted by his lack of appropriate means: he has neither boat, car nor train (5). Hihuit realises, however, that it is not 'necessary to have wings or fins to travel' (5) and that he could visit the 'the country of trees' (6). The boy is not fooled by the trees' apparent lack of movement: 'for some time when he would go walking in the forest he would feel many strange things, as if the trees wanted to speak to him, or as if the trees were moving' (6). In seeing human beings, the trees 'tighten the grip of their roots and play dead' (8). The boy whistles softly as he wanders through the forest: 'because the trees really like the music we make when whistling' (9). Gradually the trees begin to relax in the boy's company: 'the little boy noticed that the trees gradually lessened their grip. Their branches would open up a little more, like large umbrellas, and their roots would become more flexible; they would even come out of the ground, very slowly' (9), and with this came a noise: 'a loud yawning noise which came from all parts of the forest' (10). Hihuit realises that the trees have their own language which mirrors birdsong: 'if you don't pay attention, you may think that it is the birds which are singing. You have to say that it sounds very much like it. But it isn't the birds that are whistling, it is the trees' (11). The whistling of the trees is mirrored by Hihuit's own whistling. Just as for Deleuze and Guattari the song accompanies the child away from home, so Hihuit whistles to create his ritournelle or refrain.[4] His whistled ritournelle accompanies his journey into the forest and allows his deterritorialisation, his becoming-tree. Hihuit, like Grain-d'Aile, enters his becoming-tree through his desire to be close to the trees that surround him. Hihuit (his tree name means little man) sits unmoving amongst them, like 'a clandestine passenger on a motionless journey' (ATP 197E/242F). His physical journey is complete and he now becomes a *voyageur immobile* par excellence.[5] His becoming occurs in this moment of stillness, as he observes the trees' slowness and their sounds, whistling both to himself and to the trees and building his closeness to them.

Deleuze and Guattari refer to French writer André Dhôtel who

> knew how to place his characters in strange plant-becomings, becoming tree or aster: this is not the transformation of one into the other, he says, but something passing from one to the other. This something can be specified only as a sensation. It is a zone of indetermination, of indiscernibility, as if things, beasts, persons (Ahab and Moby Dick...) endlessly reach that point that immediately precedes their natural differentiation. This is what is called an affect. (WP 173E/164F)

The boy does not turn into a tree, unlike the man at the end of Miguel Angel Asturias's tale *L'Homme qui avait tout, tout, tout*, who is condemned to live as the avocado tree he has just cut down and whose toes turn into roots, body transforms into a trunk, and who has branches growing out of his arms. Such a transformation is not becoming. Hihuit desires his closeness with the trees. His imperceptible movement towards the trees is rewarded by an invitation to their dance that night. Accompanied by his refrain, he is able to leave the confines of his home and secretly slip out at night back to the forest when everyone is sleeping. Just as the animals come alive on Nurse Lugton's curtain while she sleeps, so the trees begin to dance at night. Again, the little boy does not rush in but rather enters into a period of stillness, waiting patiently before entering the dance of becoming: 'the little boy watched the trees dancing freely for a good while, and then he joined the dance' (Le Clézio 1978: 32). In *Essays Critical and Clinical*, Deleuze remarks that in his first novel, *Le Procès-Verbal* [The Interrogation], Le Clézio 'presents in an almost exemplary fashion a character taken up in a becoming-woman, then a becoming-rat, then a becoming-imperceptible in which he effaces himself' (CC 185E/12F, note 2). *Voyage au pays des arbres*, Le Clézio's only text written intentionally for young readers, provides in turn an exemplary becoming-plant. Both Hihuit and the trees lose themselves in this becoming. What passes between them is sensation, affect in Deleuzian terminology, and a zone of proximity is reached where neither entity, child and plant, is distinguishable from the other. The young reader accompanying Hihuit on this adventure is, like Hihuit himself, invited to join the dance of becoming. In doing so, a line of flight opens up – the possibility to grow in a way that surpasses typical expectations of growing up; to become other, to move away from the constraints of socially imposed majoritarian boundaries and subjectivities, to be contaminated on a truly other level, the molecular level of plantness.

Becoming-molecular, Becoming-imperceptible

For Deleuze and Guattari, becoming is to 'emit particles that take on certain relations of movement and rest because they enter a particular zone of proximity' (ATP 273E/334F). Entering into a relation of rest and movement, or speed and slowness, can facilitate becomings, as it does for Hihuit. Such movement also dominates in *Nurse Lugton's Curtain*. There are periods of absolute stillness as the animals are frozen in place on the blue stuff of the curtain. During these periods Nurse Lugton herself is awake and active. Nurse Lugton subsequently dozes off in her chair and becomes dormant once more, allowing the animals to be animated and to enter into a period of activity. Writing about Proust's *À la recherche du temps perdu*, Deleuze considers that Albertine

> can always imitate a flower, but it is when she is sleeping and enters into composition with the particles of sleep that her beauty spot and the texture of her skin enter a relation of rest and movement that place her in the zone of a molecular vegetable: the becoming-plant of Albertine. And it is when she is held prisoner that she emits the particles of a bird. And it is when she flees, launches down a line of flight, that she becomes-horse, even if it is the horse of death. (ATP 275E/337F)

In a similar vein to Albertine, Nurse Lugton's sleep moves her towards the molecular. As Carrie Rohman suggests, 'when Lugton enters an unconscious or semi-conscious state, the edicts of organic repression diminish and the affective forces of becoming are triggered' (Rohman 2013: 525). At the height of the story, she is no longer a separate, identifiable (molar/majoritarian) human being dozing in her chair but an integral part of the topography of Millamarchmantopolis. This is particularly clear in the version of the text illustrated by Julie Vivas, to accompany the following passage:

> they could see her, from their window, towering over them. She had a face like the side of a mountain with great precipices and avalanches,

and chasms for her eyes and hair and nose and teeth. And every animal which strayed into her territories she froze alive, so that all day they stood stock still on her knee, but when she fell asleep, then they were released, and down they came in the evening to Millamarchmantopolis to drink. (Woolf 2004: np)

Vivas's illustration shows Lugton 'conflated with the landscape' (Rohman 2013: 533): her neck blends with the foothills of the mountain that is her face, her nose and cheekbones are craggy and barren, towering above the town of Millamarchmantopolis. Nurse Lugton has morphed into the landscape, but her head is not a pleasant and reposing space but a rocky, inhospitable territory. Woolf's text and Vivas's illustration dehumanise and thus deterritorialise Nurse Lugton: she is no longer the familiar family nurse, but a monstrous ogress that merges with the landscape to ensnare the errant wanderer, entrapping them on the cloth of her curtain and freezing them in time and space.

In Woolf's description of Nurse Lugton, she uses *like* – 'she had a face *like* the side of a mountain' (my emphasis) – a simile indicating that Nurse Lugton resembles, bears a similarity to, or is analogous to the mountain. Such expressions are linked with the act of perception, the perceived differences or similarities between two entities and may work against becoming, for, as Tamsin Lorraine writes, 'perception involves resemblance and similarity. To be visible a becoming must already be perceivable, and to be perceivable means that it will be perceived as being like something else. Becomings are imperceptible' (Lorraine 2000: 188). In *Deleuze and Futurism: A Manifesto for Nonsense*, Helen Palmer discusses Deleuze's critique of analogy and his ensuing critique of metaphor at length (Palmer 2014: 133–57). For Palmer, whilst there are clear differences between simile and metaphor, namely the omission of the prepositions *like* or *as*, the 'ultimate goal (of both simile and metaphor) is to create a link between two disparate entities' (140–1). Indeed, Deleuze and Guattari discuss how their use of 'like' should be read, in a passage where they cite French journalist Philippe Gavi writing about the spectacle of the iron-eating performance artist Lolito:

> if we interpret the word 'like' as a metaphor, or propose a structural analogy of relations (man-iron = dog-bone), we understand nothing of becoming. The word 'like' is one of those words that change drastically in meaning and function when they are used in connection with haecceities, when they are made into expressions of becomings instead of signified states of signifying relations. (ATP 274E/336F)

Nurse Lugton need not then be perceived with respect to something else and Woolf's *like* need not be interpreted as a simile or metaphor, a binding together of entities, but as a becoming. In her dormant state, she is able to enter a period of rest and begins to emit mineral particles, which leads in turn to a becoming-mountain, becoming-mineral, becoming-molecular.

The animals in the story also escape their molar constraints and reach a becoming-molecular. Again, the image in Vivas's version evokes this further: as the animals go down to the lake to drink, Vivas provides the reader with an aerial view of the drinking-hole, a perspective favoured by Woolf 'because of its tendency to diminish the centrality of the human subject' (Levy 2004: 147). Rohman comments that 'we see only their backs, demarcated half-ways each, like cells preparing to divide. The landscape is represented almost as if sliced on a molecular level, with trees spreading out like microbial pili or flagella' (Rohman 2013: 532). This image is so unlike typical representations of animals in children's literature. The elephant in the image, for example, is no longer trapped in a stereotypical, easily identifiable, classifiable and perceptible, molar form: a large, grey beast, with big ears, the friendly sort that adorns the walls of children's nurseries. Nor is it anthropomorphised, like Babar, walking on his hind legs, wearing a green suit, forced to relinquish its bestiality and to resemble the molar human, Western colonising male. Vivas's illustration has taken the molar elephant to another level: the elephant has transformed into a molecular elephant. The elephant is no longer like anything, rather the illustration has laid bare the very essence of 'elephant'. The reader observing such an illustration is given an entirely new image of an elephant, perhaps what Deleuze and Guattari would describe as a haecceity, a thisness. The haecceity in this case is an elephantness that surpasses 'the form that we know from the outside and recognize from experience, through science, or by habit' (ATP 275E/337F). For Claire Colebrook such an image allows us to reach 'a molecular style of perception precisely because, freed from the human organism's interested and organising perception, perception can be opened up beyond itself' (Colebrook 2002: 129): the reader no longer needs to classify the elephant or respond to it in any prescribed or dogmatic way, but may embrace its elephantness on a molecular level, beyond that which is merely perceived.

In Miguel Angel Asturias's *L'Homme qui avait tout, tout, tout*, which was written for Jacqueline Duhême to illustrate, the landscape shifts and morphs without warning. The tale, which begins with the nameless man in bed being woken to an array of perceivable alarm clocks, then takes him to a crocodile park for breakfast. This is a verdant jungle-like place, evoking the rich landscape of Asturias's Guatemalan heritage, humming and crawling with insects:

> cedar, mahogany, pine, coconut trees more aerial than earthly, cacao trees earthier than aerial. Palm trees with green spreading hands. Humidity. Ant hills. Black wasps smell the acid honey. The obscurity of the undergrowth, shade in the shade of the thickets of the Crocodile park, darkness shattered by the flashes of the birds with fiery plumage. (Asturias 1999: 16)

After breakfast, the man is transported into a kaleidoscopic tunnel. Vast amounts of time pass in this tunnel, so that everything it contains merges into the kaleidoscope: 'time went by; not years but centuries. Generations and generations of kaleidoscopic stars, of man-stars, of woman-stars' (Asturias 1999: 22). Its effect on the man is that 'you saw what was behind him, through his body, and all the movement of his blood, his heart and his organs' (21). Even his dog, Trampolinet, which enters the tunnel with him, merges with the tunnel: 'he was also a dog of many colours, of changing, shimmering colours [. . .] Trampolinet disintegrated, bits of glass, bits of glass, bits of glass and little bits of every coloured glass, angles of his mirror skeleton integrated into the kaleidoscopic tunnel' (22). Trampolinet is no longer an identifiable molar dog, with four legs, a tail and a wet nose. After passing into the kaleidoscopic tunnel, Trampolinet no longer resembles anything but the kaleidoscope itself – a toy quintessentially associated with childhood. With its mirrors and multiple reflections of cascading objects, Trampolinet, like the man before him, has become-imperceptible.

For Deleuze and Guattari, all becomings rush towards becoming-imperceptible; it is their 'cosmic formula' (ATP 279E/342F). It is worth returning here to the notion of perception mentioned above in order to grasp the potential of becoming-imperceptible. To interact with a physical object, it is first perceived by the senses, and it is the perceived object that is interpreted and categorised. Our sensory perception is necessarily limited, as Deleuze and Guattari point out: 'doubtless, thresholds of perception are relative; there is always a threshold capable of grasping what eludes another: the eagle's eye...' (ATP 281E/344F). Claire Colebrook provides the example of how we perceive a plant, writing: it 'is not a static thing, although we perceive it as such. The plant is the reception of light, heat, moisture, insect pollination and so on; it is a process of becoming in relation to other becomings' (Colebrook 2002: 128). Becoming-imperceptible removes the reliance on human perception, and points to a state outside perception that both precedes and surpasses perception. Becoming-imperceptible undoes identities and requires us to 'leav[e] behind not only the perceptible boundaries of the body but also one's conventional understandings of oneself, of others, and of one's world, in order to respond to the informing impact of imperceptible encounters' (Lorraine 1999: 189). Caught in the kaleidoscope, the man's body becomes transparent, opening up to the outside and allowing it to be traversed by light, and his dog's body is effaced between the mirrors of the scope. Deleuze and Guattari tell us that 'the imperceptible itself becomes necessarily perceived at the same time as perception becomes necessarily molecular: arrive at holes, microintervals between matters, colors and sounds engulfing lines of flight, world lines, lines of transparency and intersection' (ATP 282E/346F). As the man and his dog become-imperceptible, the perceptible, physical constraints of their bodies give way to an infinitely changing geometric pattern of colour and light, allowing them, and the reader who partakes of their adventure, to embark on a path to that which is outside subjectivity, to escape on a line of flight in which the perceptible gives way to the imperceptible.

Deleuze describes his philosophy as transcendental empiricism. Empirical philosophies foreground experience, and the importance Deleuze attaches to such experience and experimentation is clear from his work, in particular with regard to literature, where he recommends, as we saw earlier, that we never ask 'what a book means, as signified or signifier', but rather 'what it functions with, in connection with what other things it does or does not transmit intensities' (ATP 4E/10F). The intensities resulting from experimentation with literature may be sensory, but the literary experience should not stop at what can be sensed or observed. Experience cannot truly occur without going beyond perception; indeed, Deleuze's empiricism becomes transcendental because of the emphasis he places on experience outside perception. The concept of becoming-imperceptible can then help us understand the *je ne sais quoi* of the reading experience, the elusive quality of reading that we are unable to classify immediately with our senses. Tamsin Lorraine writes that 'Deleuze approaches talking about the unsayable – that part of experience that cannot be talked about because it is singular, the part of experience

– no matter how ordinary or mundane that experience may be – that eludes any description we may try to give it' (Lorraine 2000: 191). Albeit somewhat idealised, a passage from Robert Louis Stevenson's 'A Gossip on Romance', equally captures the becoming-imperceptible of reading: 'in anything fit to be called by the name of reading, the process itself should be absorbing and voluptuous, we should gloat over a book, be rapt clean out of ourselves, . . . our mind filled with the busiest kaleidoscopic dance of images' (Stevenson 1908: 151). If reading leads to becoming-imperceptible – and Claire Colebrook reminds us that this is a process and 'not something that can be achieved once and for all; it is a becoming not a being' (Colebrook 2002: 132) – then the reader is 'rapt clean out of' the binary categories imposed by society. The constraints of molar subjectivities that bind the reader are shattered and new, liberating paths are opened up for the reader leading to new ways of thinking and existing.

Pure Becoming

There is one character from children's literature that for Deleuze epitomises pure becoming: Alice in Lewis Carroll's *Alice's Adventures in Wonderland*. Alice is also of particular interest from a children's literature perspective as she does not simply grow *up*: she grows both up *and* down, increasing in size and shrinking again depending on the cake she eats, the bottle from which she drinks or even which side of the mushroom she nibbles. These changes undermine Alice's sense of self and lead her to question who she is:

> I wonder if I've been changed in the night? Let me think: *was* I the same when I got up this morning? I almost think that I can remember feeling a little different. But if I'm not the same, the next question is, Who in the world am I? [. . .] 'I'm sure I'm not Ada,' she said, 'for her hair goes in such long ringlets, and mine doesn't go in ringlets at all; and I'm sure I can't be Mabel, for I know all sorts of things, and she, oh! she knows such a very little!' (Carroll 2008: 31, original emphasis)

In an attempt to confirm her identity, Alice begins to recite her lessons, but her multiplication tables are muddled as is her knowledge of capital cities and poetry, leading her to conclude 'I must be Mabel after all', then decide after this disagreeable thought that she will 'stay down here till I'm somebody else' (32). Alice's sense of self is so undermined that not only does she not know who she was, but now she believes she may be someone else and still may turn into somebody different again. For Dorothea Olkowski, this is not just pretend angst. Poor Alice has changed so much that she can no longer recite her multiplication tables, nor can she remember geography or recite a short verse correctly. In other words, the past is not carrying into the present; good sense is not functioning, and this is having an effect on her identity. (Olkowski 2008: 111)

Parodying the Cartesian *cogito*, children's literature scholar Jan Susina reads Alice's propensity to recite her lessons, whether or not she has someone to impress with her knowledge or lack thereof, as 'a form of self-validation, a sort of "I can recite, therefore I am"' (Susina 2010: 35). For Deleuze, however, it is exactly this challenge of recitation that destroys Alice's sense of self:

> the loss of the proper name is the adventure which is repeated throughout all Alice's adventures. For the proper or singular name is guaranteed by the permanence of *savoir* [. . .] This is the test of savoir and recitation which strips Alice of her identity. In it words may go awry, being obliquely swept away by the verbs. (LOS 5E/11F)

If we read Alice in this way, Alice's 'I' is not then validated by her recitation, rather Alice's 'I' dissolves through her inability to recite, and the result would appear to be, as Maria Nikolajeva somewhat bleakly suggests in *Power, Voice and Subjectivity in Literature for Young Readers*, one 'of total disempowerment' (Nikolajeva 2010: 33).

The paradoxical physical changes Alice undergoes from her arrival in Wonderland not only trigger this urge to recite, but also, as James Williams notes, 'provide Deleuze with an opportunity to explain how any such change involves all others. Alice does not grow bigger without growing smaller simultaneously' (Williams 2008: 28). Whilst common sense would seem to imply that this is impossible and goes against the notion, found especially in children's literature, that there is a forward, uni-directional movement of growing up, Williams clarifies further with the following example of the child:

> parents will recognise Deleuze's arguments and their relation to powerful emotions in the tensions collected in seeing a child grow up, between the sense of loss at the younger child growing smaller, and receding, and the sense of joy at the older version of the same child growing up and shedding its younger self. [. . .] The knot of emotions betrays the many dimensions of becoming, never a single direction in time, or a single movement, or one alteration, but all of them at different degrees of intensity. (Williams 2008: 29)

Alice paradoxically grows bigger and smaller, confused by this, she recites to confirm her identity, but instead of confirming her self-hood, her recital undoes her knowledge and dissolves her identity. All constants now effaced, Alice is now open to the possibility of pure becoming. In growing up *and* down, getting bigger and smaller, Alice no longer is, she becomes, so that her only being is that of pure becoming. If this is the case, why then does Alice have to grow *up* and up only, in order to escape Wonderland? and why does Carroll provide us with an epilogue to *Alice's Adventures in Wonderland* which would at first glance appear to overturn the pure becoming of the rest of the text?

Alice must get bigger to escape Wonderland. She physically outgrows the cards surrounding her at court, scattering them as she wakes. On waking, Alice recounts her dream to her sister, inversing the role of grown storyteller and listening child. Alice's sister in turn dreams and 'in a manner typical of closure in Victorian novels, projects the future life of the heroine' (Susina 2010: 43):

> she pictured to herself how this same little sister of hers would, in the after-time, be herself a grown woman; and how she would keep, through all her riper years, the simple and loving heart of her childhood; and how she would gather around her other little children, and make *their* eyes bright and eager with many a strange tale, perhaps even with the dream of Wonderland of long ago; and how she would feel with all their simple sorrows, and find a pleasure in all their simple joys, remembering her own child-life, and the happy summer days. (Carroll 2008: 113, original emphasis)

In this final passage where her older sister envisions Alice's growing up, the futurely direction of this growth is brought back on itself. Alice's sister brings the future grown-up Alice in contact with the present Alice: the woman in contact with the girl, the adult in contact with the child. Time and its related concept of growing up is no longer merely uni-directional but bent back on itself to allow Alice's present childhood and future adulthood to coexist in the same moment in time. There is now not just one unique futurely direction of time, but one that connects all time: that is, Aiôn.

In *A Thousand Plateaus*, Deleuze and Guattari liken Aiôn to 'the "nonpulsed" time of a floating music' (ATP 262E/320F) and refer to the compositions of Pierre Boulez in which 'sections of regularly pulsed music in standard meters alternate with sections in which performers are free to execute their parts as they see fit, the conductor providing no regular pulse' (Bogue 2010: 28). They juxtapose this 'floating time of flux' (Bogue 2010: 28) with Chronos, the 'the time of measure that situates things and persons, develops a form, and determines a subject [. . .] the "pulsed time" of a formal functional music' (ATP 262E/320F). It is in *The Logic of Sense*, however, that Deleuze explores in greater depth the subtleties of these two modes of temporality. He writes:

> *there are two times, one of which is composed only of interlocking presents; the other is constantly decomposed into elongated pasts and futures.* There are two times, one of which is always definite, active or passive; the other is eternally Infinite and eternally neutral. One is cyclical, measures the movement of bodies and depends on the matter which limits and fills it out; the other is a pure straight line at the surface, incorporeal, unlimited, an empty form of time, independent of all matter. (LOS 73E/79F, original emphasis)

Chronos is the first of these times. It is a corporeal time, burdened with physical concerns and limitations. For Alice, it is the dull, boring time she must spend sitting on the riverbank in the company of her older sister, too hot to make a daisy chain. It is the everyday time during which she will grow, mature and become adult, just as her sister imagines, for 'tomorrow will come after today just as surely as surely as Alice will age corporeally as the days go by, but this is only true according to Chronos. In Aion, the incorporeal past is simultaneous with the incorporeal future, and Alice cannot grow without shrinking, becoming larger *at the same time* as she becomes smaller than she will be' (Lundy 2012: 110, original emphasis). Aiôn is the second of these times and, as we saw in the previous chapter, is a time of pure repetition – of growing and shrinking, and of growing and shrinking again and again. Aiôn is the labyrinthine time of the caesura that Alice experiences in Wonderland. Where Chronos is corporeal, Aiôn is incorporeal, unrestrained by bodily concerns, unlimited by the directionality of growing up. It is therefore Aiôn that allows Alice to grow in two directions at once throughout the text; it is Aiôn that allows Alice's childhood to coexist with her adulthood at the same moment in time in the epilogue. It is Aiôn that divests the notion of growing up in children's literature from its bodily concerns and implicit directionality and renders it incorporeal.

Scholars of children's literature often struggle with these apparent contradictions of growth in children's texts. Maria Nikolajeva, in her seminal *From Mythic to Linear: Time in Children's Literature*, draws on C. S. Lewis's chronicles of Narnia to illustrate her frustrations with the portrayal of growth in children's literature. In the first novel of the Narnia sequence, *The Lion, the Witch and the Wardrobe* (1950), the Pevensie children, Peter, Susan, Lucy and Edmond, are evacuated from wartime London to the house of an old professor. In their games of hide and seek around the sprawling house they discover the fantasy world of Narnia accessible through the back of an old wardrobe. Like Alice, the Pevensie children grow up physically. Unlike Alice, they accomplish much more during their time in Narnia: they defeat the White Witch and become leaders of Narnia themselves, until they 'tumbl[e] out of a wardrobe door' to discover they are 'just Peter, Susan, Edmund and Lucy in their old clothes [and that it is] the same day and the same hour of the day on which they had all gone into the wardrobe to hide' (Lewis 1980: 170). For Nikolajeva, 'the children who have gone through trials in Narnia, who have proved worthy and have been crowned kings and queens, who have grown up and lived a whole life as wise and just rulers, return to their own reality as children, they lose their dearly bought knowledge and insights and therefore their accomplished initiation has no use' (Nikolajeva 2000: 134). If we read such texts through the perspective of Aiôn, we can overcome this apparent effacing of growth. The seemingly contradictory movements of growing and shrinking in *Alice's Adventures in Wonderland* or of growing into an adult and then finding oneself a child again in *The Lion, the Witch and the Wardrobe* do not negate or reverse growth – as Eleanor Kaufman writes, 'in the realm of Aion, [. . .] [t]here is a movement in two directions at once, but it is not a movement of cancellation' (Kaufman 2012: 111) – but are the essential movements of an incorporeal growth. In growing and shrinking, Alice is caught in a flux between two directions, up and down. In the pull between the two, a space opens up for Alice creating room beyond evolutionary growth for an involutionary growth: the growth of pure becoming, the growth of the molecular child. Deleuze is aware that we are conditioned into thinking about growing up and that we require an alternative to growing up:[6] 'people always think of a majoritarian future (when I am grown up, when I have power). Whereas the problem is that of a minoritarian-becoming, not pretending, not playing or imitating the child, the madman, the woman, the animal, the stammerer or the foreigner, but becoming all these, in order to invent new forces or new weapons' (D 5E/11F). We must, then, refocus our readings of growth in children's literature, away from the directional idea of growing up, to the movements of becoming and ageing in Aion. Fluid and incorporeal, the involutionary growth of becoming is bi-directional – an ageing of the simultaneous past-future event.

To age incorporeally, to grow up and down and not merely in one direction through the time of Aiôn, also requires us to rethink the presumed sequential periods of childhood, adolescence and adulthood and the memories that arise from them. In psychoanalysis, it is assumed that repressed childhood memories and traumas repeat themselves in adolescence and adulthood. In the process that Freud refers to as *Nachträglichkeit* or deferred action, experiences from infancy and childhood recur to fit in with new experiences or the attainment of a new stage of development, of adolescence for example (Laplanche and Pontalis 1967: 33), or as Ronald Bogue puts it: 'in an adult neurosis, a childhood experience suddenly takes on a new sense. The child affects the adult from a distance, retroactively' (Bogue 2010: 42). Crucial to this interpretation of memory is the idea of distance and delay: a remembered childhood experience recurs later in a sequential period of life, linearly distanced from the primary event. For Deleuze, however, 'the question then arises how to explain the phenomenon of "delay" which is involved in the time it takes for the supposedly original infantile scene to produce its effect at a distance, in the adult scene which resembles it' (DR 124E/162F). His answer lies in his conception of temporality, not in Chronos, where moments in time do succeed one another, but in Aiôn, in the unhinging of time, where childhood, or in fact any moment in time, communicates between the before and after: 'there is no question as to how the childhood event acts only with a delay. It *is* this delay, but this delay itself is the pure form of time in which before and after coexist' (DR 124E/163F, original emphasis). For Bogue 'the infantile scene does not cause the adult scene, so much as something puts the two moments in contact with one another, allowing a resonance to arise' (Bogue 2010: 42). This something Deleuze terms a dark precursor which draws these two seemingly sequential and separated states (child-adult) and times (childhood-adulthood) together, so that there is a 'communication between the basic series, that of the adult we knew as a child and that of the adult we are among other adults' (DR 124E/162–3F), and at any point in time there is a coexistence between 'the adult that we will be along with the adults that we "have been"' (DR 125E/163F). From this perspective, we can be, in a seeming paradox, the child we are and the adult we will become or the child we were with the adult we now are at any point in time. This is the realm of the molecular child where, as Deleuze says drawing on Italian film director Federico Fellini, 'we are constructed in memory; we are *simultaneously* childhood, adolescence, old age and maturity' (C2 104E/130F, original emphasis).

Deleuze is clear: our memories are not then to be teased out from our unconscious to be dissected and analysed with regard to the Oedipal triangle of mummy-daddy-me, instead 'the Freudian formula must be reversed. You have to produce the unconscious. It is not at all a matter of repressed memories or even of phantasms. You don't reproduce childhood memories, you produce blocs of child-becoming with blocs of childhood' (D 78E/96F). In *Kafka: Toward a Minor Literature*, Deleuze and Guattari contrast the limitations of Oedipal childhood memory fixed in time and which blocks desire with the childhood block 'strengthening desire instead of cramping it, displacing it in time, deterritorializing it, proliferating its connections, linking it to other intensities' (K 4E/9F). Such childhood blocks sweep up both child and adult into a block that endures across all time. Anna Hickey-Moody describes them as 'collective subjectivities that zigzag across time' (Hickey-Moody 2013: 283). The childhood block is 'the only real life of the child; it is deterritorializing; it shifts in time; with time' (K 78E/141F). In the childhood block, time is no longer linear and chronological, but now bends and warps itself to join pasts, presents and futures; childhoods, adolescences, adulthoods. The childhood block 'inject[s] the child into the adult, or the superficial adult into the real child. [. . .] the adult is captured up in a childhood block without ceasing to be an adult, just as the child can be caught up in an adult block without ceasing to be a child. This is not an artificial exchange of roles. Rather, it is the strict contiguity of two faraway segments' (K 79E/143F).

The contiguity of such distant periods in time can be seen in the letters which accompany the 1990 edition of James Joyce's *The Cat and the Devil* illustrated by Roger Blachon. In 1936, Joyce wrote a letter to his grandson and embedded his tale in it. The letter begins: 'my dear Stevie: I sent you a little cat filled with sweets a few days ago but perhaps you do not know the story about the cat of Beaugency' (Joyce 1975: 382). Joyce concludes by adding 'I hope you will like this story' (384), signing off 'Nonno', using the familiar term for grandfather in Italian. This letter is present in all editions; the 1990 edition, however, introduces a supplementary letter written by Stephen Joyce, Joyce's grandson and the original recipient of the tale. Dated 1989 and addressed to the readers of the text, this letter explains how the four-year-old Stevie now has grey hair and could be grandfather himself to the texts' readers. Whilst the purpose of Stephen Joyce's letter is to encourage young readers to pursue reading Joyce into adulthood, this mirroring of his grandfather's own letter allows Stephen Joyce to age incorporeally, to be paradoxically child and adult at the same time.

The letters which metaphorically bridge Joyce's tale; the epilogue to *Alice's Adventures in Wonderland*; the wardrobe that gives access to Narnia, are not then spaces where growth is negated or cancelled but spaces which allow the pliable time of Aiôn to open up. In Aiôn, ageing divests itself from bodily limitations and becomes incorporeal. In Aiôn, childhood and adulthood are no longer linearly separate stages of life, but are swept up into a single block. In writing his letter, Stephen Joyce becomes a molecular child. Those, whether adult or child, who read his letter are drawn into the suppleness of this childhood block of the letter. In the epilogue, Alice's sister perceives Alice as both child and adult; at once her little sister and her future grown sister, mother to her own little children. A childhood block sweeps up the young Alice of the present and the grown Alice of the future producing a molecular child, which endures in one contiguous block across all time and existing at all moments in time. In Narnia, Peter, Susan, Edmund and Lucy achieve the incorporeal growth of a molecular child, retaining their child-ness alongside their Narnian adult-ness. When they tumble out of the wardrobe, out of the caesura of Narnian time, the molecularity of the Pevensie children is not effaced but perdures. Growth in these texts is then one of Aiôn: fluid and supple, the growth of Aiôn is above all incorporeal, not one to be demarcated by fixed beginning or end points. Its bi-directionality brings the child to the adult and the adult to the child and allows for the seemingly disparate time periods of childhood and adulthood to exist in any single instant of time.

Conclusion: Beyond 'Growing up' – the Involution and Becoming of the Molecular Child

I began this chapter with the renowned line from J. M. Barrie's *Peter Pan* that all children, except the eponymous Peter, must grow up. The Deleuzian concept of becoming allows us to shift the focus of growth in children's literature from one of a linear progression to one of creative involution. Becoming effaces the binary categories that contain us, creating new assemblages and opening up other pathways or lines of flight that have no end outside themselves.

At the beginning of this chapter, I focused on becoming-animal, given that anthropomorphised animals or children mimicking animals are so prevalent in this genre. The becoming-animal of the child comes about when the child desires closeness with the animal and enters a zone of proximity with it, not when a child attempts to mimic animal traits. Becoming-animal deterritorialises the child, removing the semantic burden imposed by majoritarian adults as to what 'animal' and 'child' should be. We can, and should, then grow up to become-animal as such becomings allow the child to escape on a line of flight into new uncharted territories, embracing the animal on a molecular level.

All becomings, becoming-animal, becoming-plant, becoming-molecular, open onto the ultimate becoming: becoming-imperceptible. To become-imperceptible is to attain a state of pre-perception: the ever-changing flux that perception tries to reduce to interpretable states. Becoming-imperceptible allows what is to be rejected and shifts the focus to what becomes. As Ronald Bogue writes, 'taken together, becoming-woman, becoming-animal, becoming-imperceptible and so on, amount to a series of possible paths which lead beyond existing forms of human society towards what they call in *What is Philosophy?* new earths and peoples "to come"' (Bogue 2010: 105).

Becoming-imperceptible radically alters our reading of children's literature, by allowing us to focus on the unsayable, on the imperceptible encounters that make us involve. Shifting the focus to becoming allows us to move beyond concerns about what we change or morph into, how we reach adulthood, how successfully we navigate childhood. Becoming, then, is the new 'growing up' of the twenty-first century, affecting adult as well as the child. Becoming is not without movement or direction, however, for as Deleuze states, 'becomings belong to geography, they are orientations, directions, entries and exits' (D 2E/8F), and it is to the notion of the cartographies of childhood that we now turn in Chapter 4.

Notes

1. Wallace Hildick, who discovered the first version of the text, wondered 'if the list of animals written on the reverse side of the page indicates a potential reworking of, or alternate to, the *Dalloway* scenes at Regent's Park – as the park is not far from the Zoo' (Czarnecki 2011: 222). For a discussion of *Nurse Lugton's Curtain* see also Barai 2014.

2. Deleuze and Guattari tell us that 'Virginia Woolf experiences herself not as a monkey or a fish but as a troop of monkeys, as school of fish, according to her variable relations of becomings with the people she approaches' (ATP 239E/293F).
3. Charles J. Stivale remarks that 'for Deleuze, the importance and extreme richness of the indefinite article [...] have been overlooked as well as the fundamental value of the impersonal generally and in the indefinite article' (Stivale 2008: 130).
4. See Chapter 2 for a discussion of the refrain.
5. See Chapter 4 for a discussion of motionless journeying and cartographies of children's literature.
6. Scholars who have also suggested that we require other ways of thinking this process of growing up include queer theorist Bond Stockton 2009; Bohlmann 2012 and 2014; and Hickey-Moody 2013. I consider incorporeal ageing with regard to the British children's fantasy texts of C. S. Lewis, Philippa Pearce and Susan Cooper, in 'Temporalities of Children's Literature: Chronos, Aion and Incorporeal Ageing' (2019).

4

Lines, Maps and Islands

There is a whole geography in people, with rigid lines, supple lines, lines of flight. (*Dialogues* 10E/17F)

Maps are maps of intensity, geography is no less mental and corporeal than physical in movement. (*Dialogues* 38E/49F)

In *Through the Looking-Glass, and What Alice Found There,* Alice determines to reach the top of a hill and, after passing through the Garden of live flowers, she meets the Red Queen who asks her 'where do you come from? [...] And where are you going?' (Carroll 2008: 144). In their introduction to *A Thousand Plateaus,* Deleuze and Guattari tell us that such questions 'are totally useless [...] seeking a beginning or a foundation – all imply a false conception of voyage and movement' (ATP 25E/36F). Deleuze and Guattari offer their collaborative work, *A Thousand Plateaus,* as a pragmatic example of how to break free of such patterns of movement, telling us: 'we are writing this book as a rhizome. It is composed of plateaus [...] Each plateau can be read anywhere and can be related to any other plateau' (ATP 22E/33F). Of import is not beginning at one point and continuing logically and systematically to a second point, but to read, and by extrapolation, to move and think, rhizomatically.

Deleuze and Guattari draw their concept of the rhizome from the botanical root system. In contrast to the root system of a tree, which descends vertically into the earth and whose hierarchy of roots nourish a single plant, the rhizome is a continually growing subterranean stem which expands laterally by putting out adventitious roots at intervals: 'a rhizome has no beginning or end; it is always in the middle, between things, interbeing, *intermezzo*. The tree is filiation, but the rhizome is alliance, uniquely alliance. The tree imposes the verb "to be," but the fabric of the rhizome is the conjunction, "and ... and ... and"' (ATP 25E/36F). The fabric of the rhizome requires us to proceed differently, 'from the middle, through the middle, coming and going rather than starting and finishing' (ATP 25E/36–7F). For Deleuze and Guattari one of the principals of the rhizome is that of cartography and decalcomania.[1] The hierarchical root system of the tree 'articulates and hierarchizes tracings'. The rhizome, on the other hand, is 'a *map and not a tracing*' with 'multiple entryways' (ATP 12E/20F, original emphasis). If we are able to make maps, rather than merely follow already worn paths, we will be able to overcome these false conceptions of voyage and movement.

The Red Queen's questions capture the home-away-home motif ubiquitous in children's literature. Analyses of children's literature often consider how characters reach fabulous places such as Wonderland or Millamarchmantopolis, or the more down-to-earth Bois de Boulogne or Easter Island, and focus on the challenges characters face whilst away from home and how they return changed and more mature. From a Deleuzian perspective, this is not the journey of children's literature, however. The Deleuzian journey of children's literature surpasses journeys to and from somewhere, and even goes beyond the larger movement of growing up, of progressing from childhood to adulthood. It rises from the middle and moves rhizomatically to allow for the creation of maps that are 'impersonal and anti-commemorative' (O'Sullivan 2007: 36). These maps do not mark where characters have been or where they might go, but capture the lines and becomings that stem from their rhizomatic movements.

'To leave, to escape,' Deleuze tells us, 'is to trace a line' (D 3E/47F). In *A Thousand Plateaus* Deleuze and Guattari look to three texts, Henry James's *In the Cage* (1898), F. Scott Fitzgerald's *The Crack-up* (1936) and Pierrette Fleutiaux's work *Histoire du gouffre et de la lunette* [*The Story of the Abyss and the Spyglass*] (1976) to discuss the lines which compose us. With these texts, they identify three types of lines: lines of molar or rigid segmentarity; lines of molecular or supple segmentation; and lines of flight (ATP 195–7E/239–41F). Molar lines are 'conventional trajectories regulated by codes that impose broad social categories, fixed identities and pathways discretely divided into clear segments' (Bogue 2003: 159). On these tried and tested tracings, 'everything seems calculable and foreseen' (ATP 195E/239F), predictable and neatly packaged. Molecular lines are more fluid and supple. They create fissures, ruptures, cracks and minute disturbances in the molar regimes that contain us. Molecular lines and molar lines 'are constantly interfering, reacting upon each other, introducing into each other either a current of suppleness or a point of rigidity' (ATP 196E/240F). The third line, the line of flight, however, 'no longer tolerates segments; rather it is like an exploding of the two segmentary series' (ATP 197E/241F). Deleuze and

Lines, Maps and Islands

Guattari liken the line of flight to 'children leaving school at a run' (ATP 202E/248F): suddenly freed from the rules and regulations of the classroom, they stream noisily, joyfully out onto the playground, their zigzagging paths taking them in every possible direction. Of import is not where the children have started, nor where they are going, but 'the dynamic passage of the line [...] always between points, in the middle' (Bogue 2003: 157).

'The line of flight is a deterritorialization' (D 36E/47F). Movements of deterritorialisation[2] are in constant flux between the related movements of territorialisation and reterritorialisation. The deterritorialising movement of children leaving school 'relies on an initial territorialisation' (Colebrook 2002: 65), in this case, of being taken from the controlled, organised home environment to the more highly regulated school environment. The ringing of the school bell, signalling the start of playtime, allows children the possibility to escape the rigidity of school, to run free in the playground, to deterritorialise.

Whilst the line of flight carries us off to 'across our thresholds, towards a destination which is unknown, unforeseeable, not preexistent' (D 125E/152F), it is only *a line of escape, not freedom* (K35E/64F original emphasis); a way out that may become blocked, that may lead nowhere, that may come up against a dead end. The zigzagging lines of the children on the playground return to more rigid, molar lines as the bell rings again to mark the end of playtime, and the children line up, are silenced and move back into the school building, reterritorialised once more. At the extreme, the line of flight may veer towards absolute destruction, 'imbued with such singular despair in spite of its message of joy, as if at the very moment things are coming to a resolution its undertaking were threatened by something reaching down to its core, by a death, a demolition' (ATP 205–6E/251F), as William Golding shows in pushing the line of flight of children to its destructive end in *Lord of the Flies*.

In his essay 'What Children Say', Deleuze tells us: 'children never stop talking about what they are doing or trying to do: exploring milieus[3] by means of dynamic trajectories, and drawing up maps of them'. 'A milieu is made up of qualities, substances, powers, and events' (CC 61E/81F). To paraphrase Deleuze:[4] the playground, for example, with its materials (its tarmac surface; its climbing frames, swings and slides), its noises (the cries of children chasing each other; the rhymes of clapping games; the chants of children choosing who's 'it' – eeny, meeny, miny, mo), its animals (birds looking for remnants of snacks; the neighbourhood cat walking along a wall; a runaway dog invading the playground) or its dramas (a cut knee; an argument; a fight; the perfect goal scored) – in this milieu that is the playground, nothing is predictable. These playground movements 'never consist in running away from the world but rather in causing runoffs, as when you drill a hole in a pipe' (ATP 204E/249F). The milieu in which a child finds itself is traversed by such runoffs, such seepages. These are *lignes de fuite*, for which the standard translation is line of flight. The act of *fuir* is to flee, to escape, to leak, to seep out like *une fuite d'eau* – a water leak. *Fuir* or 'to flee is to trace a line, lines, a whole cartography' (D 36E/47F, translation altered). In these moments of flight (*fuite*), of absolute deterritorialisation, children explore mad vectors, tracing lines and composing maps.

This chapter goes on a journey through some of the rich landscapes of children's literature. In the first part, using Arthur Ransome's *Swallows and Amazons* as a starting point and drawing subsequently on Pierrette Fleutiaux's *Trini à l'île de Pâques*, I consider child cartographers: the children who create maps either literally or from within. Their cartographic activity is often represented by an endpaper map, which may allow the young reader at home perusing the map to embark on a motionless journey or *voyage immobile*. I then move on to consider perhaps the most unusual endpaper map in children's literature, that of Lewis Carroll's *Through the Looking-Glass, and What Alice Found There*. In the second part of the chapter I consider André Dhôtel's nomadic child protagonist, Gaspard, and his journey towards *le grand pays*, which by its very nature is always beyond reach. The chapter concludes by turning to the desert island of Michel Tournier's *Vendredi ou la vie sauvage* where Tournier's Robinson finds himself not only in a world without others, but also in a world out of time – a world of the incorporeal molecular child.

Cartographers

Deleuze and Guattari are clear in instructing us to 'make a map not a tracing' (ATP 13E/20F), and many characters of children's literature are actively involved in map-making processes. To capture the act of cartography and the varied functions of the map, an example from Arthur Ransome's *Swallows and Amazons* (1930) is germane. The first of a series of twelve stories set predominantly in the English Lake District, the book features four children from the Walker family, John, Susan, Titty and Roger, who captain the dingy named *Swallow*, and Nancy and Peggy Blackett, who sail the *Amazon*. The narrative depicts their sailing adventures on the lake along with camping on Wild Cat Island, a war to capture one of the boats interspersed with fishing and piracy, and a rather appropriately named uncle, Captain Flint. In the chapter entitled 'Making Ready', in which they begin their preparations for their camping trip, the following exchange takes place:

> John said: 'What about a chart?'
> Titty said that as the ocean had never been explored, there could not be any charts.
> 'But all the most exciting charts and maps have places on them that are marked "Unexplored".'
> 'Well, they won't be much good for those places,' said Titty.
> 'We ought to have a chart of some kind,' said John. 'It'll probably be all wrong, and it won't have the right names. We'll make our own names of course.' (Ransome 2012: 26–7)

This exchange between John and his ever-practical younger sister, Titty, reveals the plural functions of a map. A map is utilitarian, necessary at the outset of a voyage to guide the would-be travellers safely on their way. Yet, it must equally spark the imagination and create the desire to go beyond the already-established routes and tracings, into the unexplored and the unknown. What is *not* on the map may therefore be more compelling than what *is*, and augmenting the map as the journey progresses is a necessity.

After the war and the Swallows' victory over the Amazons, John and his crew set about finalising their map. The children actively annotate it, choosing names and symbols, and adding 'a dotted line to show the track of the *Swallow* from Wild Cat Island to the Amazon river' (355). Certain places on the Swallows' map are 'renamed in the imagined landscape of the children's make-believe, with Rio, [. . .] and the River Amazon' (Watson 2000: 110), whilst the homely family environments of Dixon's farm and Holly Howe keep their original names. The Swallows not only partake in the cartographer's charade, requiring 'the map reader to believe that a mosaic of points, lines, and areas on a flat sheet of paper is equivalent to a multidimensional world in space and time' (Muehrcke and Muehrcke 1974: 319), their map also captures an additional dimension of an imaginary fantasy world. Their map is then, as Deleuze and Guattari describe, 'open and connectable in all of its dimensions; it is detachable, reversible, susceptible to constant modification. It can be torn, reversed, adapted to any kind of mounting, reworked by an individual, group, or social formation' (ATP 12E/20F). What is more, the children add colour to their map, thereby enhancing the artistic nature of the map-making process. Deleuze writes of R. L. Stevenson, who 'shows the decisive importance of a colored map in his conception of Treasure Island. This is not to say that a milieu necessarily determines the existence of characters, but rather that the latter are defined by the trajectories they make in reality or in spirit, without which they would not become' (CC 66E/86F). Similarly to Stevenson, this addition of colour to their map does not merely capture the familiar paths or tracings used by the children, but the trajectories, real and imaginary, inherent in their adventures.

For the first edition of *Swallows and Amazons*, the children's map featured on the dust cover. In more recent editions, it appears as an endpaper. The endpaper map is something of a literary curiosity.[5] Occupying a seemingly innocuous space between the cover and the body of the text, unclassifiable as picture or illustration, the endpaper map is frequently overlooked by literary scholars, and is also at risk of being missed by the readers for whom it is destined. Its presence, when discovered, renders the fictional cartography tangible for the young reader. It allows the child reader at home to visualise and mirror the map-studying activity within the text, as Stevenson's Jim Hawkins broods over his treasure map before his voyage takes place, or as the victorious Swallows study and annotate their cartographic creation at the end of theirs. The endpaper map permits the 'motionless travel' (D 37E/49F) of which Deleuze speaks, the movement of the line of flight which 'is not exactly to travel, or even to move' (D37E/48F). The child reader of the endpaper map, a *voyageur immobile*, is not, as Mary Bryden tells us in her text *Gilles Deleuze: Travels in Literature*, 'on the trail of an explanation, of an architectural, psychoanalytical, or social history. Neither is s/he attempting to evoke or replicate cultures through the processes of imagination [. . .] Rather, s/he is entering a rhizomatic flux in which multiple becomings are potentially available' (Bryden 2007: 4–5).

In Pierrette Fleutiaux's *Trini à l'île de Pâques*, Trini, her pet mouse and her detective sister travel to Easter Island in an undercover mission to resolve the mystery of disappearing artefacts. In this volume, the endpaper map is not of Trini's own creation but rather depicts the detail of Easter Island and the sites she visits whilst there. Trini's own cartographic creation, however, arises rhizomatically, in the middle of her long journey to the Island, when she begins to consider the globe and muses on the shape of the different countries:

when you look at a globe, you see that the countries have all sorts of shapes. A hexagon: Ours [France]. A Butterfly: Guadeloupe. A boot: Italy. A triangle: Easter Island (here you need a detailed map otherwise you only see a dot). But the strangest of all, is Chile. It's a long snake down the side of Argentina, whose narrow tail sticks up under Patagonia [...] If people were formed in the image of their country, the people from here [Chile] ought to look like snakes with their ringed tails sticking up on the side. Guadaloupeans would be butterflies; Italians, ungulates, walking on the tip of Sicily; the French, pachyderms, forced to teeter on the Pyrenees and the Alps on their large feet. (Fleutiaux 1999a: 55)

In this break in her actual journey, Trini embarks on a motionless trajectory arising from her recollections of the shapes of different countries and taking her on a somewhat erratic path around the globe. Her cartographic creation and ensuing trajectory mirror the reader's motionless journey stemming from the perusal of the endpaper map depicting Easter Island. Trini's cartography is a curious blend of the geometric and the animal, as she imagines the inhabitants of these countries as creatures which mirror the shape of their homeland. Her cartographic vision reveals that becoming is never far from the trajectory, or as Deleuze puts it, it reveals the becoming that 'subtends the trajectory' (CC 65E/85F). It is, then, 'becoming that turns the most negligible of trajectories, or even a fixed immobility, into a voyage; and it is the trajectory that turns the imaginary into a becoming' (CC 65E/85F).

In his essay, 'What Children Say', Deleuze expresses an interest in the interplay between imaginary and real voyages, and those who look over the endpaper maps provided in *Trini à l'île de Pâques* or in *Swallows and Amazons* are inherently caught up in such an interplay between the real and the imaginary. The endpaper maps of children's literature are both tangible and imaginary. Held between the reader's hands, the realistic and faithful map of Easter Island captures not only Trini's fictitious journeys around this remote location, but also something of Fleutiaux's real-life voyage to the Pacific Islands, which in turn mirrors and draws on that of French explorer, Lapérouse. The fictitious Walker children, characters inspired by the real-life children of Ransome's friends, the Altounyan family, create the endpaper map depicting the voyages of the Swallows and Amazons in the real landscapes of the Lake District, nonetheless enhanced by make-believe. The endpaper maps that accompany these texts do not merely chart the characters' actual to-and-from movements but are rather 'a double map of trajectories and subtending becomings'

(Bogue 2003: 172). The dotted line on the Walker children's map captures the moment when John, Susan and Roger become-boat as they leave Wild Cat Island, as the 'fair wind' catches them and 'the little ship with her brown sail slipped swiftly away in in the sunshine' (Ransome 2012: 253–4) on their mission to capture the *Amazon*. The map of Easter Island marks the location of the great monolithic statues and the moment Trini explores the 'face-landscape aggregates' (ATP 174E/213F) in the giant heads she surveys. The maps capture the 'qualities, substances, powers, and events' (CC 61E/81F) which compose the respective milieus of Wild Cat and Easter Island: their materials (the boats, the camping paraphernalia, the leading lights; the artefacts, the lava tubes), their noises (owl call signals; the heave-ho whistle), their animals (parrots; horses, bird-men) or their dramas (octopus lagoon, an expedition to the charcoal burners; disappearing friends, a millennial sect).

Deleuze writes, 'a real voyage, by itself, lacks the force necessary to be reflected in the imagination; the imaginary voyage, by itself, does not have the force [. . .] to be verified in the real. This is why the imaginary and the real must be, rather, like two juxtaposable or superimposable parts of a single trajectory, two faces that ceaselessly interchange with one another, a mobile mirror' (CC 63E/83F). The real landscapes of the Lake District and Easter Island visited by Ransome and Fleutiaux, contain their 'own unseen, virtual landscape[s] within' (Bogue 2003: 173), disengaged from the real or revealed through the authors' act of fiction and the subsequent reading of their texts. On this fragile mirrored surface forms 'a landscape crystal in which the virtual and the actual are made to double, divide and coalesce, at once interpenetrating, passing into and out of one another, separating and cohering' (Bogue 2003: 175). Deleuze continues:

> it is not enough for the real object or the real landscape to evoke similar or related images; it must disengage *its own* virtual image at the same time that the latter, as an imaginary landscape, makes its entry into the real, following a circuit where each of the two terms pursues the other, is interchanged with the other. 'Vision' is the product of this doubling or splitting in two, this coalescence. (CC 63E/83F)

Deleuze speaks of visions in his essay 'Literature and Life,' writing that 'visions are not fantasies, but veritable Ideas that the writer sees and hears in the interstices of languages, in its intervals' (CC 5E/16F). The ceaseless pursuit of the actual and the virtual landscapes does not create a vision of something tangible appearing credibly to the mind. Nor is it a vision directed inward to the self and to one's identity, rather it is a vision that goes beyond the perceptive capabilities of the physiological organism and creates an absolute deterritorialisation, a becoming-imperceptible. Deleuze's thoughts on such visions are reminiscent of Jean-Paul Sartre who, in *Les Mots*, writes of his childhood reading experiences and his childhood books thus: 'when I opened them, I forgot about everything: was that reading? No, but it was death by ecstasy. From my annihilation there immediately sprang up natives armed with spears, the bush, an explorer with a white helmet. I was *vision*' (Sartre 1981: 74, original emphasis). Perusing the endpaper map of children's literature, the real-imaginary map, with its multiple entryways and exits, its decisive additions of colour, its trajectories and subtending becomings, creates a mobile mirror and an interpenetrating of actual and virtual landscapes – vision. Vision to take us beyond ourselves, on the path to becoming. 'And just as trajectories are no more real than becomings are imaginary, there is something unique in their joining together that belongs only to art' (CC 66E/87F). The endpaper maps of children's literature are then a 'cartography-art' (CC 66E/87F) rending both the trajectory and the becoming 'present in each other, [rendering] their mutual presence perceptible' (CC 66E/88F).

Chessboard Movements

In *Through the Looking-Glass, and What Alice Found There* the endpaper map is perhaps the most unusual of all endpaper maps in children's literature as it is a diagrammatic representation of a game of chess. After meeting the Red Queen for the first time, Alice surveys the land before her:

> for some minutes Alice stood without speaking, looking out in all directions over the country – and a most curious country it was. There were a number of little brooks running across from side to side, and the ground between was divided up into squares by a number of hedges that reached from brook to brook. 'I declare it's marked out just like a large chessboard!' Alice said at last. (Carroll 2008: 145)

From her elevated position on a hill, Alice 'appropriate[s] by her gaze what will become her territory: her looking-from-above domination is at the same time symbolic and political, as she ends up becoming queen of this country' (Peraldo and Calbérac 2014: 9). At this point the reader is offered an illustration by Tenniel of the chessboard landscape stretching out before Alice. This illustration marks a shift in perspective: the reader no longer surveys from above a diagrammatic image of the landscape, with symbols representing the chess pieces (like a key on a real map), but rather is given a mind's eye view of the scene. Yet, as if presaging the passage in *Sylvie and Bruno Concluded* where Mein Herr tells of the map that has been made 1:1 (Carroll 2008: 545–6), 'the liminal chessboard and the chessboard-landscape that Alice describes from the top of the hill are one and the same. The map is no longer a reduced representation of reality: they are two ways of representing the same thing' (Peraldo and Calbérac 2014: 10). Philip and Juliana Muehrcke comment that 'to a person who uses his imagination, a map is greater than itself, for it evokes images and emotions not apparent on the piece of paper that is called a map. But a person who does not know how to read a map or who lacks the imagination necessary to leap from the printed map to the reality it depicts will be less aware of its value' (Muehrcke and Muehrcke 1974: 320). For the young reader perusing the map of the Looking-Glass land, the paradox inherent to all maps disappears; there is no imaginative leap[6] to make. The Looking-Glass world is flat and chequered, and the map represents exactly what the world is: a chessboard.

For Victor Watson, the endpaper maps of children's literature are 'an invitation to a special kind of reading game' (Watson 2000: 110), and he suggests that these 'maps provide a shorthand version of the story in a shape dictated by geography rather than narrative sequence' (111). From a Deleuzian perspective, this reading game is one of pure repetition and the map is no longer merely a condensed geographical version of the story, rather it is a pure repetition in geographical form. The endpaper map creates a rhizomatic territory in-between, innocently placed between the cover and the body of the text. It takes the reader on a journey before the reading journey begins and reiterates that journey in geographical form once reading has started. Reading the text arising from the endpaper map repeats, in greater detail, the tracings and trajectories depicted on the map. Returning to the map at any point during the reading creates a further doubling of the journey. Each reading, of map or text, perpetuates still further repetitions.

In *Through the Looking-Glass*, Carroll adds another layer to this geographical game of pure repetition brought about by the endpaper map. In addition to the image of the chessboard, he provides the reader with a list of Dramatis Personae and the instructions: 'White Pawn (Alice) to play, and win in eleven moves' (Carroll 2008: 123). For the reader who is also skilled at chess, 'the whole action is already there, virtually contained on the chessboard and precisely detailed in the consecutive list of the moves that follows, and the novel is only a literary translation of what the reader-chessplayer could already have guessed' (Peraldo and Calbérac 2014: 13). The endpaper map, its detailed chess moves and accompanying pagination for each move are as much the story as the narrative that follows them. Where Victor Watson considers that the endpaper map invites the reader 'to read (or listen to) the text with some incomplete foreknowledge provided by the map' (Watson 2000: 11), in this case, there is nothing incomplete. The endpaper map details precisely each step of Alice's journey to come.

As Alice declares the Looking-Glass land to be a large chessboard, she also determines the nature of the land she is visiting: 'by naming the chessboard with language, she makes it real and gives new rules to the place she evolves in: the chess rules' (Peraldo and Calbérac 2014: 11). All the characters she encounters will abide by the rules of chess. Alice's role as White Pawn is assigned, and her subsequent movements are thereby predetermined. The Red Queen's earlier interrogation of Alice is indeed 'totally useless' (ATP 25E/36F) and utterly unwarranted. In her assigned role as White Queen's pawn 'she is fated to travel her predetermined course across the chessboard towards the Eighth Square' (Downey 1998: 149). Her movements comply with the rules of chess and the Red Queen explains them thus: 'you're in the Second Square to begin with: when you get into the Eighth Square you'll be a Queen' (Carroll 2008: 145). She continues:

> 'A pawn goes two squares in its first move, you know. So you'll go very quickly through the Third Square – by railway, I should think – and you'll find yourself in the Fourth Square in no time. Well, that square belongs to Tweedledum and Tweedledee – the Fifth is mostly water – the Sixth belongs to Humpty Dumpty – [. . .] the Seventh Square is all forest – however, one of the Knights will show you the way – and in the Eighth Square we shall be Queens together, and it's all feasting and fun!' (Carroll 2008: 147–8)

The Red Queen's explanations reiterate and confirm the chess moves outlined in conjunction with the chess diagram. Alice's movements are molar lines: the conventional course of the lowly pawn, determined by the rules of chess, fixed, regulated and with no room for deviation. As Alice transitions by the strange disappearing railway train[7] into the fourth square on her first move, she realises she must pass through a dark wood. She 'felt a *little* timid about going into it. However, on second thoughts, she made up her mind to go on: "for I certainly won't go *back*"' (156, original emphasis). Alice is, of course, bound to follow her molar line. This moment of decision-making is not hers: she can only go *on*.

As we have seen above, molar and molecular lines are in constant interplay, each injecting suppleness or rigidity into the other. *Through the Looking-Glass* begins with isolation and confinement: Alice is alone in the drawing-room on a snowy November day, only able to watch 'the boys getting in sticks for the bonfire' through the window (128). Despite this, she finds ways of moving without moving, slipping through the fragile surface of the looking-glass above the mantel, thereby creating a suppleness in the strict regime containing her. As is always the risk, Alice's deterritorialisation is not fully realised. Her new-found molecular line in the Looking-Glass land is soon reterritorialised as she is obliged to play the White Queen's pawn: a role that recreates the rigid segmentarity from which she has fled through the looking-glass. It appears that it is only in becoming queen, by reaching the eighth square, that Alice will regain the freedom to move in any direction she pleases. However, as we shall see in Chapter 5, Alice is able to create moments of deterritorialisation by distorting the seemingly strict rules of language the inhabitants of the Looking-Glass land try to impose on her. Her interactions with the various inhabitants of each chessboard square fissure the molar line she must follow.

If in *Alice's Adventures in Wonderland* Alice is ceaselessly changing in size, in *Through the Looking-Glass* she is ceaselessly moving, as the preposition in the title indicates. The novel depicts Alice's journey not simply through the mirror on the mantel but also through the land which she finds there. Deleuze tells us in his essay, 'What Children Say', that 'the map expresses the identity of the journey and what one journeys through. It merges with the object, when the object itself is movement' (CC 61E/81F). This is indeed the case with Alice. The purpose of Alice's journey is movement: her progression from second to eighth square. The endpaper map does not merely articulate her journey through the Looking-Glass land, it is equally the very land she is journeying through; the map and the movement coalesce.

Lines, Maps and Islands

Nomads

Gaspard, the protagonist of André Dhôtel's *Le Pays où l'on n'arrive jamais* is also a cartographer, and rather like Trini, has access to a map within. Gaspard, born to wandering parents who roam from town to town selling ties, is left in the care of his strict and conventional aunt, Gabrielle Berlicault, who owns the local *auberge*. Despite his aunt's efforts to spare him a life of 'vagabondage' (Dhôtel 2015: 7), Gaspard cannot escape his innate longing to be close to the Ardennes countryside of France, and 'would always keep an hour to himself towards the end of the day or after the evening meal to go for a walk' (17). During these walks Gaspard would find a quiet spot to observe the countryside and animals around him and feels contaminated by 'a sort of wild vigour' (19) stemming from this rural idyll surrounding him. Like Le Clézio's Hihuit discussed in Chapter 3, it is in these moments of stillness, of closeness to and affinity with nature, that Gaspard frees himself from the constraints imposed on him by his aunt, and is able to become.

On one of Gaspard's walks, his tranquillity is disrupted when he overhears a radio broadcast about a blond-haired 'runaway child' (21), approximately fifteen years old, who left Antwerp, crossed the entirety of Belgium and was last seen in the forests around Revin and Laifour, approximately twenty kilometres from Gaspard's home village of Lominval. A face appears before him through the vegetation, its piercing blue eyes have a strange 'dazzling fissure' (21) to them. This face, Gaspard discovers as he returns home to help with the evening meal, belongs to the runaway child, who appears before him shortly before being seized by the local police. As the child is captured, it 'turned its head towards Gaspard and looked at him' (23), a look that Gaspard cannot forget and that, from that moment, connects both children in their ensuing adventures.

The unnamed, androgynous child is confined in Gaspard's aunt's guesthouse until the arrival of its guardian, Monsieur Drapeur. Gaspard manages to make contact with the child through the pipes and learns that the child is looking for 'its family and its homeland'[8] (28); as a result, he determines to help the child escape. With the aid of a wire, Gaspard passes the key to the bedroom door through the guesthouse pipes to the child, so that it is able to escape once Gaspard causes a diversion at the start of his morning routine. Gaspard uses the broom, with which he should be sweeping, to dislodge an old mirror which in turns falls creating a tremendous noise.

Gaspard's aunt suspects nothing, assuming that this is just another of the unfortunate incidents that seem to plague her nephew. The ensuing commotion allows the child to escape, but Gaspard is injured in the shoulder by a shard of mirror and sent to his bedroom to rest. From the vantage point of his bedroom window, Gaspard spies the blond-haired child and realises that the child has not been able to find a suitable hiding place. Gaspard slips out unnoticed to join the child to lead it to a more favourable hiding spot in a tree. Once hidden, Gaspard's wound begins bleeding profusely again and he loses consciousness, falling out of the tree and alerting the nearby searchers of the child's whereabouts. The child, recognising Gaspard's loyalty and friendship, does not desert him and as a result, is returned to its guardian.

It is whilst Gaspard is recovering from this accident and lapsing in and out of consciousness that a map appears to him. In his hallucinations, 'Gaspard would see a forest with very tall trees. He would walk for hours in the forest, then arrive at its edge. Bright light would stream between the tree trunks. He would near the edge, then leave the forest and all of a sudden, a vast geographical map would spread out before him in the grass of the fields, with roads and real towns' (52). Gaspard who has never travelled anywhere and who barely knows the local towns mentioned in the radio alert announcing the runaway child, now accesses a vast cartography emanating from within. The apparition of this map and his subsequent encounter with an anomalous piebald horse is the catalyst for the search for the runaway child who intrigues him. It marks the beginning of an incredible journey, taking Gaspard on foot, on horseback, bicycle, canal boat and yacht, to the north through the Ardennes countryside, across the border into Belgium to Antwerp and then to Bermuda, aided by the colourful characters of Baisemain the barber, travelling musician Niklaas Cramer and his sons Ludovic and Jérôme, and the young, entrepreneurial Théodule Residore who he encounters on the way.

In the second part of the narrative, Gaspard's search shifts from finding the fugitive child from Antwerp, who he now knows as Hélène, to locating Hélène's homeland which she recalls being a curious region where oaks, birch and apple trees stand alongside palm trees on the edge of an immense sea. In one of her few childhood possessions, an old picture book, there is also the annotation 'Mummy Jenny at home in the great country' (152), followed by the words 'you will come' (153). This mysterious homeland of her early childhood seems utterly elusive and Gaspard becomes increasingly frustrated that he is merely looping back on himself in his wanderings. To assuage his doubts, Niklaas takes Gaspard up the cathedral tower of the Belgian city of Mechlin, and when Gaspard questions why this will help him, Niklaas replies:

> you need to learn how to listen [. . .] even to useless things. You need to learn how to see as well [. . .] Look at the surrounding area, and this lake over there, and the villages further out. If you want to discover what you are seeking, Gaspard, you must try to read the signs in things. Observe these gardens, these parks, with their banks of flowers, the crossings of pathways. (199)

Niklaas impresses on Gaspard the need to draw on his innate nomadism – which first revealed itself to Gaspard during his convalescence in his cartographic hallucination – and to be the nomad who, as Rosi Braidotti describes, 'knows how to read invisible maps, or maps written in the wind, on sand and stones, in the flora' (Braidotti 2011: 45).

For Deleuze and Guattari, the nomad is 'the Deterritorialised par excellence' (ATP 381E/473F). Gaspard has uprooted himself on an inexplicable urge initially to find the fugitive child and then to pursue her dream of finding *le grand pays* that both torments and fascinates her. Gaspard's encounter with the piebald horse – which 'seemed to belong to the strange world that provoked Gabrielle's indignation, and which intrigued Gaspard to the utmost' (Dhôtel 2015: 56) – whilst picking strawberries following his convalescence, allows the becoming which takes him away from Lominval, from his aunt's protective, yet restrictive home space. In symbiosis with the peculiar horse, Gaspard 'was no longer thinking about Lominval. He had the impression that he would never see the village again' (65). He feels that the horse will take him to 'the ends of the earth' (80), and in every moment that Gaspard moves further away from Lominval, his nomadism increases.

Leen de Bolle suggests that 'the nomad is indeed the person *par excellence* who encounters the new. In his travelling he leaves behind all acquired convictions and identifications. The nomad discharges himself to become empty and to travel on without roots, memories, or burdens' (De Bolle 2010: 133). Gaspard is such an empty vessel: his roots in his home village of Lominval are not truly his own, but imposed on him through circumstance, through his parents' relinquishing of their son to his aunt. During Gaspard's incredible journey, there are multiple occasions where the chance to regain his sedentary homelife presents itself. After his first night away, Gaspard impresses on Baisemain, the strange barber who accosts him in Fumay upon Gaspard and the piebald horse's tumultuous arrival there: 'in any case, I must get back to Lominval' (Dhôtel 2015: 73). Baisemain urges Gaspard to find Théodule Residore, a deaf, entrepreneurial fifteen-year-old boy who will be able to help him further. The boy Residore is convinced Gaspard must go to Antwerp even if Gaspard is not sure of it himself. His deafness means Gaspard's pleas to return go literally unheard.

Théodule Residore accompanies Gaspard on bicycle across the border. It is during this part of his journey that 'Gaspard felt carefree. It was simply life, with its many pathways' (96). 'He had nothing else to do but to let himself be led along' (97). From this point onwards, Gaspard no longer feels obliged to return to Lominval but allows himself to succumb to his nomadism and to accede to the journey unfolding before him with its 'multiple pathways' (97). This journey takes him to Hélène who is living on Monsieur Drapeur's yacht in Antwerp, and then on to Bermuda as a kitchen-hand on board Drapeur's yacht. Gaspard, with Hélène, plans and attempts to help her escape from her residence in Bermuda, but their plans fail as Hélène falls from a window and is seriously injured. As a result of this injury, Gaspard's journey loops back on itself as he and Hélène return by yacht to Antwerp. Gaspard is made to placate Hélène with a promise to find her *grand pays*, and is put on a train back to Brussels, after being threatened never to follow through with his promise. Whilst waiting for the train to depart, his thoughts turn once more to the piebald horse and he makes a decision to jump off the train, allowing his journey to burgeon once more.

By now, Gaspard is the 'subject who has relinquished all idea, desire, or nostalgia for fixity [. . .] The nomadic subject, however, is not altogether devoid of unity: his mode is one of definite, seasonal patterns of movement through rather fixed routes. It is a cohesion engendered by repetitious, cyclical moves, rhythmic displacements' (Braidotti 2011: 57–8). Indeed, there is a repetitious pattern to Gaspard's wanderings. His outward journey takes him from Lominval to Antwerp and on to Bermuda. After Hélène's accident, Gaspard is returned to Antwerp, and almost to his aunt who will be waiting for him at Brussels railway station. His escape from the train allows him to double-back on himself and he re-encounters the travelling musicians who understand his need to keep his promise to Hélène and find her homeland. Their travels return Gaspard to the forest near Lominval, the forest in which he feels most at home. There, Gaspard discovers a *château* whose grounds resemble Hélène's vision and where Jenny's name appears on a wall. The *château*'s current owner is the film producer Émile Residore, father to Théodule.

Gaspard returns to Hélène and takes her to meet Émile Residore. Convinced that she has found her homeland in his *château* grounds, Hélène remains at the *château* to begin a new life as a would-be film star. A further encounter with the piebald horse takes Gaspard back to Théodule Residore, where he discovers Hélène's guardian and Émile Residore have contacted each other and have schemed this scenario together. Hélène has not been liberated but is as much a prisoner in this new life as she was before.

In a similar vein to Carroll's *Through the Looking-Glass*, Dhôtel's novel begins with isolation and restriction. As his aunt's ward, Gaspard is removed from the deterritorialising influence of his itinerant parents. Obliged to work in his aunt's guesthouse, he is subject to the hierarchical structure of the household and made to conform to his aunt's strict social expectations. The fugitive child, Hélène, is even more closely monitored than Gaspard, given her frequent attempts to escape her guardian. When she believes she has found what she is looking for in the landscape of the *château* grounds, her deterritorialisation is, in fact, a further reterritorialisation. In 'What Children Say', Deleuze states that 'there is never a moment when children are not already plunged into an actual milieu in which they are moving about, and in which the parents as persons simply play the roles of openers or closers of doors, guardians of thresholds, connectors or disconnectors of zones' (CC 62E/82F). In *Le Pays où l'on n'arrive jamais*, substitute parental figures (Gaspard's aunt, Monsieur Drapeur, Émile Residore) are closers of doors, stifling the movement of their wards, whereas the other child figures in the text (Niklaas's sons, Ludovic and Jérôme, Théodule Residore) encourage and promote their wanderings. The itinerant adult figures (Baisemain, Niklaas), with whom Gaspard has colourful, albeit fleeting encounters, are more hesitant connectors of zones, sometimes suggesting Gaspard's reterritorialisation and his return to Lominval, before facilitating his journey. Gaspard and Hélène are therefore in a constant flux of de- and re-territorialisation with children who promote their lines of flight and adults who desire their reterritorialisation. Deleuze notes that 'children go fast because they know how to glide between' (D 32E/41F): with the aid of other children and itinerant adults, Gaspard and Hélène are able to slip through the fissures of the rigid segmentarities that attempt to contain them.

Gaspard once again helps Hélène escape, and in fleeing the confines of the *château* they encounter Niklaas, his sons and the piebald horse again. Whilst pulling Niklaas's caravan, the piebald horse suddenly takes off on its own wild trajectory, leading Gaspard and his companions to a village fair where they discover a tent with the name *Maman Jenny* on it. Hélène's search finally concludes: she finds her long-lost family, dispersed and displaced as a result of the war. Gaspard, too, reconnects with his parents, who he discovers now travel with Jenny. Deleuze and Guattari question whether 'voyages are always a return to rigid segmentarity? Is it always your daddy and mommy that you meet when you travel, even as far away as the South Seas, like Melville?' (ATP 199E/244F). In the case of Gaspard and Hélène, however, the children have not returned to their stifling adoptive homes, but have found a nomadic home, with parents who inhabit a supple space, devoid of all constraints. With no fixed abode and no fixed identities, Gaspard and Hélène's families are free to uproot themselves and move off at any time. Their itinerancy places them on a perpetual line of flight, in the middle, between points.

Even though Gaspard and Hélène reach their destination in some respects, they discover that *le grand pays* is always beyond reach. Their vagabond movements link them inextricably to the landscape they are seeking, and yet, by its own nature, this landscape permanently escapes them. Gaspard realises as the novel concludes that 'the great country's horizon is constantly receding in the depths of space and time' (Dhôtel 2015: 229). Freed from restrictions of place, their past identities effaced, Gaspard and Hélène find their place whilst realising that their place will always be elsewhere in the temporal and spatial fissure that is the *grand pays*. Danielle Henky considers that for Dhôtel's protagonists 'it is possible to live the adventure endlessly whilst never giving up their childhood universe' (Henky 2012: 75). Such a view aligns itself with the difficulties of the growing-up motif in children's literature discussed in the previous chapter. The fissures in the rigid segmentarity that the search for the elusive *grand pays* creates, however, permit a temporal unhinging. Rather than being stuck in a perpetual childhood, Gaspard and Hélène – on the cusp of adulthood, aged fifteen, and in their pursuit of the *grand pays* – discover access to Aiôn and the contiguity of their child and adult selves.

Desert Islands: Worlds Without Others, Worlds Out of Time

In his essay entitled 'Causes and Reasons of Desert Islands' dating from the 1950s, Deleuze writes of Daniel Defoe's *Robinson Crusoe*: 'one can hardly imagine a more boring novel and it is sad to see children still reading it today' (DI E12/15F), adding quite gleefully 'any healthy reader would dream of seeing [Friday] eat Robinson' (DI E12/15F). In her reading of Tournier's *Vendredi ou les limbes du Pacifique* Mary Bryden notes that 'Deleuze's jocular comment [...] made many years before *Vendredi ou les limbes du Pacifique* was written, [...] might be seen to anticipate it' (Bryden 2007: 103). With the advent of Tournier's two *Fridays*, *Vendredi ou les limbes du Pacifique*[9] in 1967 and *Vendredi ou la vie sauvage*[10] in 1971, 'Deleuze's dream come[s] true. Although no cannibalism is practised between the two men, there is a certain reciprocal ingestion that characterises' both novels (Philippopoulos-Mihalopoulos 2012: 92). With Vendredi now in eponymous position in Tournier's texts, Robinson, after an initial period of isolation on Speranza, his remote island, and after the violent explosion that destroys all his attempts at recreating civilisation, finds himself swept up, consumed by Vendredi's way of life and vision of the world. 'Tournier's Vendredi *does* eat Robinson, in a sense, in that he assimilates him into his own life and manner of being' (Bryden 2007: 103, original emphasis). Vendredi's manner of being is one of becoming and is aligned with the nature of the island. This Tournier evokes in the title of his second *Friday*, *Vendredi ou la vie sauvage*[11] – Friday or the untamed life.

Vendredi begins to pull away from Robinson's attempts at civilisation, shortly before the dramatic explosion, when Robinson retreats to the island's cave for the first time after Vendredi's arrival. 'Since Robinson was not there, all these white-man obligations disappeared and Vendredi had only to obey his Indian heart' (Tournier 2012: 86). Vendredi embarks on an adventure, free from Robinson's stratifying demands. Finding a chest of rich fabrics and jewels, Vendredi sets about dressing up cactuses with 'vaguely human forms' (87). Once finished he contemplates his handiwork: 'this crowd of ladies, of prelates, of major-domos and of quirky monsters who in their sumptuous finery seemed to contort themselves, to bow and curtesy to each other, to dance a fantastic and motionless ballet. [Vendredi] laughed very loudly and imitated these absurd figures by gesticulating and jumping on the spot' (87). After this entertaining episode, Vendredi moves into the forest, where Robinson eventually finds him.

> The Indian had hidden his head under a hat of plants and flowers. All over his body, with jenipapo juice – a plant which gives a green ink when one of its stems is broken – he had drawn branches and leaves which climbed, winding up his thighs and his torso. Disguised in this way as a plant-man and still roaring with laughter, he performed a triumphant dance around Robinson. (Tournier 2012: 93)

These entertaining, almost childlike episodes in which Vendredi rediscovers the joy of island life, firstly augmented by civilisation's adornments and secondly drawn from the island itself, anticipate Robinson's liberation to come. After the explosion, which 'entrains a literal *devenir-elementaire* [becoming-elemental], in that it fragments and molecularises the solid accumulations which have bolstered Robinson's sense of well-being up to now' (Bryden 2007: 111), Robinson begins a new life. He takes siestas as he feels the need, cuts his beard and lets his hair grow long: 'he seemed much younger, almost Vendredi's brother. He no longer looked like a governor and even less like a general' (Tournier 2012: 101).

With Vendredi, Robinson learns the simple pleasures of shooting arrows, not for any practical necessity but merely 'for the pleasure of seeing them soar in the sky, like seagulls' (Tournier 2012: 103). Together they discover the silent beauty of gunpowder. Since Robinson's weapons were destroyed in the explosion, there is no need to store the gunpowder salvaged from the shipwreck. One evening, Vendredi takes a handful of gunpowder from a keg and throws it into the fire. 'Robinson had stepped backwards fearing an explosion. There was no explosion, only a large green flame that rose up in a storm-like puff of wind and disappeared instantly' (116–17). Mixing the remaining gunpowder with resin, they rub it onto the island's dead trees, setting them alight so that a 'whole tree was covered with a palpitating golden shell, and it burned until the morning like a great fiery candelabra' (117).

In the years preceding the explosion, Robinson had taught Vendredi English by showing him an object, saying its name and having Vendredi repeat it. On one occasion afterwards, Vendredi notices a small white spot in the grass and the following exchange occurs:

> – Daisy.
> – Yes, replied Robinson, it's a daisy.
> No sooner had he uttered these words, than the daisy flapped its wings and flew off.

> – You see, he said straightaway, we were wrong. It wasn't a daisy, it was a butterfly.
> – A white butterfly, replied Vendredi, it is a daisy that flies. (Tournier 2012: 119)

In his previous existence, Robinson would have become angry with Vendredi. He would have persisted and forced Vendredi to admit his error, but after the explosion, in the realisation that 'he had had enough of this boring and problematic organisation, but that he hadn't the courage to destroy it' (99), Robinson does not seek to argue with Vendredi. Robinson only desires closeness to Vendredi and it is this proximity that facilitates his becomings. In no longer keeping Vendredi a subservient figure, distanced and remote, to be educated in Robinson's westernised ways, Robinson is gradually contaminated by Vendredi. Vendredi 'alone is able to guide and complete the metamorphosis Robinson began and to reveal to him its sense and its aim' (LOS 354E/367F). His laughter, his joyfulness, his oneness with nature lead Robinson to his own becomings: becomings-aerial, as he observes the flight of the arrows; becomings-fire as he watches the resin-covered trees burn in the liberation of the gunpowder; becomings-daisy, as he appreciates the indistinction of the daisy-butterfly.

Vendredi 'restores the earth, but also water and fire, to the sky. It is he who makes the dead goat (=Robinson) fly and sing' (LOS 354E/367F). The dead goat in question is the anomalous leader of the herd of goats inhabiting the island, named Andoar by Vendredi. The 'king-goat' (Tournier 2012: 128) is antagonised by Vendredi's intimate and sensual relationship with the she-goat: 'Vendredi and Anda were inseparable. At night, Vendredi would cover himself with the warm and living fur of Anda, spread out on him. During the day, she never left his side' (130). Their ensuing battle culminates in Vendredi and Andoar locking together, Vendredi clinging to the beast's back. Despite Vendredi's attempts to stop Andoar and Andoar's attempts to throw Vendredi from his back, both plummet off a precipice: a failed flight pre-empting Andoar's flight to come and Robinson's 'aerial-oriented life phase' (Bryden 2007: 113). Vendredi recognises that 'the great goat died saving me' adding, to Robinson's bemusement, 'but I will soon make him fly and sing' (Tournier 2012: 137). Deleuze, recognising the importance of Vendredi's curious undertaking, describes it at the start of his essay on Tournier thus:

> in the first stage of the project, he makes use of the skin. The hair is removed, the skin is washed, pumiced, and spread out on a wooden

structure. Bound to a fishing pole, the goat amplifies the least movement of the line, assumes the role of a gigantic celestial bobber, and transcribes the waters onto the sky. As for the second stage, Friday makes use of the head and the gut and fashions from them an instrument; he places it in a dead tree in order to produce an instantaneous symphony whose sole performer must be the wind. [...] In these two ways, the great goat frees the Elements. (LOS 341E/350–1F)

Through Vendredi's lengthy preparations, the once earth-bound dead goat is transformed into a dancing kite[12] and an aeolian harp, and from these, into pure states of air-borne movement and sound: 'thus flying-Andoar and singing-Andoar appeared reunited in the same sombre celebration. And above all, there was this deep and beautiful music, so harrowing that one would have said it was the lament of the great goat, who died, saving Vendredi' (Tournier 2012: 147). In life, Andoar could not tolerate his rider; in death he 'becomes the vehicle for Robinson's travel towards the solar element' (Bryden 2007: 113).[13]

Deleuze's treatment of Tournier's *Vendredi ou les limbes du Pacifique* is an interrogation of what happens when Others are removed from the structure of the world. For Deleuze, when this is the case, 'there reigns alone the brutal opposition of the sun and earth, of an unbearable light and an obscure abyss' (LOS 345E/355F). This opposition is most starkly illustrated with the episode of Robinson's exploration of the cave in the centre of the isle. Despite using it as a storage facility, for food, clothing, tools, weapons, and further back his barrels of gunpowder, Robinson had never explored the depths of the cave. Determined to undertake this exploration but unable to take a torch with him for fear of making the gunpowder explode, Robinson has no choice but to 'accept the darkness and try to get used to it' (Tournier 2012: 59). As the last rays of daylight penetrate the cave, Robinson slips into a cycle of sleeping and eating, which lasts for several days. Then, having lost all notion of time, he goes further into the cave where he finds a 'sort of tepid niche' (60). To access this niche, he must undress and rub himself in his remaining goat's milk, which enables him to slip inside, 'hunched up on himself, his knees tucked up to his chin, his shins crossed, his hands placed on his feet' (60). In this foetal position, he falls asleep only to find on his waking that '*the darkness had become brightness around him. He was still not able to see anything there, but he was immersed in brightness and not in darkness*' (60, original emphasis).

This brightness makes Robinson think of his mother, of being cradled in her arms, and allows him to recall his childhood memories of the preparation of the *gâteau des Rois*,[14] the traditional cake for the feast of Epiphany: 'it seemed to Robinson that the whole isle of Speranza was an immense cake and that he was himself the little bean hidden deep down in the crust' (61). The psychoanalytic undertones of this passage are clear: Robinson wallows in the womb-like comfort of the cave and relishes 'the marvellous peace of his childhood' (63) that he discovers there. Casting himself a 'little bean' allows him to both impregnate his luscious Speranza and to be birthed by the island as he overcomes the temptation to remain there and emerges from the cave. The ingestion of Robinson into the island which in turn pre-empts Vendredi's ingestion of Robinson to come; the repetitive cycles of eating and sleeping that precede the discovery of the womb-like niche; the coating of goat's milk that Robinson requires to enter the niche, return Robinson to an infantile state of oral fixation. For Deleuze, 'this is a regression much more fantastic than the regression of neurosis inasmuch as it reaches back to the Earth-Mother – the primordial Mother' (LOS 353F/365F). In his a-temporal and a-spatial cave, Robinson is utterly alone and 'attempts to compensate for the absence of real Others by [. . .] organising a superhuman filiation' (LOS 353E/366F) with the very fabric of the island that envelops him.

But what of this curious inversion of perception that Robinson encounters in the cave, where he perceives the absolute darkness of the cave as a bright whiteness all around him? In a situation such as Robinson's, there is no Other who can ground his perceptions, who can stop day slipping into night; dark becoming light. This is 'the adventure of depth. The structure-Other organizes and pacifies depth. It renders it livable' (LOS 353E/366F). Without the structure-Other everything is in disarray: we cannot make sense, we cannot perceive.

> *The Other* is the structure that conditions the entire field of perception. The Other renders perception possible, along with its functioning, and renders possible *ab initio* the constitution and application of the categories of subject and object [. . .] The Other renders perception possible because it spatializes (forms, unforms, or coordinates spaces) and temporalizes. Without this, perception would not be possible. (Boundas 1994: 112, original emphasis)

The only salvation possible for Robinson, like Lewis Carroll's Alice, after her sojourn in the depths of Wonderland, is to 'return to the surface and discover surfaces' (LOS 354E/366F). After Vendredi's arrival Robinson only returns the cave to wallow in its tranquillity once more. It is, then, Vendredi who brings Robinson out of the abyss, out of the intoxicating, perception-altering depths of the cave. It is Vendredi who draws him to the surface and facilitates not only Robinson's movement towards the surface but beyond towards the sky and towards becoming-aerial.

'When Robinson encounters Friday, he will no longer apprehend him as an Other' (LOS 348E/359F), writes Deleuze; rather Vendredi 'presents to Robinson the image of the personal double' (LOS 354E/367F). In *Vendredi ou la vie sauvage*, Vendredi introduces Robinson to two games of doubles. Robinson, physically sickened at the fricassee of python Vendredi presents him, knocks his plate onto the floor. Rather than coming to blows, the furious Vendredi disappears and returns with a mannequin-like figure fabricated from coconuts and bamboo canes which he introduces to Robinson as 'Robinson Crusoe, governor of the Isle of Speranza' (Tournier 2012: 110). Vendredi picks up the discarded plate, cracks it over the mannequin's head, and bursts out laughing before embracing the real Robinson. Robinson in turn sculpts a sand statue of Vendredi upon which he takes out his frustrations. 'From that moment on, there were four of them living on the island. There was the real Robinson and the doll Robinson, the real Vendredi and the doll Vendredi and anything that the two friends may have done to upset each other, insults, blows, fits of anger – they aimed at the copy of the other' (111). This precedes another game which takes this reciprocal doubling further still. In this second game invented by Vendredi no physical likeness is produced. Instead, Vendredi pretends to be Robinson, leaving Robinson to assume to role of Vendredi. In the same way that the game of mannequins allows the friends to vent their frustrations with each other, this second game allows Vendredi in particular to dominate Robinson, as Robinson first did with Vendredi on his arrival on the island.

These amusing and inventive games of mimicry have clear 'psychotherapeutic purposes' (Beckett 2009: 76), and whilst they introduce a notion of the double, they are nonetheless firmly anchored within the structure-Other that organises the world. Robinson perceives the collection of bamboo canes and coconuts as an imitation of himself. It is Vendredi's intention that Robinson takes this collection of sticks and nuts to resemble him. The Other 'sets up a world in which desire is constrained by a field of possibilities adumbrated by what is possible for others' (Bourassa 2015: 145). Vendredi, however, is not of this structure. Vendredi is 'not an Other, but something wholly other (*un tout-autre*) than the Other; not a replica, but a Double: one who reveals pure elements and dissolves objects, bodies, and the earth' (LOS 355E/368F). Vendredi is the great liberator, freer of the elements, who permits self and other to dissolve in his presence. He is not an Other to confirm that light is light or dark is dark, but the Other than Other who liberates in Robinson these previously trapped elemental forces, forces of lightness and darkness, fire and air.

Not only is Vendredi Robinson's Double, he is also a child. Indeed, Deleuze briefly recognises the child-like surface nature of Vendredi, writing: 'what is to be said of Friday, if not that he is a mischievous child, wholly at the surface' (LOS 355E/367F). Like an untamed, unsupervised child, he laughs, dances and covers himself in dye. His games of make-believe, of dressing up, his creativity and ingenious ideas, render him a ludic presence on the island. Whilst Sandra Beckett notes that '*Vendredi ou la vie sauvage* bestows particular importance to the child and its universe' (Beckett 1997: 138), few critics pursue this aspect of the novel. Not only does Vendredi draw Robinson out of the depths of a futile regression to a lost, past childhood, up to the surface, he puts him in touch through becomings-elemental with his molecular child. In emerging from the cave, Robinson relinquishes the child he once was, about whom he phantasises; he rids himself of this molar child whose adult future he is now experiencing. Robinson moves away from a personal childhood to an indefinite, impersonal childhood open to experimentation and creativity. Robinson reaches his molecular child through entering into a zone of proximity with Vendredi, the creative, unpredictable surface-child.

Robinson's molecular child unsettles his pre-established structures and allows him to shed the corporeal time of his clepsydra, his water-clock which drives him to observe strict routines and to striate the island around him. Robinson can now enjoy the incorporeal time of the island, far from the dictates of an enforced civilisation. In this island Aiôn, he changes physically, ageing in reverse to resemble Vendredi's brother. Newly liberated on the island, Robinson becomes a molecular child, the adult he is with the child he was, enjoying a contiguity of childhood and adulthood. Hints of this temporal limbo enjoyed on the island are more evident in *Vendredi ou les limbes du Pacifique*: the title of Tournier's first *Friday* 'points to an alignment with Limbo, itself an intermediate dwelling place' (Bryden 2007: 114) out of normal time. Aiôn, as we have seen, is never fully without

Chronos, and Chronos erupts into the Aiôn of Speranza at the arrival of the *Whitebird*. On meeting the *Whitebird*'s captain for the first time, Robinson immediately asks him the date and discovers that he has been on the island for 'exactly twenty-eight years, two months and twenty-two days' (Tournier 2012: 150). Robinson quickly calculates that he is therefore fifty years old, and yet 'thanks to the free and happy life he was leading on Speranza, thanks above all to Vendredi, he felt younger and younger' (151). Similar to Lewis Carroll's Alice, Robinson is pulled in two directions at once: there is no directional impetus to Robinson's ageing on Speranza, rather, as a molecular child, Robinson undergoes an involutionary growth, a simultaneous past-future ageing in Aiôn.

The arrival of the *Whitebird* entrains the sudden departure of Vendredi, who succumbs to the pull of the 'beautiful sailing boat, svelte, light and white, [it] was certainly the most marvellous aerial thing he had ever seen' (154). Distraught by Vendredi's departure and by the idea that the liberating Vendredi will now be enslaved by the crew of the *Whitebird*, Robinson has only one thought: to return to his cave and await death, having lost his Double and rejected the Structure-Other that the *Whitebird* represents. On his way to the cave Robinson discovers the ship's boy who has escaped the brutal treatment on board and taken refuge on the island. In *Vendredi ou les limbes du Pacifique*, Robinson names the ship's boy *Jeudi* or Thursday: 'You will be called Thursday. It is the day of Jupiter, god of the sky. It is also the Sunday of children' (272). This child 'descended from the sky, not grown from the earth or in woman [...] Created from a union between Robinson and the sky, Jeudi, son of Jupiter, is a solar miracle [...] he is the apotheosis of Robinson's own metamorphosis' (Jardine 2001: 1141). In *Vendredi ou la vie sauvage*, however, Robinson decides to name him 'Sunday. It is the day of feasts, of laughter, of games. And for me you will always be the Sunday's child' (Tournier 2012: 165). In both texts, childhood wins out, but in *Vendredi ou la vie sauvage*, Tournier shifts the focus subtly from the sky to that of the essence of childhood. Tournier's desert island is, then, a world of Doubles, of child-Doubles and a world out of time, where childhood endures across all time.

Conclusion: Moving Rhizomatically

The home-away-home motif so prevalent in children's literature perpetuates a false impression of journeying and movement. Travelling

Lines, Maps and Islands

with Deleuze requires us to forego fixed starting and end points and to move rhizomatically, from and through the middle, not tracing well-known routes and paths, but creating new lines and composing maps.

We are all traversed by various types of line: rigid molar lines which contain us, regulate us, fix us into discreet identities and onto predetermined pathways; supple molecular lines which create cracks within the regime, which act upon the molar to disrupt it and interfere with it; and lines of flight – dynamic, zigzagging lines which carry us off towards unknown, unpredictable destinations. The milieus or environments in which children find themselves are traversed by lines of flight, possibilities for deterritorialisation, for seeping out and for breaking free.

Children are always making and modifying maps of their environments or *milieus*, as the endpaper maps of children's literature depict. These are real-imaginary maps, open and connectable, with varied entryways and exits. Additions of colour and other annotations capture real and imaginary trajectories and the becomings that lie beneath them. These coalesce to form a 'mobile mirror' of actual and virtual landscapes – vision – to take us beyond ourselves, on the path to becoming.

Children who have access to a map within, like André Dhôtel's Gaspard and Hélène, are caught in an ongoing flux of de-and re-territorialisation. Parental figures in their lives attempt to block and cut short lines of flight promoted by other children and itinerant adult figures. Drawing on their innate nomadism, these children are able to slip between the confining, stratifying lines imposed on them. Their 'return home' is a liberating one: a new nomadic home devoid of fixity of time, place or identity.

The faraway landscape of the *grand pays*, like Tournier's desert island, is a place beyond time. A landscape of Aiôn where childhood endures. A landscape of the creative and capricious surface-child, whose ageing is no longer a concern. Rather, in these incorporeal landscapes, childhood concerns move from the personal to the impersonal, from the definite to the indefinite, from the depths to the surface. The following chapter takes up this concept of surface to consider how language can be pushed through its own fragile surface of sense to its outside, and allows a new perspective on the notion of (non)sense in children's literature.

Notes

1. In distinguishing between these two terms of cartography and decalcomania (a process of transferring pictures from a specially prepared paper to surfaces such as glass or porcelain), Deleuze and Guattari are careful to point out that they have not 'reverted to a simple dualism' (ATP 13E/21F): the map may break down and turn into a tracing and conversely the tracing may and should feed back into the map, only then are the inherent blockages of the tracing overcome and transformed. A tracing is a molar line, a pre-prescribed pathway in containable, definable categorises. A tracing should not be confused with the expression *to trace a line* which occurs throughout Deleuze's work and which is a liberating action.
2. The French prefix *dé-* expresses the notions of distancing, removal, withdrawal, destruction. *Terre* is French for earth, but also for soil, ground, land. The verb *dé-terrer* means to pull up, to uproot (as in potatoes from the ground).
3. *Milieu* is French for environment, but also has a rhizomatic meaning of the middle.
4. Deleuze's example of a child's milieu comes from Freud's case study of Little Hans' fear of the horses he sees on the streets. Freud interprets this as a manifestation of the castration complex. Deleuze reads the horses Hans encounters as elements of the milieu he occupies.
5. The endpaper map is found in many iconic children's texts such as A. A. Milne's *Winnie-the-Pooh*, Kenneth Grahame's *The Wind in the Willows*, and Tove Janesson's *Moominland Midwinter*, etc. For a detailed account of the many maps in children's literature see Pavlik 2010.
6. The reader's imagination is called upon when reading the text, as transitions between the squares of the board landscape are marked by ****.
7. See Lecercle (2002) for a reading of Alice's nonsensical train as a collective assemblage of enunciation.
8. It is worth considering the meaning of the French *pays*. This masculine noun has many translations, including 'country' (*un pays scandinave*, a Scandinavian country); 'land', 'region' or 'area' (*un pays montagneux*, mountainous region). The phrase *avoir le mal du pays* means to be homesick whilst *etre un enfant du pays* implies being local to a given area. Hélène is looking for *le grand pays* – her homeland, and thanks to the descriptions that come with it, there is a sense of greatness to this homeland, vastness and immensity.
9. In the appendices to *The Logic of Sense*, Deleuze includes an essay entitled, 'Michel Tournier and the World without Others', about Tournier's first Friday, *Vendredi ou les limbes du Pacifique*. This has been included

as a postface in Folio's paperback edition of the text since. Tournier's text is, for Deleuze, 'an extraordinary novel' (LOS 359E/372F), where 'the isle is as much the hero of the novel as Robinson or Friday' (LOS 342E/351F). For Tournier, the addition of Deleuze's postface to the first Friday was a source of 'pleasure and pride' (Beckett 2009: 78). Sandra Beckett continues to cite Tournier, who claims that '"the proof of the novel's success is the response that it was able to elicit from two readers at opposite poles of sophistication: a child at one end of the scale, a metaphysician at the other"' (78). Tournier's comments once more bring the presumed child-adult binary and the otherness of the child to the fore, as discussed in the Introduction.

10. In the years that followed the publication of *Vendredi ou la vie sauvage*, a shift in Tournier's nomenclature for the text occurs. Sandra Beckett outlines the transition in his own classification of the text in *Crossover Fiction: Global and Historical Perspectives*. It merits quoting at length, to capture the looking-glass logic of Tournier's reasoning: 'initially, he himself called the novel "the children's version" of the first Friday and an article published at the time of the book's launching was titled "When Michel Tournier rewrites his books for children." [...] The author describes [a] step that preceded the actual rewriting. An unformulated "children's version" of the novel had somehow pre-existed the adult versions in his mind: "Translating Friday into Friday and Robinson, I had the distinct feeling I was taking a path already travelled in the opposite direction ... in a sense, I was only able to derive a children's novel because the latter had itself been taken from the former in the first place." By the 1980s, Tournier regretted that his bestselling novel was classified as a "children's book," insisting that the shorter text is not an adaptation for children but rather a new and improved version. The author continues to maintain that there are merely two Fridays, and that the shorter one is the result of an evolution of his art toward a more perfect text that appeals to a crossover audience' (Beckett 2009: 75).

11. Whilst I focus solely on Tournier's second *Friday*, *Vendredi ou la vie sauvage*, it is worth noting some key differences between the two volumes which serve to muddy the classification of this text further. Although Tournier's second *Friday* is substantially shorter than his first, he nonetheless wrote new material for the second version which, in turn, made its way into the adult version, as Beckett describes: 'some scenes were introduced into the revised adult paperback edition in 1972, notably the highly significant game of effigies [...]. Tournier claims that these appropriations make it difficult to say whether the adult version or the children's version is really the original' (Beckett 2009: 76). Another notable difference between the two texts is the absence of the scenes of a sexual nature, depicting Robinson and

Vendredi's carnal relationship with Speranza. In his second *Friday*, Tournier replaced many of the more explicit scenes of *Vendredi ou les limbes du Pacifique* with more ambiguous, sensual scenes of Vendredi and the she-goat, Anda, leaving Tournier accused of 'bowdlerizing his own books by critics who disapprove of the self-censorship [he] applies when he rewrites an adult novel for a young audience' (Beckett 2009: 77). Unlike the game of effigies, the scenes where Vendredi and Anda sleep together have not been retrospectively included in subsequent editions of the adult version. It is precisely 'the absence of this passage in the adult Friday that makes *it* the bowdlerized version, according to the author' (Beckett 2009: 77 my emphasis), further blurring the boundaries between the two texts.
12. Bryden (2007) points out that the kite episode is curiously absent in the adaptation of the children's version for television.
13. Bryden notes that 'later Robinson will record in his log book: "Andoar, c'était moi"' [Andoar was me] (Bryden 2007: 113). Tournier omitted the log book from the children's novel and this direct connection between Robinson and Andoar is not as distinct.
14. A *fève* (literally a bean) is hidden in the *gâteau des Rois* (cake of the Kings) eaten in France to celebrate the arrival of the three Wise Men in Bethlehem. The *fève* is typically a small ceramic charm and the person who finds the *fève* in their slice of cake is crowned 'king'.

5
Stuttering, Nonsense and Zeroth Voice

> For the disadvantages of the Author are constituting a point of departure or of origin, forming a subject of enunciation on which all the produced utterances depend, getting recognized and identified in an order of dominant meaning or established powers: 'I in my capacity as . . .' (*Dialogues* 27E/35–6F)

For Deleuze, to write in 'one's capacity as' is one of the difficulties of authorship. To write children's literature then amplifies this difficulty and returns us to the paradox of children's literature as the adult author must write in his or her capacity as a child. There is not simply the voice of the speaking character or third person narrator to consider, however; these voices contain echoes of the other individuals involved in children's book production and provision: editor, illustrator, teacher, librarian, parent and so on. In trying to form a subject of enunciation, in trying to emulate the voices of young people in their writing, adult writers of children's literature can only produce a preconceived notion of young people's language to give them voices to read that purport to be their own but never can be.

Deleuze, with Guattari, provides us with the concepts of major and minor literature which can help us think through this paradoxical question of voice in children's literature. Those who occupy *majoritarian* positions in society have power and exercise control; those who, because of race, gender, age and so on, do not occupy this privileged position, are *minoritarian*. Deleuze and Guattari tell us that 'a minor literature doesn't come from a minor language; it is rather that which a minority constructs within a major language' (K 16E/29F). As a Prague Jew writing in German, Kafka's literary output exemplified minor literature for Deleuze and Guattari. He was, in this respect, 'like a foreigner in [his] own language' (D 4E/10F), able to deterritorialise language by abstracting it from the dominant social structures in which it finds itself and 'forcing [it] to do things its guardians never expected it could do' (Saldanha 2013: 17). Kafka therefore minorises language, 'much as in music, where the minor mode refers to dynamic combinations in perpetual disequilibrium

[. . .] he carves out a nonpreexistent foreign language *within* his own language. He makes the language itself scream, stutter, stammer, or murmur' (CC 109–10E/138F original emphasis). For Deleuze and Guattari, major literature creates individuated enunciation: in major literature there are great masters or towering individuals who dominate, whom others try to copy and imitate. Minor literature, however, is not about the single voice of some great master, but rather is the voice of collectivity, of the group who are detached from the perceived norm.

For Deleuze and Guattari, 'the three characteristics of minor literature are the deterritorialization of language, the connection of the individual to the political immediacy, and the collective assemblage of enunciation' (K 18E/33F). The first term in the phrase 'children's literature' speaks to the collective: children's literature is fundamentally about young people and is read predominantly by them. Children are also minoritarian, not necessarily in number, but in contrast to the dominant, adult world around them. Like Kafka, and many other groups in the world today, they have no language that is truly their own, but rather must negotiate the majoritarian norms that control language to find their own voice. Where deterritorialisation in Kafka is produced through his use of a language that was both his own and yet never could be, deterritorialisation occurs in children's fiction not because young people are writing it, but precisely because they are not. These majoritarian voices are problematic for children's literature: voices in children's fiction may be highly didactic and often convey distinct ideologies. Third-person narrators can clearly tell the reader what to think, and although first-person narrators can only describe what they know, they often cannot resist the urge to tell the implied reader what they have learnt (Trites 2000); children's literature cannot, therefore, be read in isolation from the socio-political environment within which it is published.

Traditional approaches to voice in children's literature attempt to position the child within ideological discourses and focus on the creation or silencing of the child's voice. In this chapter, however, I consider the child in children's literature which succeeds in minorising language, in carving out a foreign language within language and making it stutter. In the first part of this chapter, I turn to Lewis Carroll's Alice in both *Alice's Adventures in Wonderland* and *Through the Looking-Glass and What Alice Found There*. In these texts, Alice is acutely aware of the majoritarian requirements for language, but in her ambitions to demonstrate her knowledge, she succeeds in creating her own style and making language stutter. I go on to contrast Alice's surface use of language to the eponymous Devil from James Joyce's *The Cat and the Devil*, whose use of language is more guttural. The chapter then goes on to consider the surfaces on which sense is created in Carroll's texts, before moving on to analyse the figure of Humpty Dumpty who claims famously to master meaning and who, with his use of esoteric and portmanteau words, succeeds in pushing language through its fragile surface of sense to its outside. I conclude the chapter by advocating for the zeroth voice of the molecular child: a voice called out of the reading of texts which forms at the zero point of thought, as (non)sense is created.

Stuttering, Persiflage and Howl-words

When we first meet Alice, she is sitting on the riverbank with her sister, occasionally peeping into the book her sister is reading silently. The book does nothing for Alice for it has 'no pictures or conversations in it' (Carroll 2008: 23), and as a result Alice is distanced from her sister and the literary, majoritarian world she represents. To escape the boredom of her sister's silent literary world, she follows the White Rabbit down the rabbit hole, and as the rabbit hole-tunnel turns into 'a very deep well' (24), her leisurely fall gives her the chance to use her previously silenced voice, to monologue and wonder out loud. During her soliloquy, Alice attempts to demonstrate her knowledge of the major language from which she felt alienated on the riverbank. She wonders 'what Latitude or Longitude [she has] got to?' (24–5), but the meaning of these words is lost on her; for Alice, they are merely 'nice grand words to say' (24–5). As her fall continues, she wonders if she will appear on the other side of the world, in 'The Antipathies' (25) rather than in the Antipodes. Alice's ruminations reveal her awareness of another language, one which she feels the need and the desire to access, but which remains beyond her grasp. She tries, in vain, to show that she, like her elder sister, belongs to the majoritarian norm, through her mastery of the molar language, but the child's mouth deterritorialises these major words and they exit minorised: jumbled, distorted and confused.

Not only does Alice realise that she should use an elegant and precise vocabulary, she also knows that she ought to understand the rules and structures that govern this majoritarian, adult language. Obeying the grammatical terms of one's language, in both speech and writing, 'means to submit to the societal laws of one's culture, since grammar expresses the appropriate and accepted means of expression' (Albrecht-Crane 2007: 123), but as Alice's journey into Wonderland continues, she soon loses her grip on grammar and her ability to 'speak good English' (Carroll 2008: 29). Her limited knowledge slips away from her too, as she desperately attempts to cling to what she has learnt, be it multiplication tables, geography or poetry. As she begins to recite the first of the verses that permeate the text ('How doth the little – '), her voice soon 'sound[s] hoarse and strange, and the words [do] not come the same way they used to do' (31). For scholar of children's literature, Jan Susina, 'Carroll is satirizing the practice of forcing children to memorize and recite instructional verse' (Susina 2010: 39), demonstrating how such hollow exercises do not enhance a child's understanding of the subject matter. Meeting the aloof, hookah-smoking Caterpillar, for example, brings about her inventive, irreverent and amusing parody 'You Are Old, Father William'. The majoritarian caterpillar tells her 'It is wrong from beginning to end' (Carroll 2008: 54), but Alice, albeit timidly, defends her recital. Later, when the Mock Turtle tells Alice to repeat ''Tis the Voice of the Sluggard', she recognises a bastion of the majoritarian language in him and by extension the other creatures: the berating school master figure, thinking to herself: 'How the creatures order one about, and make one repeat lessons [...] I might as well be at school at once' (96). The 'uncommon nonsense' (96) that she creates despite the creatures' remonstrations and scolding, reveals Alice's non-conformity and the creative potential of her own voice. Carroll's parodic verse therefore goes beyond a mere commentary on the flaws of the contemporary system of education. In Deleuzian terms, it, along with her attempts to use a refined vocabulary, allows Alice to stutter and to make language vibrate and 'trembl[e] from head to toe' (CC 109E/137F). This stuttering initially worries Alice; she is concerned about being mistaken for Mabel who 'knows such a very little' (Carroll 2008: 31) and the social implications of this. Her muddled knowledge will mean she is 'defined as an "out-law[]", as [a] social misfit[], as other' (Albrecht-Crane 2007: 123), as a poorly educated, minoritarian child not an erudite majoritarian adult.

Whilst Alice's stuttering begins before her interaction with the various inhabitants of Wonderland, as she encounters more creatures, so her stuttering grows. The first creature she encounters is the Mouse in the pool of tears. Alice calls out: 'O Mouse! (Alice thought this must be the right way of speaking to a mouse: she had never

Stuttering, Nonsense and Zeroth Voice

done such a thing before, but she remembered having seen in her brother's Latin Grammar, "A mouse – of a mouse – to a mouse – a mouse – O mouse!"' (Carroll 2008: 34). She attempts to address the creature in an English based on a vague recollection of Latin declension: the archetypal majoritarian language to which she would be denied access based on her gender. When this Latin-based English fails her, she tries French instead, uttering 'Où est ma chatte?' (34, original italics), blindly repeating a memorised phrase without thinking of its meaning and the consequences of its use. Alice, then, mixes her child's knowledge of English, still nascent and unsure, with her even more limited knowledge of other languages, producing a bizarre and unreliable form of polyglottism. Whilst Deleuze is clear that mixing languages is not the same as minorising language – Kafka 'is a foreigner in his own language: he does not mix another language with his own language' (CC 110E/138F) – Rosi Braidotti suggests that

> the complex muscular and mental apparati that join forces in the production of language combine in the polyglot to produce strange sounds, phonetic connections, vocal combinations, and rhythmic junctures. A sort of polymorphous perversity accompanies a polyglot's accent, which reveals the capacity to slip in between the languages, stealing acoustic traces here, diphthong sounds there, in a constant and childlike game of *persiflage*. (Braidotti 2011: 40)

Braidotti's use of the French word *persiflage* fits well with Deleuze's vibrating concept of stuttering and allows Alice's stuttering to include multi-lingual elements. Persiflage is a frivolous bantering talk, mocking and light-hearted, derived from the French verb *siffler*, meaning to whistle. Alice's banter, like a whistle, is not always fully enunciated, escaping from the corners of her mouth, often in undertones either in conversation with herself or in retort to the comments of the creatures she meets. Alice's persiflage or stuttering, composed of her imperfect use of English, with hints of Latin and French, creates a unique style.

In this, Alice resembles a little-known character from children's literature, the eponymous Devil in James Joyce's *The Cat and the Devil*. Speaking primarily in English, the Devil resorts to poor French as he splutters with rage when tricked by the mayor of the town of Beaugency. In this short fairy tale, written in a letter to Stevie, Joyce's grandson, the Devil agrees a Faustian pact with the mayor: in payment for building the bridge across the wide river Loire that the people of Beaugency desperately need, the devil will take the soul of the first being to cross it. As the townspeople gather to see the new bridge, the mayor of Beaugency arrives curiously holding a white cat under one arm and a bucket of water in the other hand. After the appropriate fanfares, the mayor tips the bucket of water over the cat which, in disgust, runs across the bridge and into the arms of the Devil waiting on the other side. The Devil, in his fury, bellows at the townspeople:

> Messieurs les Balgentiens, [. . .] vous n'êtes que des chats! And he said to the cat: Viens ici, mon petit chat! Tu as peur, mon petit chou-chat? Tu as froid, mon pau-petit chou-chat? Viens ici, le diable t'emporte? On va se chauffer tous le deux. (Joyce 1975: 383)

In the edition illustrated by Rose, there is no further explanation of this outburst in French. In the edition illustrated by Erdoes, a footnote translation is provided. The Blachon edition also has such a footnote but goes further to explain that the purpose of the footnote is to help those readers who 'cannot understand very bad French very well' (Joyce 1990: np). The French translation of the text, illustrated by Corre, keeps the Devil's outburst in French and gives a footnote explanation to this effect. Joyce's original letter, and all editions of it, concludes with a postscript explanation of the Devil's linguistic abilities, and reads thus: 'the devil mostly speaks a language of his own called Bellsybabble, which he makes up himself as he goes along, but when he is very angry he can speak quite bad French very well, though some who have heard him say that he has a strong Dublin accent' (Joyce 1975: 384). Unlike Alice's persiflage, which escapes from the corners of her mouth, the Devil's own language is tied to the depths of the body. His guttural Bellsybabble[1] 'emerges ex nihilo, less an act of conscious deliberation than an almost bodily pulsion, a "belly's babble"' (Thurston 2004: 112). His cries of rage, rising from the literal depths, resemble the *mots-cris* or howl-words Deleuze sees in Antonin Artaud's schizophrenic language. For Deleuze, Artaud's language is 'carved into the depths of bodies' (LOS 96E/103F) because the surface on which sense circulates, the plane or frontier separating 'propositions and things' (LOS 99E/105F), has been prised open for the schizophrenic, leaving only a 'gaping depth' (LOS 99E/106F) from which an entirely other language emerges, with 'its consonantal, guttural, and aspirated overloads, its apostrophes and internal accents, its breaths and its scansions' (LOS 101E/109F), producing 'many active howls in one continuous breath' (LOS 102E/109F). Whilst the schizophrenic Artaud produces such howl-words as the result of intense suffering, the Devil's Bellsybabble has a more playful, almost childlike side. In a similar vein to Alice's bantering talk, the Devil's babble implies a rapid speech, silly or excited, potentially incomprehensible. A babble that is often associated with the sounds an infant makes in the early stages of language acquisition. What is more, its anagrammatic nature, which allows Bellsybabble to form *belle syllabe*, implies that even the smallest part of the Devil's utterance can create a beautiful sound. For Marie-Dominique Garnier, 'Joyce's devil speaks [...] a prototypical Wakean tongue or "belzey babble" (FW 64.11), [...] which sounds like the end product of a disassembly-line distorting Beaugency into belles gens ("Balgentiens") and "bellsy" – where Beelzebub overlaps with balls, bells and belles' (Garnier 2003: 101). Quite what this invented language may look or sound like remains unknown, for as Amanda Sigler remarks:

> we do not have any samples of Bellsybabble in Joyce's 1936 letter, except perhaps for the word 'Bellsybabble' itself. Yet illustrators such as Erdoes, Corre, and Torres have often portrayed the devil with an array of nonsensical symbols or letters emanating from his mouth. Sometimes these symbols include characters from the English alphabet; at other times (such as in Erdoes), they suggest characters from Asian and Native American languages. (Sigler 2008: 548)

Whilst representation of the Devil's Bellsybabble is unnecessary, since, in these howl-words, 'all literal, syllabic, and phonetic values have been replaced by *values which are exclusively tonic* and not written' (LOS 101E/108F original emphasis), these images nevertheless reinforce the Devil's polyglottism. The Erdoes illustration of Bellsybabble, in addition to the characters mentioned above, includes hieroglyphs and pictographs. In the illustration by Corre, a complete menagerie of animals also appears in the Devil's Bellsybabble speech bubble. Amongst the snakes, hedgehogs, fish, owls and crocodiles, suggesting an array of animal becomings brought about by these howl-words, there are also witches in flight. In *A Thousand Plateaus*, Deleuze and Guattari align the figure of the Devil to that of the witch; both being capable of transporting us to strange becomings (ATP 252–3E/309–10F). The Devil's howling then makes 'language take flight, [...] send[ing] it racing along a witch's line, ceaselessly placing it in a state of disequilibrium, making it bifurcate and vary in each of its terms, following an incessant modulation' (CC 109–10).

Alice's stuttering style, the Devil's often inaccurate use of major codes and the howling language of his own creation, reveal 'the moment when language is no longer defined by what it says, even less by what makes it a signifying thing, but by what causes it to move, to flow, and to explode – desire' (AO 145E/158F). Alice and the somewhat childlike Devil find their voice by playing with language and languages in all their forms, unburdened by grammatical rules, shunning all established codes and inventing anew. The Devil's howling is produced from the depths whereas Alice's stuttering is tied to the surface, letting language seep out from the mouth that produces it to follow its own rhizomatic course, for 'creative stuttering is what makes language grow from the middle, like grass; it is what makes language a rhizome instead of a tree' (CC 111E/140F). In his Bellsybabble, in her muddling up words, in her mis-recital of lessons and poems, in playing with other languages, language in both Alice's and the Devil's mouth becomes free, expressive, rich and creative. Alice's voice, previously silenced by her status as a child and by societal etiquette, not interrupting her older, reading sister, is reinstated. The Devil's voice, previously curbed by the cunning mayor, is ready to race off on its own devil's line with its own unique style.

Surfaces of Sense: Dry Ta[i]l[e]s

Throughout her journey in Wonderland and through the Looking-Glass land, Alice encounters the continual modulating flow of meaning in language through Carroll's constant play on words, either with words that have sense but are imbued with ambiguity as either homophones or homonyms, or with words that have no sense outside themselves, or words 'called by names which are quite indeterminate' (LOS 53E/59F). At the outset of *Through the Looking-Glass*, Alice is confined inside on a snowy November afternoon, and ponders the possibility of passing through the looking-glass and into the house she observes on the other side. Imagining the glass to be soft and gauze-like, she soon discovers it 'beginning to melt away, just like a bright silvery mist' (Carroll 2008: 132). One of her first discoveries in this mirrored reality is that 'the very clock on the chimney-piece (you know you can only see the back of it in the Looking-glass) had got the face of a little old man, and grinned at her' (133). In the Looking-Glass world, the typically expressionless face of a clock, devoid of human-like eyes, nose and mouth, suddenly takes on a smiling human face. It is worth pausing here to consider Deleuze's

Stuttering, Nonsense and Zeroth Voice

undertaking in *The Logic of Sense* and how Carroll's play on words throughout his texts speaks to Deleuze's understanding of sense. Jean-Jacques Lecercle writes that

> in *Logique du Sens* Deleuze develops and transforms the concept [of series]: the image of two parallel lines fails to insist on the contact between the two (halves of the) series. So the best image is that of the mirror, and we can understand why Deleuze is so keen on Lewis Carroll, for the looking-glass is indeed a good example of a frontier, a surface which both links and separates two series, distinct yet similar. On the other side of the mirror, Alice finds the same objects as in her mother's sitting-room, but with a slight difference: on the face of the looking-glass clock there is a broad smile (I have chosen this example to show that what links the two series is not only a physical process – reflection – but also an ideal one: the pun on 'face', or rather Carroll's decision to take a dead metaphor literally). (Lecercle 1985: 94–5)

We can liken this fragile surface of the mirror which simultaneously links and separates two series of sense, in this case the human face and the face of the clock, to another fragile membrane: the bubble. In the Looking-Glass land, these two spheres of sense (human face/ clock face) converge, in the same way that two bubbles touch and form a shared surface. This shared surface between the two bubbles simultaneously joins and separates them: permitting 'the coexistence of two sides without thickness' (LOS 25E/33F). When two bubbles join, the fluid that is contained in each of them is shared at the point of contact, in the shared membrane. It inheres in both and yet is also distinct to each individual bubble. For James Williams, such a surface is 'independent of both, yet also the medium for their mutual transformations' (Williams 2008: 80): the shared surface which links the separate meanings of human face and clock face now permits the meaning of human face to transform the meaning of clock face, and vice versa. If we imagine this in two dimensions, with circles instead of spheres, this interdependent, shared frontier appears as a straight line between two circles on which meaning may glide in either direction. This is problematic, however, because it creates the image of a uniquely bi-directional movement of meaning – up and down, backwards and forwards, dependent on the orientation of the circle. In three dimensions, a smooth plane forms at the point of intersection between two spheres where sense is free to circulate in multiple directions. It is on this plane that the separate meanings of face converge, coexist and transform each other (the surface of the human-clock/ clock-human face). When spheres of sense converge in this way, meaning can be pushed to what Deleuze terms in *Essays Critical and Clinical* 'its Outside' (CC 72E/94F). Ronald Bogue writes:

> the outside that is proper to language is like the linguistic surface of *The Logic of Sense*, the surface between words and things, the *limit* of language that puts language in contact with the nonlinguistic. If language is seen as a sphere, the sphere's outer surface is the sphere's outside, but it is also that which touches on the nonlinguistic (that which is outside the sphere) and allows the linguisitic and the nonlinguistic to communicate with one another (the sphere's surface as a membrane, or permeable limit common to inside and outside). (Bogue 2003: 163, original emphasis)

When two of these spheres or bubbles collide, two outside surfaces join to form a new internal surface common to both. In this way, the sense of each separate sphere is able to contaminate or influence the other. It is on this conjoined surface that we move away from the constraints of denotation, of what something points to specifically, and get closer to its true sense, as Deleuze writes:

> to pass to the other side of the mirror is to pass from the relation of denotation to the relation of expression – without pausing at the intermediaries, namely, at manifestation and signification. It is to reach a region where language no longer has any relation to that which it denotes, but only to that which it expresses, that is, to sense. (LOS 31E/38F)

Thus, in pushing language to its Outside, in pushing meaning to converge with other meanings, it does not matter what 'face' denotes or refers to (human face or clock face) but only that which it expresses.

Sense is not something static but rather something that moves, and we can only understand this mobility of sense by referring to the original French. Deleuze's eponymous *sens* in French can translate as meaning or sense, as in common sense. It can also refer to our senses, our sense of smell or touch, for example. The French *sens* also has an implicit directionality to it. As Jean-Jacques Lecercle puts it '"*bon sens*", good sense, puns on the French word "sens" in its meanings of both "meaning" and "direction". Good sense, therefore, is the right direction (which is also a one-way street) – it is the direction of right thinking (do not stray to the left!), and also of the inevitability, from right to left, of time's arrow' (Lecercle 2002: 121). Ronald Bogue also points to this dual meaning of *sens*, writing: 'Deleuze argues, good sense, *le bon sens*, is simply limited sense, sense in one direction' (Bogue 2003: 25). For Lecercle, 'Deleuze relies on this ambiguity' contained in the word *sens*; it enables him to 'develop his spatial metaphor: the frontier between the two series [of signifying and signified] is conceived as a line along which the paradoxical (the nonsensical) element glides in both directions, giving sense, but indifferent to the direction taken' (Lecercle 1985: 103). This line of which Lecercle talks is somewhat deceptive. As mentioned above, a two-dimensional plane that exists through the joining of spheres, on which sense is free to move in many possible directions, is more appropriate. The Mouse's tale in *Alice's Adventures in Wonderland* allows us to see how surfaces of sense converge and have mobility and directionality.

When Alice begins to listen to the Mouse's tale two different spheres of sense exist based upon the homophone tale/tail. The passage reads as follows:

> 'Mine is a long and a sad tale!' said the Mouse, turning to Alice, and sighing.
> 'It *is* a long tail, certainly,' said Alice, looking down with wonder at the Mouse's tail; 'but why do you call it sad?' And she kept on puzzling about it while the Mouse was speaking, so that her idea of the tale was something like this: (Carroll 2008: 38–9, original emphasis)

The Mouse is telling his story, a 'sad and long tale', whereas Alice perceives a 'long tail': each approaches the homophone with a different signified. Each is pursuing a different *sens*, sense in a different direction. As the story progresses, however, the two independent spheres of meaning (tale/tail), with their unique directionalities, converge. The tale becomes a tail. This is represented visually for the young reader, who, with 'perhaps the best-known example in English of emblematic, or figured, verse: poems printed in such a way that they resemble something related to their subject matter' (Carroll and Gardner 2000: 34), can see the physical tail as the tale unfolds. The conjoined spheres of sense form a surface on which meaning circulates in multiple directions. What would lack sense now gains sense. Conversely, when the Mouse reprimands Alice for her inattentiveness, she tells him that he had reached the fifth bend and when the Mouse denies this ('"I had not!" cried the Mouse, sharply and very angrily' (Carroll 2008: 40)) Alice perceives a knot, pulling the converging spheres of meaning apart and sending meaning off, along with the affronted Mouse, in opposing directions.

Before the Mouse can recount his own tale/tail, the animals must dry off. Here, Carroll's play on the homonym dry creates a communicative breakdown over the best way to get dry after swimming in Alice's Pool of Tears, and seems for Dorothea Olkowski 'to be related to the question of distinguishing sense and reference' (Olkowski 2008: 111). The wet and cold Alice wishes simply to be dry, whereas the Mouse 'connect[s] different ideas to the name *dry*' (112). The Mouse is convinced that by recounting a tedious story, 'borrowed from a primer in history', (Lecercle 2002: 123), his auditors will dry off. His story begins thus, with interruptions from the Duck:

> 'Edwin and Morcar, the earls of Mercia and Northumbria, declared for him: and even Stigand, the patriotic archbishop of Canterbury, found it advisable – '
>
> 'Found *what*?' said the Duck.
>
> 'Found *it*,' the Mouse replied rather crossly: 'of course you know what "it" means.'
>
> 'I know what "it" means well enough, when I find a thing,' said the Duck: 'it's generally a frog or a worm. The question is, what did the archbishop find?'
>
> The Mouse did not notice this question, but hurriedly went on, ' – found it advisable to go with Edgar Atheling to meet William and offer him the crown.' (Carroll 2008: 36 original emphasis)

In recounting his historical anecdote, reminiscent of Alice's ponderings during her fall down the rabbit hole, the Mouse creates a surface where the distinct meanings of dry (not wet) and dry (dull and uninteresting) can merge, irrespective of sense and reference. When Alice declares she is 'as wet as ever' and that the Mouse's interpretation of dry 'doesn't seem to dry me at all' (36), the creatures embark on their raucous and chaotic Caucus race and, like the once conjoined meanings of dry, pull apart and go hurtling off in their own individual directions.

In the Mouse's story, we not only see converging spheres of meaning coming together, contaminating each other, overthrowing denotation and permitting meaning to circulate freely in whichever direction it chooses, then pulling apart assuming individual directionality. We also see the presence of what Deleuze terms an *aliquid*. Derived from the Latin *aliquis*, this denotes something indefinite: a something, an anything, or as Markus Bohlmann puts it, 'this "aliquid" refers to the realm of sense that slips away from being accurately pinned down' (Bohlmann 2014: 407). Deleuze writes about this passage as follows:

> in *Alice*, the characters have only two possible means of drying themselves after falling into the pool of tears: either to listen to the Mouse's story, the 'dryest' story one could be acquainted with, since it isolates the

sense of a proposition in a ghostly 'it'; or to be launched into a Caucus Race, running around from one proposition to another, stopping when one wishes, without winners or losers, in the circuit of infinite proliferation. At any rate, dryness is what shall later on be named impenetrability. And the two paradoxes represent the essential forms of stuttering. (LOS 39E/45F)

This 'ghostly "it"' (LOS 39E/45F) haunting the Mouse's dry tale pops up in the middle of the story and is an example of what Deleuze refers to as a word that 'is called by names which are quite indeterminate: *aliquid*, it, that, thing, gadget, or "whatchamacallit"' (LOS 53E/59F). 'It' has sense for everybody listening (who does not understand such a simple word as 'it'?, as the Mouse somewhat pompously points out), and for the Duck, 'it' is usually something edible (Carroll 2008: 36). Deleuze's reads this passage as follows:

> it is clear that the Duck employs and understands 'it' as a denoting term for all things, state of affairs and possible qualities (an indicator). It specifies even that the denoted thing is essentially something which is (or may be eaten). [. . .] But the Mouse made use of 'it' in an entirely different manner, as the sense of an earlier proposition, as the event expressed by the proposition (to go and offer the crown to William). The equivocation of 'it' is therefore distributed in accordance with the duality of denotation and expression. The two dimensions of the proposition are organized in two series which converge asymptomatically, in a term as ambiguous as 'it,' since they meet one another only at the frontier which they continuously stretch . . . These two dimensions converge only in an esoteric word, in a non-identifiable *aliquid*. (LOS 32E/39F)

Lecercle takes up Deleuze's reading of this 'it' passage in both his *Philosophy through the Looking-Glass* (1985) and his later *Philosophy of Nonsense* (1994). For Lecercle, this passage 'can be fully understood only in the light of Chomskyan linguistics – although Carroll was in no way a grammarian or a philologist himself, he was a century in advance of contemporary specialists' (Lecercle 1994: 2). Lecercle pursues this analysis in his *Deleuze and Language* (2002), writing:

> it is clear for the Duck, who is the representative of common sense, 'it' should be bearer of denotation (this is helped by Deleuze's translations of 'it' as '*ceci*', a deictic). But the Mouse, even if he is not aware of the complexities of Chomsky's generative-transformational grammar, is aware that the function of 'it' is not to denote, that is has no referent. Or, rather, that the only referent of this 'it' is not an edible object, but the event expressed by the proposition, incarnated by the verb, temporarily absent

but coming later, as the Mouse insists on finishing, if not the story, at least the sentence. [...] So the event is expressed by a verb in the infinitive and the 'it' is the ambiguous term in which the two series of denotation and expression paradoxically diverge (there is expression but no denotation) and converge (the 'it', as the Duck is aware, suggests or maintains the possibility of denotation). (Lecercle 2002: 124)

The Duck and the Mouse have, then, two different interpretations of what they hear. The Duck has a common-sensical approach: 'it' must denote something, must refer to something tangible, preferably edible. The Mouse ties 'it' to the infinitive-driven verbal phrase not yet uttered (to go and offer). In the Mouse's dry tale, these separate spheres of meaning converge: 'it' can be both denotation and expression when 'it' meets on the surface membrane of the conjoined spheres of sense. Unlike 'dry' or 'face', which have specific meanings, 'it' is indeterminate and ambiguous and as such makes the Mouse's tale stutter and vibrate. As an *aliquid*, 'it' bolsters the fragile surface, rendering it impenetrable, as it paradoxically allows both specific denotation and expressions of events to come to circulate freely on its surface. This impenetrable surface of multi-directional sense takes on its own temporality, that of Aiôn, which I will return to in more detail later in this chapter. There is one character in *Alice Through the Looking-Glass* which epitomises this impenetrability: Humpty Dumpty.

Humpty Dumpty: The Impenetrable

Transitioning from the fifth square, trying to capture the egg she has bought from the Sheep's shop, which gets 'larger and larger, and more and more human' (Carroll 2008: 181), Alice recognises the nursery rhyme figure of Humpty Dumpty (for '"It can't be anybody else!"' (181)), poised cross-legged on a high and narrow wall. She recites the famous nursery rhyme to herself, completing the short verse without recourse to parody – a unique achievement for Alice in her combined journeys through Wonderland and the Looking-Glass land. This accurate recital may be due, in part, to the fact that the rhyme is itself a riddle. As such the rhyme presages the conversation in which Humpty Dumpty takes everything Alice says as a riddle, ironically not realising he is the subject of one, and oblivious to its outcome, or, as David Rudd remarks: 'perilously ignoring the discursive chain in which he [is] positioned' (Rudd 2005: 23). Humpty Dumpty's rhyme contains no answer itself because 'the reason the king's men could not put him together again is known to everyone' (Opie and Opie 1997: 252): following nursery rhyme lore, Humpty Dumpty is of course an egg, and this he finds *'very provoking'* (Carroll 2008: 181, original emphasis). Here, we come up against the first impenetrable element of Humpty Dumpty's being: 'Humpty Dumpty is the character who blurs all distinctions, and therefore causes uneasiness (is he an egg or a man? Is this his waist or his neck?) (Lecercle 1985: 73). Humpty Dumpty is a quandary: egg or man? Both views are for Lecercle 'entirely rational, i.e. coherent and textually founded. Humpty Dumpty's *cogito*, "I think, therefore I am not an egg", is opposed to Alice's conventional reasonings: the nursery rhyme says this is an egg, *ergo* it *is* an egg' (Lecercle 1994: 142–3). Humpty Dumpty is an augmented egg, an egg with intellect, an over-inflated one at that, and at the same time a diminished man, a human reduced to the fragility of an egg. Within Humpty Dumpty, the separate spheres of meaning (egg/man) converge to form a new surface of sense: the plane of Humpty Dumpty. Maria Nikolajeva considers that Humpty Dumpty is 'an empty signifier' (Nikolajeva 2010: 27), for, as a nursery rhyme character, his name does 'not have a meaning. It is a signifier without the signified' (28). His name does, however, have an agreed-upon meaning, one which Humpty Dumpty assigns himself: 'my name means the shape I am' (Carroll 2008: 183). The words *humpty dumpty* express a haecceity, simply humpty dumptyness – an egg-like shape with human features; fragility and precariousness; ignorance of potential hazard, and the delusion that salvation is possible. Unlike most words which 'presuppose[ ] other words that can replace [them], complete [them], or form alternatives with [them]' (CC 73E/94F), the words *humpty dumpty* are utterly self-referential. They cannot be substituted or replaced by another single word. They therefore exist in a zone independent of and impenetrable by the language that has created them.

Humpty Dumpty's use of language is as impenetrable as his name, as the conversation that follows reveals:

> 'When *I* use a word,' Humpty Dumpty said in rather a scornful tone, 'it means just what I choose it to mean – neither more nor less.'
>
> 'The question is,' said Alice, 'whether you can make words mean so many different things.'
>
> 'The question is,' said Humpty Dumpty, 'which is to be master – that's all.'
>
> Alice was too much puzzled to say anything, so after a minute Humpty Dumpty began again. 'They've a temper, some of them – particularly

verbs, they're the proudest – adjectives you can do anything with, but not verbs – however, I can manage the whole lot of them! Impenetrability! That's what *I* say!' (Carroll 2008: 186, original emphasis)

For many scholars of children's literature, this dialogue shows Humpty Dumpty employing a majoritarian language, arbitrarily manipulating the rules to suit himself. Nikolajeva, in particular, considers that this dialogue demonstrates how 'language is a vehicle of power, and whoever possesses this power can also suppress and govern other people' (Nikolajeva 2010: 27). Nikolajeva reads Humpty Dumpty as a majoritarian figure, controlling language, denying others, and Alice in particular, access to it. Teresa de Lauretis's reading of Humpty Dumpty is more nuanced, writing in *Alice Doesn't: Feminism, Semiotics, Cinema* that Humpty Dumpty only '*thinks* himself the master of language' (de Lauretis 1984: 1, my emphasis), but by randomising the meaning of words, by choosing meaning arbitrarily, he reveals himself not so much as master but as minoriser of language, for as Patricia Pisters puts it: 'would a master look like an egg? [...] Would a master take seriously playful words like "Jabberwocky," "'twas brillig" and "borogrove"? Would he propose playful ideas like "un-birthday presents"?' (Pisters 2003: 115). In this way Humpty Dumpty resembles another literary character to whom Deleuze refers in *Essays Critical and Clinical*: Bartleby. Deleuze calls Bartleby's repeated phrase *I would prefer not to* a formula, writing 'perhaps it is the formula that carves out a kind of foreign language within language' (CC 71E/93F); the effect of this formula is 'to sweep up language in its entirety, sending it into flight, pushing it to its very limit in order to discover its Outside' (CC 72E/94F). Humpty Dumpty, like Bartleby, creates 'bloc[s] of words which fascinate[] with [their] impenetrability, [their] inscrutability, [their] implacable deflection of meaning' (Buchanan et al. 2015: 1). Humpty Dumpty is then 'the Giver of sense' (LOS 91E/98F): his egg-like shape creates its own sphere, or more precisely ovoid, of sense: a surface without thickness on which language 'immunizes itself against interpretation' (Buchanan et al. 2015: 2) and sense permanently slides and rebounds. Humpty Dumpty pushes language through his own impenetrable yet fragile outside, and does so predominantly through his use of esoteric and portmanteau words.

Stuttering, Nonsense and Zeroth Voice

Esoteric and Portmanteau Words

In *The Logic of Sense*, Deleuze distinguishes between the esoteric and portmanteau words to be found in Carroll's *œuvre*. Esoteric words belong to the select few: they are what we imagine makes up the Devil's personal Bellsybabble; they are Humpty Dumpty's unique inventions in the Looking-Glass land. Esoteric words can include those such as 'y'reince' appearing in *Sylvie and Bruno*: a syllabic contraction which sums up the entire sense of the phrase 'Your Royal Highness' 'with a single syllable – or an "Unpronounceable Monosyllable"' (LOS 52E/58F). These are *'contracting* words', (LOS 55E/62F) 'in which the sense is squeezed from several lexemes into one' (Palmer 2014: 28). Esoteric words may also be 'denotative and expressive' (LOS 53E/59F), such as 'the Phlizz [which] is almost an onomatopoeia for something vanishing' (LOS 53E/59F). Or again the *aliquid*, which as we have seen, captures that indeterminate thingumajig floating in phrases.

Portmanteau words 'are themselves esoteric words of a new kind' (LOS 53E/59F). They appear in the Jabberwocky poem, the poem Alice first discovers in the Looking-Glass room; and it is no coincidence that to make its sense appear she must hold it up to a mirror, for its nonsense words will only begin to make sense on such a surface. The first two verses read as follows:

> Twas brillig, and the slithy toves
> Did gyre and gimble in the wabe;
> All mimsy were the borogoves,
> And the mome raths outgrabe.
>
> Beware the Jabberwock, my son!
> The jaws that bite, the claws that catch!
> Beware the Jubjub bird, and shun
> The frumious Bandersnatch! (Carroll 2008: 137–8)

When Alice later meets Humpty Dumpty, she requests he explain the meaning of the Jabberwocky to her. His explanations begin, thus, after Alice recites the first verse:

> '"Brillig" means four o'clock in the afternoon – the time when you begin broiling things for dinner.'
> 'That'll do very well,' said Alice: 'and "slithy"?'
> 'Well, "slithy" means "lithe and slimy." "Lithe" is the same as "active." You see it's like a portmanteau – there are two meanings packed up into one word.' (Carroll 2008: 187)

Deleuze warns us however, that despite 'a great number of words [which] stretch out a fantastic zoology' (LOS 53E/60F) not all the words in the Jabberwocky poem form portmanteau words: '"toves" (badgers-lizards-corkscrews), "borogoves" (birds-buoys), "raths" (green pigs) and the verb "outgribe" (bellowing-whistling-sneezing)' (LOS 53E/60F), whilst playful and irreverent, and thoroughly deterritorialising of the mouth that utters them, cannot be considered portmanteau words following Humpty Dumpty's definition. Then, there are words such as Snark, the physically and linguistically monstrous snake-shark creature of Carroll's *The Hunting of the Snark*, which appear to adhere to Humpty Dumpty's definition, but which are not true portmanteau words. Deleuze describes such words as '*circulating* words' (LOS 56E/62F) conjoining two heterogeneous propositions. The circulating presence of the elusive Snark holds the poem together: 'this mysterious element reoccurs in the story; each stanza repeats something about the Snark, which generates a sense of connection' (Faulkner 2006: 143): a synthesis of conjunction.

Jean-Jacques Lecercle takes a position over the inconsistency and arbitrariness of Humpty Dumpty's explanations: 'Humpty Dumpty's explanations are semantic, whereas the rules for the formation of portmanteau-words are morphological' (Lecercle 1994: 44). He continues, drawing on Almuth Grésillon's study of portmanteau words *La Règle et le monstre: le mot-valise*: 'the *sine qua non* for the formation of a portmanteau word, [is] the presence of a string of phonemes common to the two words that have merged into one. [. . .] Thus, the presence of "hol" makes "alcoholidays" immediately understandable' (44). In the preface to *Looking-Glass*, Carroll 'himself plays a second Humpty Dumpty for the benefit of the readers' (Lecercle 1994: 46), offering a phonetic guide to the pronunciation of portmanteau words which serves to undermine Humpty Dumpty's semantic one: 'the new words in the poem "Jabberwocky" have given rise to some differences of opinion as to their pronunciation [. . .]. Pronounce "slythy" as if it were the two words "sly, the"; make the g hard in "gyre" and "gimble"; and pronounce "rath" to rhyme with "bath"' (Carroll 2008: 125). Indeed, Deleuze comments that

> Humpty Dumpty offers as portmanteau words the words 'slithy' (=lithe-slimy-active) 'mimsy' (=flimsy-miserable), etc. Here our discomfort increases. We see clearly in each case that there are several contracted words and senses; but these elements are easily organized into a single series in order to compose a global sense. We do not therefore see how

the portmanteau word can be distinguished from a simple contraction or from a synthesis of connective succession. (LOS 54E/61F)

For Deleuze, the portmanteau word par excellence is frumious. This is explained by Carroll in the preface to *The Hunting of the Snark*, and represents for Lecercle an additional 'psychological' (Lecercle 1994: 47) account for the portmanteau word:

> for instance, take the two words 'fuming' and 'furious.' Make up your mind that you will say both words, but leave it unsettled which you will say first. Now open your mouth and speak. If your thoughts incline ever so little towards 'fuming,' you will say 'fuming-furious'; if they turn, by even a hair's breadth, towards 'furious,' you will say 'furious-fuming'; but if you have the rarest of gifts, a perfectly balanced mind, you will say 'frumious'. (Carroll 2008: 756)

Frumious, for Deleuze, reveals that the true 'portmanteau word is grounded upon a strict disjunctive synthesis' (LOS 55E/61F): 'the necessary disjunction is not between fuming and furious, for one may indeed be both at once; rather, it is between fuming-and-furious on one hand and furious-and-fuming on the other. In this sense, the function of the portmanteau word always consists in the ramification of the series into which it is inserted' (LOS 55E/62F). Deleuze's disjunctive synthesis allows two separate terms (fuming-and-furious and furious-and-fuming) to be brought together in a synthesis (frumious) that paradoxically reaffirms the separation or disjunction between them (frumious meaning fuming-and-furious, is not the same as frumious meaning furious-and-fuming). This disjunctive synthesis is a zigzagging flash that simultaneously brings together and forces apart two heterogeneous series of sense, creating ripples in each separate series into which the portmanteau is inserted.[2]

The cumulative effect of Humpty Dumpty's use of esoteric and portmanteau words and Alice's stuttering which brings her to meet Humpty Dumpty is, of course, nonsense, but as Kimberley Reynolds points out, 'the term "nonsense" is something of a misnomer' (Reynolds 2007: 47).[3] Nonsense for Lecercle is 'a kind of textual double-bind, or paradox' (Lecercle 1994: 25), and as such is as paradoxical as the synthesis that creates the words which compose it. 'It tells the reader to abide, and not to abide, by the rules of language' (25). Its words appear to have no sense, but nevertheless 'these nonsense words structure the text: they have no meaning, but they prevent the text from lacking sense' (Lecercle 1985: 104). Nonsense returns us to the idea of the directionality of sense; nonsense does not imply no-sense whatsoever, but rather not the typical direction of good sense, as Ronald Bogue comments: 'even sequences of nonce words ("Twas brillig, and the slithy toves...") all have sense, just not good sense' (Bogue 2003: 25). Without nonsense, language remains trapped in a self-referential bind, for 'we can never formulate simultaneously both a proposition and its sense; we can never say what is the sense of what we say [...] There is only one kind of word which expresses both itself and its sense – precisely the nonsense word: abraxas, snark or blituri' (DR 155E/201F). Nonsense with its esoteric and portmanteau words allows language to push through the fragile surface of sense and to 'get outside of itself to speak about itself, to say its sense' (Buchanan et al. 2015: 2). When language is able to speak itself, it is able to precede and surpass the organs of perception that produce it. Nonsense is therefore the becoming-imperceptible of language; it bypasses the need for meaning and it 'functions as the zero point of thought' (LOS 279E/281F). This zero point of thought is not a moment of nothingness, of emptiness, but rather a moment which 'enacts the creation of sense' (Pebesma 2017: 11). The zero's shape (0) – Humpty Dumpty-esque in appearance – allows us to envision the surface of sense cracking asunder and revealing its double-sidedness: we cannot have sense without nonsense, nor nonsense without sense. At the moment of this crack, we have access to Aiôn, Deleuze's pure form of time which arises from the caesura. At this zero point of thought, or as Lecercle frames it, in 'the hesitation between sense and nonsense' (Lecercle 1985: 109), 'the world becomes in all directions in the same Aion' (Bogue 2003: 25). Nonsense words, created in the zigzag of disjunctive synthesis, with their ramifications in the individual series into which they are inserted, become blocs of pure impenetrability circulating like 'a refrain' (DR 123E/161F), resonating verbally across time and space, crystallising time. This refrain or becoming-imperceptible of language I term the zeroth voice of childhood, and it is to this notion that we now turn.

Zeroth Voice

I prefaced this chapter with a short passage from *Dialogues* in which Deleuze discusses the disadvantages of authorship, and to reach my notion of the zeroth voice, it is necessary to return to this passage now. Deleuze tells us: 'the disadvantages of the Author are constituting a point of departure or of origin, forming a subject of enunciation on which all the produced utterances depend, getting recognized and identified in an order of dominant meaning or established powers: "I in my capacity as ...".' He goes on to make one of his most radical claims, namely that 'there is no subject, but instead collective assemblages of enunciation' (D 28E/36F). This declaration shakes traditional literary approaches, where some of the first questions typically asked of narrative are 'who speaks?', 'who sees?' and 'whose story is it?' To look for voice in written narrative is, traditionally, to look for the style or manner of expression that distinguishes author, narrator, or character. Deleuze, with Guattari, admits that even Kafka, the author who epitomises the creation of the collective assemblage of enunciation, would have certainly reflected on these modes before rejecting them: 'undoubtedly, for a while, Kafka thought according to these traditional categories of the two subjects, the author and the hero, the narrator and the character' (K 18E/F32). This move away from traditional literary categories, and in particular from the subject, encapsulates Deleuze's philosophical purpose, as Joff Bradley suggests: 'throughout his *œuvre*, Deleuze looked to forge a philosophy to dislodge and decentre the "I" or speaking subject' (Bradley 2015: 189); or as Gregg Lambert remarks, 'Deleuze and Guattari's entire theory of language is made to answer this provocation, to prove that the subject is not the master of the word it chooses to express its beliefs or its desires' (Lambert 2007: 37). Deleuze tells us that 'to the question "Who is speaking?", we answer sometimes with the individual, sometimes with the person, and sometimes with the ground which dissolves both' (LOS 159E/166F). The concept of the assemblage is this ground that overcomes all forms of subjectivity and that which creates enunciation:

> it is always an assemblage which produces utterances. Utterances do not have as their cause a subject which would act as a subject of enunciation, any more than they are related to subjects as subjects of utterance. The utterance is the product of an assemblage – which is always collective, which brings into play within us and outside us populations, multiplicities, territories, becomings, affects, events. The proper name does not designate a subject, but something which happens, at least between two terms which are not subjects, but agents, elements. (D 51E/65F)

For Claire Colebrook, 'it is in free-indirect style that literature discloses language as a "collective assemblage"' (Colebrook 2002: 112). Free-indirect style provides an indirect representation of characters: pronouns and tags do not indicate who owns the narration; instead there is a distortion of character and narratorial perspectives. Access to the character's mind is given but without loss of authorial control. Colebrook goes on to write that free-indirect style

> frees language from its ownership by any subject of enunciation, we can see the flow of language itself, its production of sense and nonsense, its virtual and creative power. This is why free-indirect style merges with stream of consciousness. Free-indirect style uses the third person to describe single characters from the point of view of a received and anonymous language. (Colebrook 2002: 114)

Whilst it might be understandable to assume that children's literature more typically makes use of third-person narrators who can clearly tell the reader what to think, and first-person narrators who, whilst they can only describe what they know, often cannot resist the urge to tell the implied reader what they have learned, the genre of children's literature, as Maria Nikolajeva explains, increasingly makes use of free-indirect discourse:

> if we take a closer look at the narrator of modern children's fiction, we note several significant shifts. It is commonly believed that young readers prefer dialogue to description and that dialogue is an effective device to develop a plot. In many contemporary children's novels, dialogue – that is, direct speech representation – is supplanted by free indirect discourse. (Nikolajeva 1998: 228)

Elsewhere, I have shown how the complexities of narration in children's literature can lead to a multitude of self-reflecting voices which join together to compose the voice of the protagonist in fiction for young people. Drawing on Deleuze's concept of the simulacrum, I show how these simulacral voices free narration from any form of ownership and create a collective enunciation (Newland 2009). Here, I wish to focus on nonsense, as 'a mode of writing that has come to be associated with children's literature' (Reynolds 2007: 45) and is so prevalent there. In this way, I will build on Jean-Jacques Lecercle's assertion that 'nonsense is the literary name for the assemblage of enunciation' (Lecercle 2002: 55) and Claire Colebrook's claim about free-indirect discourse, quoted above, and add that it is also in nonsense that literature reveals not merely its collective assemblage but also its own voice.

Referring to James Joyce's *The Dead* and his use of free-indirect discourse in the first line of this text ('Lily, the caretaker's daughter, was literally run off her feet'), Lecercle writes: 'it is the text that speaks, and not Lily, nor Gabriel, nor the anonymous narrator (who may or may not be Gabriel), nor Joyce himself. Or rather every single one of those various voices, a Babel of voices convoked by the *sense* of the utterance: sense is the voice of the text' (Lecercle 2002: 136). If, for Lecercle, sense is the voice of the text emerging through free-indirect discourse, can we make the same claim for a text composed of nonsense? At the end of *Alice's Adventures in Wonderland*, the Knave of Hearts stands trial for stealing the Queen of Heart's tarts. During the trial, the White Rabbit presents an unopened letter as new evidence and proceeds to read its verses as follows:

> They told me you had been to her,
> And mentioned me to him:
> She gave me a good character,
> But said I could not swim.
>
> He sent them word I had not gone
> (We know it to be true):
> If she should push the matter on,
> What would become of you?
>
> I gave her one, they gave him two,
> You gave us three or more;
> They all returned from him to you,
> Though they were mine before.
>
> If I or she should chance to be
> Involved in this affair,
> He trusts to you to set them free,
> Exactly as we were.
>
> My notion was that you had been
> (Before she had this fit)
> An obstacle that came between
> Him, and ourselves, and it.
>
> Don't let him know she liked them best,
> For this must ever be
> A secret, kept from all the rest,
> Between yourself and me. (Carroll 2008: 109)

Throughout *Alice's Adventures in Wonderland* and *Through the Looking-Glass*, the real-world Charles Dodgson writes 'in his capacity as' Lewis Carroll, narrator of Alice's curious adventures, and the persona who tells us 'these were the verses the White Rabbit read' (Carroll 2008: 108). The dizzying swirl of personal pronouns in the verse, however, means we are no longer able to identify this 'in his capacity as', for 'it is clear that the principal difficulty of the text is that its author remains unknown: it is read by the White Rabbit, the prosecution maintains that it was written by the Knave of Hearts, who denies this and advances as proof the fact that the poem is not in his handwriting' (Lecercle 1985: 76). We are bombarded with pronouns (I, you, he, she, it, we, they, me, mine, yourself, ourselves, us, them), lost as to where to position ourselves as readers. What is more, a doubling of locutor-auditor occurs: the White Rabbit voicing the verses of uncertain authorship to the listening jurors mirrors the real-world situation where a parent may be reading out loud to a listening child. The *aliquid* second-person pronoun which circulates throughout the poem, rather like the Mouse's 'it', further interpellates the 'you' outside the text,[4] drawing the reader into the text and conflating readerly and narrative persons, thereby facilitating the creation of the assemblage, for, as we saw in the Introduction, we cannot create an assemblage when we are a distanced observer (D 52E/66F). There is no longer one distinct subject either inside or outside the text – all that remains is a collective assemblage producing utterances. Through the creation of nonsense, language has been pushed outside itself and 'speaks directly, in its own right' (Lecercle 1985: 76), stripped of all subject imposition. What surfaces at this zero point of thought, the point at which all (non)sense is created, is the becoming-imperceptible of language, the pure voice of the text, and this I call *zeroth* voice.

Deleuze uses the term 'the fourth person singular' (LOS 118E/125F),[5] to describe such a voice. This he borrows from poet Lawrence Ferlinghetti, whose *Her* (1960) was translated into French as *La quatrième personne du singulier* (1961). More recently, Ferlinghetti incorporated the notion of the fourth person singular into his poem 'To the Oracle at Delphi'. The verse in which it occurs reads,

> Far-seeing Sybil, forever hidden,
> Come out of your cave at last
> And speak to us in the poet's voice
> the voice of the fourth person singular
> the voice of the inscrutable future
> the voice of the people mixed
> with a wild soft laughter –
> And give us new dreams to dream,
> Give us new myths to live by! (Ferlinghetti 2001: 93)

This verse captures the essence of the fourth person singular: a multiple voice of 'people mixed', creative and dynamic, full of laughter and humour, and hopeful futurely promise. It is 'a way of getting outside of the enchained interiority of the oneself (the "I") [... it] is neither you nor me, or even them and us, but a dissolution of the very idea of the self, a splendid "they" that is impersonal and pre-individual' (Buchanan 2000: 17). In order to speak to the moment in which this voice is formed, at the zero point of thought, I have taken the liberty of adapting Deleuze's term and calling it *zeroth* voice. Following the principle of the zeroth law of thermodynamics,[6] coined when a more fundamental principle was discovered, underlying the three established laws already in use, this zeroth voice is more fundamental than the voice of a first, second, or third person, both preceding and superseding other grammatical persons. It exists in the absence of, or before the imposition of, any defined grammatical person, in the flow that is the assemblage. Zeroth voice is not negative in the sense of being null and worth nothing, but is rather groundless, containing all other voices but not imposing any one of them. Zeroth voice overcomes any authorial voice, any narratorial voice, any readerly voice, reaching a voice that precedes all of these. It is a voice that is inherently enabling and liberating because it goes beyond the limited horizon of the self, beyond the need for identification with another, and endows us with possibilities of as yet non-realised potential. Zeroth voice forms then 'a new type of esoteric language [. . .] which is its own model and reality' (LOS 159E/166F), the language of the assemblage, the voice of becoming, but, more specifically, the voice of becoming-imperceptible, avoiding any reduction to one given person only.

Concerned that when young readers progress towards such private reading, they may lose the ability to hear a voice in texts, children's literature scholar Roderick McGillis remarks in his paper, 'Calling a Voice Out of Silence: Hearing What We Read': 'to save the reader from the reign of awful darkness and silence, we must give him voice; to save the text, we must save its voice' (McGillis 1984: 25). Here he evokes the dreary texts 'without pictures or conversations' (Carroll 2008: 23) read by Alice's sister on the riverbank. Alice does not 'hear' the zeroth voice when glancing over her sister's shoulder on the riverbank; her sister's fiction does not 'work' for Alice. As we have seen previously, Deleuze tells us the only questions we should ask of a book are 'does it work, and how does it work?' (N 8E/17F). When Deleuze asks such questions of literature, he is asking if a voice can be called out of the silence of the text; he is asking if this intense zeroth voice is created and can be 'heard'.

It is, then, the zeroth voice that surfaces from, for example, the pure repetition of Ionesco's *Contes*: the parent and child who share the story at home outside the text mirror the storytelling father and daughter within the text. In the myriad Jacquelines uttered by the reading parent, by the storytelling father, by Josette, it becomes impossible to impose a defined speaking subject distinct from one or other Jacqueline; rather, a collective assemblage of enunciation with its zeroth voice emerges as language is pushed to its outside through pure repetition. In Pierrette Fleutiaux's corpus for children, as we have seen, a heave-ho refrain permeates. This reassuring whistle, akin to Alice's *persiflage*, reaches into her corpus for adults. This repeated code-word calls out, in its zeroth voice, to a reader of Fleutiaux whose readings stretch over time from childhood to adulthood, and joins them in Aiôn in a childhood block. The zeroth voice is not then simply a child voice or an adult voice, but one that allows both child and adult to coexist in one pure moment of time and in one voice stripped of a distinct subject position: it is the voice of the molecular child that emerges in the space of children's literature. The zeroth voice is not simply a human attribute, but may arise from something non-human, typically devoid of voice. The zeroth voice is the only voice that we can hear in our becoming-plant with Le Clézio's Hihuit or in our becoming-molecular with Asturias's man who has everything. It is, therefore, this zeroth voice that we should hope will prevail when reading. Where Roland Barthes is renowned for requiring the death of the author and the birth of the reader (Barthes 1977: 148), with Deleuze, I believe we can insist on the next step, the death of the subject and the birth of the imperceptible assemblage and its unique voice, the zeroth voice.

Conclusion: The (Non)sense of Zeroth Voice

In this chapter, we have seen a progression from the majoritarian language forms used by those who are in authority and wield power, and which are demanded of others, to a minoritarian use of language. *Alice's Adventures in Wonderland* and *Through the Looking-Glass and What Alice Found There* provide many examples of this minorisation of language. Alice is keenly aware of the demands of the major codes of language and has even learnt certain phrases and expressions through her schooling, but she does not master it. In trying to use majoritarian forms, appropriate grammar and even foreign languages, she minorises language. Words become jumbled

Stuttering, Nonsense and Zeroth Voice

and distorted in her mouth and Alice begins to stutter. Alice's stuttering is not a speech impediment in the traditional sense but rather what occurs when she attempts to remember her lessons, recite learnt verses and follow the prescribed rules of grammar. As her knowledge crumbles around her and her voice becomes strange and unfamiliar, so she produces a persiflage, a whistling, childlike banter that escapes from the corners of her mouth. This is Alice's new style, which breaks away from majoritarian constraints and limitation. Like Joyce's playful Devil, who creates a new style, exploding from the depths of his belly in his fury, Alice is finding her own voice: playful, irreverent, impervious to established codes and norms. In her stuttering and persiflage and in his guttural Bellsybabble, Alice and the Devil send language racing on a witch's line to create their own distinct style.

In *Through the Looking-Glass*, the egg-man paradox Humpty Dumpty epitomises the creation of (non)sense. He is a haecceity: expressing and denoting only humpty-dumptyness. He is in and of himself a fragile surface on which sense slips and slides, allowing separate meanings to converge and pull apart again. With his creation of esoteric and portmanteau words, Humpty Dumpty is able to push language through to its own outside, to let language escape itself and express its own sense.

The nonsense in Carroll's work is not devoid of sense, it just does not have the directionality of good, common sense. In the nonsense created by Humpty Dumpty and other characters from the Alice texts, we are able to see language speaking itself, no longer limited to organs of production and perception. This is, then, the becoming-imperceptible of language which occurs at the zero point of thought, as the egg cracks open ($0 => ( )$), as the double sidedness of sense is revealed. This zeroth voice of the becoming-imperceptible of language overcomes any authorial voice, any narratorial voice, any voice reading the text aloud, but reaches a voice that precedes all of these. It is a voice that is inherently enabling and liberating because it goes beyond the limited horizon of the self, beyond the need for identification with another, and endows us with possibilities of as yet non-realised potential. It allows readers to escape the bounds of the imposed voices of the text and to go beyond the imposition of grammatical persons. The zeroth voice exists in the flow of assemblage: it is what we hear when literature works for us.

My next chapter considers a most unique children's book, *L'Oiseau philosophie*, created from Deleuze's own writings. This unassuming text – Deleuze in picture-book form – lays bare what Deleuze 'does' to literature and to children's literature in particular, with its visuals of the non-linear growth of the molecular child.

Notes

1. It is interesting to note that the Blachon edition of *The Cat and the Devil* contains a typing error. The original Bellysbabble is rendered Bellysbabble in this version of the text. In the French edition, illustrated by Corre, Bellysbabble is translated as *le diababélien*, which keeps a notion of the babbling aspect of the language (*babiller*: to babble, *Babel*: Babel) but loses its relationship to the guttural.
2. For further discussion of disjunctive synthesis in Deleuze, see also Lecercle 2012 and Palmer 2014.
3. For a detailed discussion of the history of literary nonsense, see Reynolds 2007.
4. In A. A. Milne's *Winnie-the-Pooh*, Pooh visits Christopher Robin and requests a balloon; the following exchange occurs:

   > 'Good morning Christopher Robin,' he said.
   > 'Good morning Winnie-ther-Pooh,' *said you*.
   > 'I wonder if you've got such a thing as a balloon about you?'
   > 'A balloon?'
   > 'Yes, I just said to myself coming along: "I wonder if Christopher Robin has such a thing as a balloon about him?" I just said it to myself, thinking about balloons and wondering.'
   > 'What do you want a balloon for?' *you said*. (Milne 1973: 8–9; my emphasis)

   This is another example of the interpellation of a 'you' external to the text.
5. The term 'fourth person singular' resonates across the Deleuzian *œuvre*, appearing in *The Logic of Sense*, *Negotiations* and *Desert Islands*. Until Joff Bradley's recent 'The Eyes of the Fourth Person Singular' (2015) it has received little critical attention.
6. In thermodynamics, the zeroth law 'states that if two objects, A and B, are at thermal equilibrium with each other and if B is at thermal equilibrium with a third object, C, then A is also at thermal equilibrium with C. This fact is important enough to be called a law of thermodynamics, and is so basic that it needs to precede the other laws, but the other laws had already been numbered before people figured out how important this law is, so it is called the zeroth law' (Mortimer 2000: 100).

6

Painting the Imperceptible: Deleuze in Picture-book Form

> Ce livre me satisfait d'autant plus que j'y vois une intention merveilleuse où je veux me reconnaître d'autant plus que j'y agis moins. [This book particularly pleases me as I see in it a marvellous plan where I recognise myself in it all the more that I am less involved.] (*L'Oiseau philosophie*)
>
> it is part of the charm of many of the most interesting picture books that they so strangely combine the childlike and the sophisticated – that the viewer they imply is both very learned and very ingenuous. (Nodelman 1988: 21)

In 1997, two years after Deleuze's death, Éditions du Seuil published a small picture book entitled *L'Oiseau philosophie*. Unlike the other children's texts written by Deleuze's favoured authors that I have considered thus far, *L'Oiseau philosophie* is a picture book, not written by Deleuze, but created from Deleuze's own writings and illustrated by his long-time friend, Jacqueline Duhême, with the subtitle *Duhême dessine Deleuze* [Duhême draws Deleuze]. Classified by the Bibliothèque nationale de France as both a work of philosophy and a children's book, it is therefore a paradox in and of itself: one that remains curiously overlooked by Deleuzian scholars and practically unknown in the field of children's literature. Of its thirty-two excerpts, nineteen are drawn from *Dialogues*, written with Claire Parnet and published in 1977, and thirteen from *What is Philosophy?*, written in collaboration with Félix Guattari[1] and published in 1991. Each excerpt is centred on the page, on a back drop of Duhême's images. *L'Oiseau philosophie* conforms to Perry Nodelman's categorisation of 'picture book', as illustration dominates over the text, 'tak[ing] up most of the space and bear[ing] the burden of conveying most of the meaning' (Nodelman 1988: viii), and yet it is an unusual children's text, for it tells no story and does not have its 'culmination and termination points' (ATP 22E/32F), or a linear path to follow from beginning to end. *L'Oiseau philosophie* is then, like Deleuze and Guattari's own text *A Thousand Plateaus*, 'composed of plateaus [. . .] Each plateau can be read starting anywhere and can be related to any other plateau' (ATP 22E/33F). What is more, the creation of *L'Oiseau philosophie* marks a Deleuzian plateau in the pictorial life of Duhême,[2] not a space of respite or for calmly pausing, but rather, as Brian Massumi describes in his foreword to the English translation of *A Thousand Plateaus*, a point 'when circumstances combine to bring an activity to a pitch of intensity' (ATP xivE). In 2015, Gallimard Jeunesse republished *L'Oiseau philosophie*. This edition features new cover art and an additional dedication to the memory of 'Gilles et Jean-Pierre', alluding to Jean-Pierre Bamberger, Deleuze's closest friend, who died in 2014.

Jacqueline Duhême's (1927–) career[3] as a children's book illustrator spans more than sixty years and is marked by fortuitous encounters. As an illegitimate child, Duhême was passed from orphanage to convent, around France and then to Greece in the hope of locating her Greek father. The onset of the Second World War transformed Duhême firstly into a shepherdess then into a factory worker, with a period of convalescence that took her to the south of France. Working subsequently as a children's nanny, she met Henri Matisse – who had at that time begun his work on the Chapelle du Rosaire in Vence – and was able to take her drawings to him. On her return to Paris, Duhême was given Paul Éluard's *Dignes de vivre* by a friend and asked to take it to a signing. Éluard mistakenly dedicated the book to Duhême and this chance encounter blossomed into a long-lasting friendship. An invitation from Matisse to work as his assistant took Duhême back to the south of France in the late summer of 1948, and she began her now prestigious artistic career.

With Matisse, Duhême learnt the techniques of her trade, from the care of brushes to the preparation of his coloured papers from which he would make his *découpages*. She also posed as his model for the Virgin Mary for the Chapelle du Rosaire. Matisse, Duhême recalls, was very similar in character to Deleuze: 'they both had the same view of work, a type of willingness to work. Nothing would stop them from getting to work, they loved working, it was like a duty for them' (Newland 2016: 80).

In addition to working with Matisse and Éluard, other prestigious artistic and cultural figures Duhême has worked with include poet Jacques Prévert, novelist Maurice Druon, Nobel laureate Miguel Angel Asturias and first lady Jackie Kennedy. Duhême has, as a result, become one of the most well-known and influential contemporary children's illustrators in France. Her images grace the pages of many more writers, such as Raymond Queneau (*Zazie dans le métro*),

Blaise Cendrars (*Petits contes nègres pour les enfants des Blancs*), Vercors (*Camille ou l'enfant double*), Jules Supervielle (*L'Enfant de la haute mer*), Joël Sadeler (*Le voyage du chariot à mots*), Élisabeth Badinter (*Le Voyage en Laponie de Monsieur de Maupertuis*) and Susie Morgenstern (*Comme il faut*). Éluard described her as *l'imagière des poètes* – the poets' illuminator – a whimsical term which simultaneously captures the idea of a picture book for children (*l'imagier*), its illustrator (also *l'imagier* in French, with the feminine form *l'imagière*) and illuminators of ancient manuscripts (also *l'imagier*).[4] Her *œuvre* may be situated within the tradition of naïve art, not in any pejorative sense but rather for its apparent simplicity and for Duhême's penchant for the child figure and for fabulous birds and animals. Duhême's universe therefore corresponds perfectly to Deleuzian philosophy, itself interspersed with witches and sorcerers: figures which are more typically at home in the genre of children's literature.

The extracts included in *L'Oiseau philosophie* were selected by Martine Laffon. Laffon, an editor and philosopher herself, had previously edited *Le Monde de Sophie*, by Norwegian author Jostein Gaarder (1952–), originally published as *Sophies verden* in 1991, a text about a little girl, named Sophie,[5] who is fascinated by the complexities of the universe and wide-ranging philosophical questions. According to Duhême, Deleuze was 'very happy with *Le Monde de Sophie*, with people's curiosity for philosophy, young people's, children's' (Newland 2016: 82). Indeed, Jean-Jacques Lecercle comments on Deleuze's pleasure in the reception of his own philosophy by a wide audience, writing that 'Deleuze was duly proud of this and rejoiced in the fact that *The Fold* had been appreciated by Japanese paper folders and Australian surfers' (Lecercle 2012: 13). *L'Oiseau philosophie* follows in these footsteps and brings Deleuzian thought to a new, younger, uninitiated audience. For Douglas Ord, 'it makes for "a Deleuze" accessible through bite-sized texts – Deleuze of the aphorism – *and* through Duhême's visual dialogue with these texts' (Ord 2014: 87, original emphasis). The text is dedicated to Lola, Deleuze's granddaughter who, rather like Gaarder's Sophie, loved to ask him questions and who was, rather like the fictional Alice who fascinated him, aged seven or eight at the time of the book's publication (Newland 2016: 79).

L'Oiseau philosophie is prefaced by Martine Laffon and includes extracts from correspondence with Deleuze. Whilst he never saw the finished text, he had clearly enthused about its creation. His comments included in the preface read as follows: 'this book particularly pleases me as I see in it a marvellous plan where I recognise myself in it all the more that I am less involved (LOP: np). Duhême completed *L'Oiseau philosophie* 'in tears, having lost Deleuze for whom I cared deeply. I was overcome with grief' (Newland 2016: 81). *L'Oiseau philosophie* is, then, homage to a friendship between Gilles Deleuze, Jacqueline Duhême and Jean-Pierre Bamberger, and images of this friendship permeate the entirety of the text. Notably absent are images of Félix Guattari with whom Deleuze enjoyed an intense collaboration.

The first part of this chapter considers the presence of the bird in *L'Oiseau philosophie*, from its title and cover art to more subtle representations within the text. Birds, coupled with children and witches, other recurring figures within the text, are endowed with a latent potential: each may embark on a line of flight at any moment. In *L'Oiseau philosophie*, these three elements come together to draw readers of the text towards their own liberating deterritorialisations. In the second part of the chapter, I consider the child-figure throughout the text and Duhême's portrayals, refreshing for children's literature, of ambiguous, androgynous children. The indefinite molecular child figure in the text, along with the humorous ways Duhême captures Deleuze's distaste for the tree and the rhizomatic structure of *L'Oiseau philosophie* itself, reveal the malleability of time and make childhood a force that flows through all moments in life and something that is always accessible to us, not merely a transitory stage. The final part of this chapter sheds light on a little-discussed, yet deeply important friendship in Deleuze's life, that with Jean-Pierre Bamberger. To conclude, the chapter considers that Duhême in her portrayal of Deleuze in picture-book form is able to attain one of his most profound wishes: she is able to paint the imperceptible.

A Bird

A bird graces the cover of *L'Oiseau philosophie*. It is a flamboyant, colourful bird, similar to the bird of paradise, with a long narrow beak reminiscent of a humming bird. The original edition sees the philosophy bird set on a pale blue background; its multi-coloured wings pre-empt the vibrant colours of the endpapers and Duhême's images inside the text. For the 2015 edition, Duhême provides a new image of the philosophy bird: now more evidently in flight, its wings spread to enhance its vivid colours. This philosophy bird faces the opening of the book, as if directing its reader to open up the text and begin reading. The bird is a recurrent motif throughout Duhême's œuvre, and Jean Perrot, who sees echoes of the baroque in her technique, comments specifically on the recurrence of the bird of paradise in Duhême's work:

> the bird, the wing, spirals of plants, seeds from bouquets carried by the wind, flamboyant sunrises and sunsets and still many more elements constitute so many emblems of allegories that the illustrator has enriched and developed with age. Particularly revealing is this technique of an expression indirectly derived from the practices of baroque art which is the use of the image of the bird of paradise that can be found in J. Duhême's œuvre. (Perrot 1991: 31)

Duhême's use of the bird originates from her friendship with French poet Paul Éluard and her first children's book which Éluard wrote for her to illustrate: *Grain-d'Aile*. The eponymous Grain-d'Aile longs to have wings and to fly like a bird, and, as discussed in Chapter 3, she undergoes a becoming-bird through her desire and proximity to the birds in her garden. *Grain-d'Aile* is accompanied by a preface by the writer and poet, Lucien Scheler, in which he describes Grain-d'Aile's discovery of two fabulous beings, 'the lyrebird and the bluebird' (Éluard 1997: np). Duhême is the artistic bluebird (*oiseau bleu*) to Éluard's poetic lyrebird (*oiseau-lyre*). Her œuvre, replete with birds and flying creatures, anticipates the creation of *L'Oiseau philosophie* in 1997, which marks a further metamorphosis of the artist and of the bird: from bluebird (*oiseau bleu*) to philosophy bird (*oiseau philosophie*). Duhême derived the playful title from a conversation with Deleuze, explaining:

> when Gilles passed away, the book didn't have a title and I had wanted to talk about it with him. But in fact, I remembered what he said to me one day when I said to him 'But philosophy is difficult for me, I don't have the right words for it.' He replied, 'But you do, it is very pretty Jacqueline, it's a bird's name . . . philosophy.' So, I put the name of a bird. (Newland 2016: 78)[6]

Duhême, recalling her friend's poetic description, renders visible not any specific bird but rather a philosophy bird, like that Deleuze and Guattari describe in *What is Philosophy?*: 'the concept of a bird is found not in its genus or species but in the composition of its postures, colors, and songs' (WP 25E/20F). Duhême's philosophy bird is indefinite, it cannot be identified as any bird in particular, although it has features of the humming bird and the bird of paradise. Rather it captures the very essence of a bird: its flamboyant plumage, its ability to spread its wings and fly and attain a liberating line of flight.

The bird, for Deleuze and Guattari, is also a creator of refrains, and in putting the name of a bird as the title of her tribute to Deleuze, and creating the image of the philosophy bird, Duhême allows a ritournelle to pervade the text. This ritournelle sweeps up other iterations of the bird in both Deleuze and Duhême's *œuvres*: the stylistic 'bird of fire' (N 166E/225F) to which Deleuze refers in his 1989 letter to Réda Bensmaïa; the birdsong pervading the work of Messiaen; Hitchcock's intensive, vibrating portrayal of birds; the fluttering vibrancy of birds present in Matisse's cut-outs; the flamboyant birds present in *Grain-d'Aile, Tistou les pouces vertes, L'Homme qui avait tout, tout, tout*. This ritournelle resonates and intersects across the breadth of both artist and philosopher's work. The ritournelle, as we have seen previously in Chapter 2, is essentially linked to the child: it is the comforting ditty the child sings when far from home; it is the humming, vibrating sounds of the home that help create its circular boundaries and regulate its diverse time frames; and it is the crack in this circle through which others enter and the child may venture out. In returning in both the title of this tribute to Deleuze and its cover art, the philosophy bird brings in this other aspect of the ritournelle, the child for whom the text is destined, and who peruses the text. The ritournelle, like the heave-ho chorus resonating through Fleutiaux's work, gathers up birds in other childhood and adult readings, and presages the presence of birds to come within the text itself, crystallising these iterations of bird into its own unique interconnective temporality and transforming them all in a creative deterritorialisation.

In the cover image of the original edition, Duhême is also present, in her *bleu de travail*, her painters' overalls,[7] arms outstretched, encouraging the philosophy bird to fly off and embark on its liberating line of flight. In *A Thousand Plateaus*, Deleuze and Guattari ponder the notion of an artist who paints a bird, writing:

> suppose a painter 'represents' a bird; this is in fact a becoming-bird that can occur only to the extent that the bird itself is in the process of becoming something else, a pure line and pure color. Thus imitation self-destructs since the imitator unknowingly enters into a becoming that conjugates with the unknowing becoming of that which he or she imitates. (ATP 304–5E/374F)

In creating the cover image of the philosophy bird, Duhême sets the bird off on its line of flight, on its deterritorialising path of becomings-other, and because all becomings are inherently double, Duhême herself is drawn into this reciprocal movement of becoming. The creation of the image of the philosophy bird therefore forms a block which captures both bird and illustrator. Duhême can never imitate because that which she is attempting to imitate is already becoming-other, as is the painter in her attempt.

Within the text, there is one image where birds dominate. In this image appearing across a double page, pale blue birds, with pencil detail on their plumage, fly from both pages inwards towards the centre fold of the book over two seated figures. These birds are devoid of the flamboyant plumage of the philosophy bird of the cover. In their beaks, they carry small human-shaped figures, stylised child figures, which appear to have been plucked from a pile of cut-outs or *découpages* resembling those by Duhême's former employer, Matisse. The birds are accompanied by another figure in flight: the witch. The following extracts complement this image: on the left-hand page, 'thinking provokes general indifference. It is a dangerous exercise nevertheless'; on the right-hand page, 'to think is always to follow the witch's flight' (WP 41E/44F). In *What is Philosophy?* these two extracts frame a longer paragraph which reads as follows:

> precisely because the plane of immanence is prephilosophical and does not immediately take effect with concepts, it implies a sort of groping experimentation and its layout resorts to measures that are not very respectable, rational, or reasonable. The measures belong to the order of dreams, of pathological processes, esoteric experiences, drunkenness, and excess. We head for the horizon, on the plane of immanence, and we return with bloodshot eyes, yet they are the eyes of the mind. Even Descartes had his dream. (WP 41E/44F)

A reader familiar with Deleuze's work may recognise the missing text in the image. Duhême's illustration not only repeats the 'hermetic impulse' (Ramey 2012: 6) within Deleuzian thought but conjures images of the missing text. The seated figures appear entranced or dreaming in some way. The eyes of the figure on the right dominate, bloodshot, perhaps Deleuze's 'eyes of the mind'. The head of the seated figure on the left is sunk into its chest whereas the figure on the right stares open-mouthed to the ceiling, its head lifted, observing the mad vector of the witch's flight accompanied by birds. Image and text not only reiterate each other on these two pages, giving a visual image to Deleuze's thought, but are also able to capture text that is absent or text that appears in Deleuze's broader work.

Duhême's images accompanying these phrases equally evoke a passage from *Kafka: Toward a Minor Literature* where Deleuze and Guattari discuss bent and straightened heads. They link the image of the bent head to all that blocks and stifles desire, and that reduces our ability to make connections. The straightened head, however, is liberating and deterritorialising and opens us up to new connections (K 5E/8–9F). This notion occurs later in *What is Philosophy?*, when Deleuze and Guattari tell us that

> art is continually haunted by the animal. Kafka's art is the most profound meditation on the territory and the house, the burrow, portrait-postures (the inhabitant's lowered head with chin sunk into their chest, or on the contrary, 'Shamefaced Lacky' whose angular head goes right through the ceiling) [. . .] All that is needed to produce art is here: a house, some postures, colors, and songs – on condition that it all opens onto and launches itself on a mad vector as on a witch's broom. (WP 184–5E/175F)

In Duhême's images, the figure with the bent or sunken head on the left-hand page is coupled with a bird that is particularly remarkable. In the lower right-hand corner of the left-hand page, a bird has fallen from its flight and lies upside down, its claws rigidly sticking into the air. One of the paper-like child figures has fallen or been dropped from the beak of the bird flying directly above and is falling head-first towards the rigidly prostrate bird. In their section on becoming-music in *A Thousand Plateaus*, Deleuze and Guattari question: 'why does the child die, or the bird fall as though pierced by an arrow? Because of the "danger" inherent in any line that escapes, in any line of flight or creative deterritorialization: the danger of veering toward destruction, toward abolition' (ATP 299E/367F). Deleuze and Guattari's lines of flight have great potential for change and transformation, but they are not without risk. The dangers of such liberating thought stated in the text are reiterated in this image and bring in the other flying element of both image and text: the witch. Joshua Ramey considers that 'thought is a "witches' flight" in the sense of carrying us to beyond the frontier of what the body and mind have been presumed able to do' (Ramey 2012: 18). Duhême's witch is not out of place in children's literature, but she is not the typical witch of the genre, malevolent and menacing, she is rather a witch who takes us beyond ourselves, beyond the physical limitations of both mind and body. Deleuze's text coupled with Duhême's images force readers, young or old, nascent or learned, out of their comfortable mould and, like a cut-out snipped from its page of conformity, project readers on a new line. Image and text push the reader to follow the liberating mad vector of the witch's flight, even if the inherent risks are great.

A Child

The child figure features prominently throughout *L'Oiseau philosophie*. The first image of the text, which accompanies Deleuze's plea that we treat the book 'as you would treat a record you listen to, a film or TV programme you watch' (D 3–4E/10F), portrays three unclothed child-like figures. These images set the tone for the entire book. One is lying on its stomach reading, its reading posture therefore rendering it androgynous. The other two figures are upright and frame the citation. Whilst Duhême has made no attempt to hide representations of gender, there is only the merest suggestion from the depiction of the standing figures that one figure may be male. Duhême's images are purposefully ambiguous and, like the excerpt they accompany, imply that we need to strip ourselves bare and shed our preconceived notions of what reading should be. Whether adult or child, to read in a Deleuzian way that will not condemn the book, is to come to the reading experience naked, not weighed down by traditional reading conventions.

Whilst depictions of unclothed children are present in children's literature,[8] from the outset of *L'Oiseau philosophie* Duhême presents us with an image of the child that is completely unusual for the genre. Aside representations of Deleuze and Bamberger, to which I will turn later in this chapter, there are two other groupings of figures in *L'Oiseau philosophie*: child figures with bodies of various sizes which appear as central 'characters' dominating a page or as minor figures around the borders; and miniature more mature figures who appear solely in the periphery of pages. Duhême's child figures, whether large or small, show no physical signs of ageing or maturation. Often unclothed and always gender ambiguous, these child figures capture the essence of any child whatsoever (*un enfant quelconque*) that Deleuze seeks. Lacking in distinct facial characteristics and indeterminate with regard to age, gender and race, Duhême's figures are not the molar child of children's literature to be guided and shaped through didactic texts and imbued ideologies to a predetermined future adulthood, rather they are bodies 'without any personal coordinates' (CC 166E). Duhême's child figures are not specific, discrete persons with their own individual subjectivity indicated by a definite article, but are indefinite and non-specific, devoid of subjectivity but open to the potential of becoming: a molecular child par excellence.

The prevalence of this molecular child in *L'Oiseau philosophie*, coupled with the proximity between portrayals of figures of all sizes and the lack of a linear progression from child to adult, reveals only involution not evolution. This involution is reinforced by the nature of the text itself. As a rhizome book, a text composed of plateaus, *L'Oiseau philosophie* has no directional impetus: it can be opened at any page and the extracts read in any order. Deleuze and Guattari are well known for stating in *A Thousand Plateaus* that 'we have had enough of trees. We should stop believing in trees, roots, and radicles. They've made us suffer too much' (ATP 15E/24F), and there is one image in particular in *L'Oiseau philosophie* which captures their dislike of the tree in a literal yet playful way. Duhême depicts the tree on the left-hand side of a double-page spread as a fixed, archaic, Jurassic image of thought. This is juxtaposed, on the facing page, to a liberating image of the rhizome.[9] Duhême captures with clarity and humour the essence of this concept: there are dinosaurs in the branches of the staid tree, whose arm-like branches hold brooms to sweep away this archaic way of thinking. Vivid red triangular borders create depth on the facing page and draw the viewer into the middle of the page: obliging the reader's eye to move in the way that Deleuze and Guattari desire, rhizomatically, 'from the middle, through the middle' (ATP 25E/36F). The naked, amorphous figures, dancing and skipping, balance their laterally connecting rhizomes on their heads on the facing page and point to the cathartic nature of the rhizome, freeing us from our out-dated arborescent thought. This image pre-empts the extract and accompanying image five spreads later, stating: 'we have grass in our heads and not trees' (D 39E/51F). This particular image is reminiscent of Andy Warhol's Pop Art *Marilyn* images. Duhême creates a double diptych where pairs of child figures, devoid of facial characteristics or other distinguishing features but with grass-like hair, appear above and below the extract.

These literal depictions of the rhizome and the tree reveal, then, the implications of Deleuze and Guattari's concept for children's literature. Duhême's indefinite molecular child figures, coupled with the lack of directional impetus within the text, allow *L'Oiseau philosophie* to critique the teleological model that dominates Western childhood as discussed in Chapter 3, that we must grow *up*. Duhême's rhizome-book, with its ambiguous child figures, allows us to move from an arborescent notion of childhood to a rhizomatic one. *L'Oiseau philosophie* therefore gives us an image of a rhizomatic childhood, dominated by a malleable time which is no longer uni-directional, but may be bent backwards and forwards and around itself, as Alice discovers in her adventures in Wonderland, and which makes room for other becomings outside of a Chronos-driven growing up. The adult-child binary that typically pervades all children's literature has been swept away and replaced by a connectivity between old and young, adult and child, on the labyrinthine time line of Aiôn. One border image captures this connectivity perfectly: a contented child figure skips towards the centrefold of the page, holding on each side the hand of a dancing skeleton. These joyful figures, accompanied by a bird and a skeleton-bird in flight, remind us that, unbounded from Chronos and its regulatory constraints, we are 'simultaneously childhood, adolescence, old age and maturity' (C2 104E/130F). They remind us also that childhood, rather than being seen merely as an initial and transitory stage of life, should be understood as 'a specific strength, force or intensity' (Kohan 2015: 57) which inheres throughout our entire lifetime.

The playfulness of Duhême's child figures evident throughout *L'Oiseau philosophie* also speaks to a passage in Deleuze's earlier text, *Nietzsche and Philosophy*, where he writes of the game and the child at play:

> affirming becoming and affirming the being of becoming are two moments of a game which are compounded with a third term, the player, the artist or the child. The player-artist-child, Zeus-child: Dionysus, who the myth presents to us surrounded by his divine toys. The player temporarily abandons himself to life and temporarily fixes his gaze upon it; the artist places himself provisionally in his work and provisionally above it; the child plays, withdraws from the game and returns to it. In this game of becoming, the being of becoming also plays the game with itself; the aeon (time), says Heraclitus, is a child who plays. (NP 24E/28F)

The child engrossed in this innocent play for play's sake exists in its own bubble of time and space, out of sync or disconnected with ordinary time moving chronologically forward around it. The child may equally retreat from this play to enjoy, as Bogue puts it, 'a moment of distanced contemplation of the game' (Bogue 1989: 29). Time is fractured here in this dual dynamic of play, in these ever-returning moments of participation in and reflection upon the game. Time no longer moves in a simple linear fashion but rather loops back on itself in these repeated moments of the game. According to Bogue, 'the thought of the eternal return may be understood in terms of these two moments. One first participates in becoming and thereby affirms it; then one recognizes that all moments in the world are moments of becoming, that the very being of the world is becoming' (Bogue 1989: 29). It is this conceptualisation that allows Deleuze to state that 'return is the being of becoming itself, the being which is affirmed in becoming' (NP 24E/28F).

Becoming, as we have seen previously, is not a mere transformation and does not concern resemblance, imitation or identification, but takes us into the secretive world of sorcery, of contamination and contagion, brought about through desired proximity with an anomalous other. As Samantha Bankston reminds us: 'through the passage of Aion, or the eternal return, the double movement of becoming is laid bare. That which one becomes is subjected to becoming just as the one that becomes is simultaneously subjected to becoming. The "I" is dissolved in the double process of absolute becoming of Aion' (Bankston 2017: 40). Duhême illustrates becoming and its effect on the self alongside the following extract from *What is Philosophy?*: 'we write and think for animals themselves. We become animal so that the animal also becomes something else. The agony of a rat or the slaughter of a calf remains present in thought not through pity but as the zone of exchange between man and animal in which something of one passes into the other' (WP 109E/105F). Her image of becoming seems at first glance utterly un-Deleuzian: a 'child' and a 'tiger' stand opposite each other, but their heads are switched so that the child's head is that of a tiger and vice versa, in a curious game of dressing up. Below the child lies a dead bird, which like its counterpart in this text discussed above is pictured on its back with its claws sticking directly up. Below the tiger lies a dead rat on its side, its paws reaching out towards the reader. This switching of heads appears to provide a far too literal representation of an exchange between child and animal. In this image, however, the child and the tiger can no longer be read as molar entities in binary opposition to each other. Rather the reader is presented with monstrous, mutant figures, abnormalities in every way. Rosi Braidotti considers that 'the proliferation of monstrous social imaginary calls for [. . .] a form of philosophical teratology which Deleuze is in a unique position to provide' (Braidotti 2000: 165) with his philosophy of becoming. Duhême's image is also reminiscent of another child-tiger pairing in children's literature: Rudyard Kipling's Mowgli and Shere Khan from *The Jungle Book*. Mowgli is the feral child, raised by wolves, and whilst children's literature scholar, Amy Ratelle, considers that Mowgli's 'animalism remain[s] more a performance than a replacement' (Ratelle 2015: 50), Patricia Pisters's analysis of the 1942 film adaptation of Kipling's *Jungle Book* by Zoltan Korda reads Mowgli's hybridity thus: 'it is mainly his motor system, the way he moves lightly, and his athleticism (the way his body moves and rests, slows down, and speeds up), that shows he is in a state of becoming-animal' (Pisters 2003: 154). Duhême's image is not of course a moving image but a static one. She nonetheless places one of the child's feet in front of the other, as if stepping towards the tiger, whose paw reaches out to the child opposite. In these gestures, Duhême creates a movement that sweeps up the two heterogeneous parts, child and animal, and brings them together through a longing for closeness on a molecular level.

Reading the child in Duhême's image as a feral child such as Mowgli reveals him not to be undergoing becoming-wolf, however, but a becoming-tiger, with the anomalous other: his nemesis Shere Khan, the ageing, but deadly tiger. Just as Captain Ahab's becoming 'bypasses the pack or the school, operating directly through a monstrous alliance with the Unique, the Leviathan, Moby Dick' (ATP 243/298F), so this Mowgli-child's becoming bypasses the pack with whom he was raised and is feline not lupine. His becoming-tiger occurs in the attraction they have to each other throughout the text and not in the moment when Oedipal desire surfaces and reterritorialises the becoming as Mowgli finally kills Shere Khan and returns to the village wearing the tiger's skin. Duhême's image alludes to such a risk, with the failure of becoming reiterated by the dead animals at the feet of the child-tiger characters. Duhême's illustration therefore goes beyond the anthropomorphised image of child-animal exchange typified in children's literature, beyond the typical child in the tiger-suit image. Instead, her illustration captures the closeness and molecular exchange of becoming-animal where 'it is a question of composing a body with the animal, a body without organs defined by zones of intensity or proximity' (ATP 274E/335F). Duhême's image captures something of the Body without Organs (BwO) that Deleuze and Guattari propose as their antidote to psychoanalysis and towards which becoming-animal moves us.

Psychoanalysis, for Deleuze and Guattari, reduces childhood imaginings, utterances and desires to Oedipal lack within the daddy-mummy-me triangle of the nuclear family. In *Anti-Oedipus* Deleuze and Guattari consider 'a child at play, or a child crawling about exploring the various rooms of the house he lives in. He looks intently at an electrical outlet, he moves his body about like a machine, he uses one of his legs as though it were an oar, he goes into the kitchen, into the study, he runs toy cars back and forth' (AO 50E/55F). This observation reveals the constant machining of the child; its exploration of the world as a constant desire to be plugged in, to be connected with external things. Deleuze and Guattari do not deny its parents a role in this, writing 'it is obvious that his parents are present all this time and that the child would have nothing were it not for them' (AO 50E/55F). However, they refuse to see all the child's external experiences as 'representative of his parents' (AO 50E/55F), feeding back into the Oedipus complex. To provide an example of the child's 'wide-ranging life of desire – [its] whole set of nonfamilial relations with the objects and the machines of desire' (AO 51E/56F), they reference Richard Lindner's painting *Boy with Machine* as an example of the desiring-machines created by the child. This 'turgid little boy has already plugged a desiring-machine into a social machine, short-circuiting the parents' (AO 392E/429F), and is as such moving towards what Deleuze and Guattari refer to as a BwO: a term borrowed from Antonin Artaud and used initially by Deleuze in *The Logic of Sense*.[10] The BwO is not literally a body devoid of internal organs, nor is it something that can ever be attained in its entirety, for in pushing the BwO to the limit, as, for example, drug addicts, alcoholics or anorexics may do, we risk its destruction. Rather the BwO is brought about through desire: it is in fact 'the degree zero of desire, it is what desire desires when it no longer wishes to desire [. . .]. In effect, this is what desire *desires* the most, not to desire; or, more accurately, to be in a state in which desire is unable to exert any pressure' (Buchanan 2015: 28 original emphasis). The BwO is not a closed, self-contained organism, but one that is open to multiple outside connections through bodies assembling with a heterogeneous external other. It overturns the organising social, biological, psychological and cultural structures that contain us; as Patty Sotirin explains, a BwO is 'a body that is not organized in accord with Oedipal relations, biological functions, organic forms, or cultural-historical values. Rather a BwO deconstructs these seemingly inviolable arrangements, deterriorializing particles, intensities, energies in molecular lines of flows, thresholds and becomings' (Sotirin 2007: 101–2). In Duhême's head-swap image, the molar classifications of child and tiger are displaced. We cannot look at her image and see two distinct and fixed subjects, child and tiger, imbued with preconceived socio-cultural values. Instead we are confronted with a BwO 'crisscrossed by particles and fluxes which break free from objects and subjects' (D 89E/108F). These are teratologic bodies: they are not particularly appealing to look at, yet they are nonetheless vital. In *Essays Critical and Clinical*, Deleuze makes such an observation in his reading of D. H. Lawrence's work. He considers that 'Lawrence ceaselessly describes bodies that are organically defective or unattractive – like the fat retired toreador or the skinny, oily Mexican general – but that are nonetheless traversed by this intense vitality that defies organs and undoes their organization' (CC 131E/164F). Their vitality stems from their abnormality. They are vital but not in any traditional sense. In head swapping, Duhême's BwO redefines the limits of the child's and the tiger's organisms and opens up each body to connections beyond the normal organic limits of the body. As Patricia Pisters suggests, 'the BwO does not oppose the organs: it opposes the *limits* of the organism and makes multiple connections that go beyond the organism's organization as it is traditionally defined' (Pisters 2003: 110, original emphasis). In the introduction to his translation of *Critique et Clinique*, Daniel W. Smith likens the BwO to 'what is "seen," for example, in the phenomena known as internal or external "autoscopia": it is no longer *my* head, but I feel myself inside *a* head' (CC xxxviiE). The BwO towards which we move through becoming is no longer governed by subject-specific pronouns or possessive adjectives – these are displaced by the indefinite article. Like the zeroth voice that speaks it, discussed in Chapter 5, in becoming, it is no longer *my* body but *a body* in symbiosis with an external other which itself is changed by the double capture of becoming. This displacement creates 'a field of intensities that works purely on the sensitive, the invasion of the affect' (Pisters 2003: 68) that precedes and supersedes the *I* that feels or experiences it.

A further image which captures something of the BwO appears later in the text, where a pale green circle fills the centre of the page and contains the extract: 'we are not in the world, we become with the world; we become by contemplating it. Everything is vision, becoming. We become universes. Becoming animal, plant, molecular, becoming zero' (WP 169E/160F). As we progress through such becomings, the organism that contains us fuses with external others. In becoming, the organism can no longer be described through traditional means, the physical limits of the organism are effaced through desire and opened up to the creation of a BwO. In this image, four figures are caught up in an assemblage. These figures are placed at each quarter of the circle. The head of each figure, the cognisant part of each body, is no longer visible but subsumed into the egg-like shape which they encircle, with only the body, arms and legs of each figure visible. The arms of each figure reach out to another object placed in between each figure: a fern-like leaf, a cow, a translucent body, and a string of DNA, each representing the different types of becoming mentioned in the text. The BwO towards which animal, vegetal and molecular becoming are moving us is therefore not to be understood through reason or cognition, but is something to be felt intensively. This new 'intensive reality' (ATP 164E/202F) is created 'where things and organs are distinguished solely by gradients, migrations, zones of proximity. The egg is the BwO. The BwO is not "before" the organism; it is adjacent to it and is continually in the process of constructing itself' (ATP 164E/202F). The image here captures the nature of *L'Oiseau philosophie*: it is not a book destined for interpretation but a book to be experienced intensively; an a-signifying machine to be plugged into other things. Like the BwO, it is all that is left when interpretation is removed, when 'no longer are there acts to explain, dreams or phantasies to interpret, childhood memories to recall, words to make signify; instead, there are colors and sounds, becomings and intensities' (ATP 162/200F).

Life, Death and Friendship

L'Oiseau philosophie pays homage to a friendship – a long-standing, intense friendship between Gilles Deleuze, Jean-Pierre Bamberger and Jacqueline Duhême. This particular 'fold of friendship' to use Charles Stivale's term, brings in two other more well-known friendships that marked Deleuze's life through the texts chosen for inclusion in *L'Oiseau philosophie*: *What is Philosophy?* representing Deleuze's last collaboration with Félix Guattari, and *Dialogues*, written with Claire Parnet, with whom he shared a unique student-professor bond.

It was in the years following the Liberation that Jean-Pierre Bamberger met Deleuze, according to Claire Parnet writing on behalf of the 'collective friends of Jean-Pierre Bamberger' in his obituary of 2014. For Parnet, Deleuze was Bamberger's double, 'with whom he began an infinite and daily conversation until the last days of the philosopher' (Parnet 2014: np). Deleuze attests to the fidelity of this friendship in *Dialogues* stating 'Jean-Pierre, the only friend whom I have never left and who has never left me' (D 11E/18F). Duhême describes the friends as 'poets' who both had 'visions' (Newland 2016: 77), and yet, despite his 'philosophical background' (TRM

204F), Bamberger was 'the creator who [did] not want to write' (Parnet 2014: np). It was whilst working as an 'illustrating-reporter' (Duhême 1998: 62) for Hélène Lazareff, founder and director of the magazine *Elle*,[11] that Duhême had a fortuitous meeting with Bamberger. She describes their encounter as follows:

> Jean-Pierre Bamberger was a great friend of Hélène Lazareff who was my employer. Once he came to see her. [...] and I, I thought he was nice and he lived in the same area as me. So, we left together by bus. We became friends, and then when you know Jean-Pierre Bamberger, you know Gilles – it doesn't happen any other way. They were like two peas in a pod, they were like that right to the end, he [Jean-Pierre] never got over Gilles's death, he adored Gilles... he was... I wouldn't say his best friend, he was his alter-ego. They were always together. (Newland 2016: 77)

It is not surprising then, that images of Deleuze and Bamberger permeate *L'Oiseau philosophie*. Duhême pictures them together, in conversation, or alone, appearing both young and vital, and more mature; like the child-figures in the text, these are non-linear images of Deleuze and Bamberger at different stages of life.

The most vibrant and prominent representation of this friendship appears in the final third of the book: Deleuze and Bamberger are drawn in semi-profile walking hand in hand as if exiting the book to the left. Duhême, a tiny figure at the bottom, gazes up in awe at her two friends, her palette and paintbrush in her hands. Youthfulness and vitality dominate this image of the encounter between Deleuze and Bamberger in their prime: a contrast to the way in which Deleuze was known to '[cast] himself and Jean-Pierre Bamberger (one in weakened health, the other a hypochondriac) as the "pale reproduction" of Beckett's Mercier and Camier' (Stivale 2008: 120), and to the other key images of Deleuze in *L'Oiseau Philosophie* which show an older Deleuze, or a Deleuze deceased. In likening Bamberger and himself to Beckett's comedic duo, Deleuze captures the essential aspects of friendship: charm and madness. In Charles Stivale's readings of Deleuze's *Abécédaire* he writes:

> Deleuze says that the charm that people reveal only comes through their madness (*folie*), through the side of someone that shows they're a bit unhinged. He maintains that if you can't grasp the small trace of madness in someone, you can't be their friend. But if you grasp that small point of someone's insanity (*démence*), the point where they are afraid or even happy, that point of madness is the very source of their charm. (Stivale 2008: 35)

Duhême's image of the two friends roaming – rather like Beckett's other well-known nomadic duo, Vladimir and Estragon – out of the book speaks to the passage in *Dialogues* in which Deleuze questions what such an encounter brings about: 'what precisely is an encounter with someone you like? Is it an encounter with someone, or with the animals who come to populate you, or with the ideas which take you over, the movements which move you, the sounds which run through you?' (D 11E/17F). Duhême, who depicts her friends covered in exotic animals, plants and flowers, as they are reborn 'as public garden or zoo' (WP 71E/73F) in their interaction with each other, captures this radiating, penetrating idea of friendship. 'Before we even have time to formulate specific thoughts or opinions about a person', Frida Beckman notes, drawing on Deleuze's comments in his *Abécédaire,* 'we may perceive a gesture, an opening, an awakening that goes to the very root of perception, and this [Deleuze] explains to Parnet, constitutes a friendship' (Beckman 2017: 46). Friendship, *folie* and perception, like Duhême's image of Deleuze and Bamberger, go hand in hand.

The final image of text, which accompanies the citation 'any event is a fog of a million droplets' (D 65/79), depicts Deleuze's unclothed corpse lying beneath a tree-like shape, as rain pours down. Death, for Deleuze, 'has two aspects. One is personal, concerning the I or the ego [. . .] The other is strangely impersonal, with no relation to "me", neither present nor past but always coming' (DR 112E/148F). As with the idea of childhood, we should not be fascinated by the circumstances of Deleuze's death as an individual, with the end of 'a life in a particular organism' (Beckman 2017: 109), but, as Frida Beckman points out, 'Deleuze's death should perhaps also be seen as "a death"' (110) – an indefinite, impersonal event of the infinitive 'to die' which does away with possessive indicators and in which becoming inheres. James Williams notes that 'a personal death is an end. It is a final destruction and passing away. Impersonal death is a living on through participation in a cycle of dying. Everything dies and because everything dies we live on in the dying and living of others' (Williams 2011b: 173). Personal death is firmly fixed on the time-line of Chronos – the ending of a specific life at a given point in time. Impersonal death belongs, however, to the realm of Aiôn and to the eternal return, and it is this dual aspect of death that Duhême captures with this final image of *L'Oiseau philosophie*: the personal, impactful death of a dear friend and an impersonal life-affirming death.

On the one hand, this image evokes the mourning and the sorrow felt by Duhême creating the images for the text: the deluge of raindrops symbolising her chagrin at the loss of her friend. Yet, Deleuze's corpse, lying at the foot of this isolated tree standing in a fog of raindrops on a blue-grey background, is accompanied by another figure. At the top of the tree, a small, white, almost iridescent figure dances, its arms open wide, like the spread of a bird's wings, giving, on the other hand, another face to this final image of *L'Oiseau philosophie*: that of joy, with the molecular child dancing atop the tree under which Deleuze's corpse lays. To counter the apparent incongruity of this tree image, Douglas Ord reads it as 'an incorporeal eruption – a sort of rhizomatic mushroom cloud' (Ord 2014: 92). It also can be read as an image of the resurrection of Deleuze, what Ord calls, drawing on Deleuze's *Nietzsche and Philosophy*, a '"résurrection dionysiaque" in the form of a child' (92). This co-presence of corpse and molecular child can, however, be read as a visual of Aiôn, of the connectivity of time and of the simultaneity of all stages of life at any point in life. Beaulieu and Ord have likened the circumstances of Deleuze's own death, his defenestration on 4 November 1995, to the fictional Alice's passage through the mirror, occurring on the day before Bonfire Night, also 4 November. They speculate as follows: 'could it be that Deleuze's last gesture, in tracing that of Alice, permitted him to renew ties with the world of children regarding which he avowed an infinite admiration and of which the measure has not yet been taken?' (Beaulieu and Ord 2017: 134). Their insight ties the final stage of Deleuze's death to a fictional childhood that dominated his early thinking and, like Duhême's image, reinforces the idea that without the limitations of Chronos, time escapes its linear impetus, allowing childhood and death to be one and the same moment in time in Aiôn, the joyous child who plays.

Conclusion: Painting the Imperceptible

L'Oiseau philosophie is a truly unusual text: defying the logic of the academe, it slips between strata of classification into a smooth space projecting those who encounter it and those who created it onto dizzying lines of flight. In this text, the binary categories of children's literature and of philosophy become, breaking free of their molar constraints, and like the caged bird suddenly freed or the child dismissed from school onto the playground, are propelled into a new colourful and vibrant space, full of vitality and utterly deterriorialising. There is no logic to this text, and indeed, there does not have to be one, as Deleuze himself considers in the preface to *L'Oiseau philosophie*: 'there need not be a logical sequence, just an aesthetic cohesion' (LOP: np). The point of this text is not to analyse, or to seek meaning, but to lay ourselves bare to the reading experience and to open ourselves up to becoming.

Duhême's illustrations may appear at first glance to be childlike or even simplistic, at times even un-Deleuzian. Yet, this simplicity of Duhême's illustrations marries well with Deleuze's thought, which, as Frida Beckman notes, has itself 'a certain innocence' (Beckman 2017: 124). Behind this innocence of her work there nonetheless lies much training and a wealth of literary and cultural experience, as Duhême states in *Passion Couleurs*: 'everything is thought through despite any obvious spontaneity' (Duhême 1998: 45). Indeed, this text marks an apogee in Duhême's artistic career, and bears the hallmarks of her sixty years of experience with great masters such as Matisse, Éluard, Prévert and Druon. It is this wealth of experience which allows Duhême not only to 'paint words' (LOP: np), as Deleuze describes it, but also to 'liberate philosophical concepts of pure events, that is to say capable of moving a little girl without logical consequence' (LOP: np). Indeed, for Deleuze, Duhême's illustrations are 'able to provide both a rigorous clarity and a tenderness' to the text (LOP: np), and like any great artist, Duhême 'make[s] perceptible the imperceptible forces that populate the world, affect us, and make us become' (WP 182E/172F).

In the introduction to his translation of *Francis Bacon: The Logic of Sensation*, Daniel W. Smith writes that we are conditioned to 'heed what artists do, not what they say' (FB xiE). Deleuze, Smith explains, 'insists that we do not listen closely enough to what painters have to say: "The texts of a painter act in a completely different manner than the paintings," he [Deleuze] notes. "In general, when artists speak of what they are doing, they have an extraordinary modesty, a severity toward themselves, and a great force"' (FB xiE). Duhême in her *Passion Couleurs* interviews with *Le Monde* journalist Florence Noiville, responds to Noiville who asks her if she has a message she hopes to transmit to children. Duhême replies: 'the idea that you have to feel things intensely? That painters and poets are the only people who invite us to leave ourselves? Absolutely' (Duhême 1998: 102). These words show that Duhême is as conscious of the logic of sensation created by art as her friend. Her images not only capture and render Deleuze's concepts visible, but also help us to leave ourselves and move beyond the limitation of our bodies. In *L'Oiseau philosophie*, Duhême paints the imperceptible and gives us an image of what children's literature should be: pure becoming which opens up the molecular child to us all.

Notes

1. François Dosse makes the claim that *Qu'est-ce que la philosophie?* 'was manifestly written by Deleuze alone, but [that] he agreed to a coauthor credit with Guattari, as a tribute to their exceptionally intense friendship, suggesting too that the ideas developed in the book and its language were the fruit of their common endeavour since 1969' (Dosse 2010: 456). This argument is taken up in Ord 2014 and Beckman 2017.
2. In *Passion Couleurs: Entretiens avec Florence Noiville*, Duhême describes the creation of *L'Oiseau philosophie* as 'un bouleversement, un palier dans la vie de mes images' (Duhême 1998: 48). *Palier* translates literally as a landing between two staircases, but also has the sense of new level attained; in this context, the Deleuzian concept of plateau would seem an appropriate translation.
3. For an analysis of Duhême's cultural influence see Newland 2016.
4. Duhême always refers to herself as *imagière* rather than the more pedestrian *illustratrice*.
5. In naming his heroine Sophie, Gaarder alludes to the Comtesse de Ségur's well-known Fleurville trilogy, which includes *Les Petites Filles modèles, Les Malheurs de Sophie* and *Les Vacances*. Ségur's Sophie is anything but a model child, unlike Gaarder's Sophie.
6. In French, the expression *donner à quelqu'un des noms d'oiseaux* exists, implying to offend or insult someone.
7. This self-portrait is also recalling the photographs of Duhême at Matisse's villa, in overalls perched on a tall step-ladder whilst helping him prepare the windows for the Chapelle du Rosaire in Vence.
8. For an extended discussion of the portrayal of naked children in picture books see Nodelman 1988: 121–4.
9. For Deleuze, 'the rhizome includes the best and the worst: potato and couchgrass, or the weed' (ATP 13E/7F). Duhême's mother would also describe her daughter in a similar vein: despite various attempts to abort her pregnancy, Jacqueline survived and subsequently her mother would refer to her as 'weeds, couchgrass, it just grows and you can't get rid of it' (Duhême 1998: 14).
10. Buchanan 2015 provides a genealogy of the BwO throughout Deleuze's *œuvre*, highlighting its literary inception in *The Logic of Sense* and its transformations throughout his collaboration with Guattari.
11. Working at *Elle*, Duhême had the opportunity to illustrate Jacqueline

Kennedy's visit to Paris in 1961. Her illustrations so delighted Kennedy that Duhême accompanied her on subsequent foreign tours, to Rome, India and Pakistan. She also covered Pope Paul VI's visit to the Holy Land and Charles de Gaulle's visit to South America, both in 1962.

7

Conclusion: Children's Literature on a Witch's Broom

To think is always to follow a witch's line. (*What is Philosophy?* 41E/44F)

In this study we have taken what at first might seem an unlikely step, taking Deleuze into the genre of children's literature. But there Deleuze, whose philosophy often speaks of witches and sorcerers, is quite at home; all the more so because, despite the simplicity implied by its specific readership, children's literature is in fact fraught with paradox. As we have seen, Deleuze sits well in this Looking-Glass genre which paradoxically pulls us towards both child and adult. With Deleuze, we have explored an eclectic variety of little-known children's texts written by some of the authors who fascinate him. We have seen how inviting Deleuze into this genre can invigorate our readings of it. We have taken his advice and thought about children's literature following an unpredictable, exhilarating witch's line.

Mounting the witch's broom alongside Deleuze in these readings of children's literature has brought forth intensive encounters and propelled us in unusual directions. The bizarrely repetitious *contes* of the absurd dramatist Eugène Ionesco have swept us up in the dizzying swirl of pure repetition and opened up for us the malleable time of Aiôn. The ritournelles of Pierrette Fleutiaux's young detective Trini have resonated through time and space, gathering up disparate time frames of childhood and adulthood and allowing a supple molecular child to emerge through their presence. We have grown otherwise, becoming-animal with the scurrying vermin of high modernist author, Virginia Woolf; becoming-plant with the dancing trees of contemporary author J.-M. Gustave Le Clézio; becoming-molecular as Woolf's Nurse Lugton merges with the mountains of Millamarchmantopolis; becoming-imperceptible in the kaleidoscopic tunnel of Miguel Angel Asturias's nameless man who had everything. We have relinquished our to-and-from journeys and made nomadic excursions into the landscapes of André Dhôtel's elusive *grand pays*. We have journeyed to Michel Tournier's desert island to discover a world out of time. We have learnt to stutter with Lewis Carroll's

Alice and enjoyed the howling language of James Joyce's Devil, before pushing language through its fragile surface to the point at which all (non)sense forms. Our zigzagging witch's broom has taken us to the wildest arc of its trajectory: the becoming-imperceptible of language – the zeroth voice.

Of all the texts discussed in *Deleuze in Children's Literature*, Deleuze only ever wrote extensively on Lewis Carroll's Alice books. Whilst he discussed Tournier's *Vendredi ou les limbes du Pacifique*, there is no record of him commentating on Tournier's second Friday, *Vendredi ou la vie sauvage*. We know for certain that Deleuze read another of these texts, Asturias's *L'Homme qui avait tout, tout, tout*, having corresponded with its illustrator, Jacqueline Duhême, regarding her images for the text. We can speculate that Deleuze may also have been aware of Dhôtel and Le Clézio's contributions to children's literature: *Le Pays où l'on n'arrive jamais* (1955) and *Voyage au Pays des Arbres* (1978) were both published in Deleuze's lifetime, as were the first two *contes* written by Ionesco, with *Conte 1* appearing in same year as Deleuze's *The Logic of Sense*. Equally, Deleuze may have been aware of Woolf's and Joyce's short texts for children which were both translated into French.[1] Pierrette Fleutiaux's Trini sequels appeared after Deleuze's death, as did *L'Oiseau philosophie*; yet it is clear from the preface of this picture book that Deleuze knew of the intention to create it but did not live to see its publication. We also know anecdotally that Deleuze was certainly fond of telling children stories: his autobiographer refers to the stories of Monsieur Idiot that Deleuze would tell the daughters of his supervisor, Maurice de Gandillac (Dosse 2010: 107).

This wide-ranging corpus with its very particular range of authors by no means represents the limitations of the possibilities for Deleuzian readings of children's literature. Whilst the field of Deleuze and education is well-advanced, there is still a pressing need to introduce the scope and potential of Deleuzian readings to the field of children's literature. In his 2013 *Reading the Child in Children's Literature: An Heretical Approach*, David Rudd, whilst not engaging deeply with Deleuze, nonetheless finds himself 'attracted by Gilles Deleuze's notion of theory' in which 'all texts offer possibilities for developing new "flights" of thought' (Rudd 2013: 3). His plea to 'celebrate the "energetics" of texts' (3) perhaps comes closest to the witch's line that I have sought in my study. To seek the witch's line when reading is, by its very nature, not something that is comfortable or reassuring, but a way of thinking that sends us zigzagging into the unknown as if propelled by an invisible force. It speaks to the vitality of children's literature, the *je ne sais quoi* that keeps us reading, that 'feeling of a gust of air from behind each time you read' (D 15 E/22F). *Deleuze in Children's Literature* has demonstrated how we may 'do' children's literature with Deleuze and equally what Deleuze 'does' to children's literature. It is my hope that this will encourage more scholars of children's literature to explore the richness of Deleuze's concepts in their own readings.

To close this study, it is then fitting to repeat and turn again to Lewis Carroll's Alice books and Deleuze's own *L'Oiseau philosophie*. Alice has, like a haunting refrain, permeated each chapter of this text. Her descent into Wonderland and her passage through the fragile surface of the mirror into the Looking-Glass land epitomises the invigorating witch's line that we seek in our reading experiences. Her becomings, repetitions and stutterings alongside the cartographies she composes reveal the potential of the molecular child to shake the status quo and destabilise the socially ingrained structures, binaries and practices that define us. This molecular child is open to experimentation and creativity: a child open to becoming; a child of the 'people to come' (C2 228E/288F). *L'Oiseau philosophie*, this unassuming picture book, is the ideal molecular text for this new collectivity.

Alice: Molecular Child

Alice is a molecular child par excellence. She is big, then she is small; she believes she is Alice, but she could well be Mabel. Her recital of rhymes and poems, which in Wonderland and the Looking-Glass land morph into inadvertent and amusing parodies, should reaffirm her ever-changing identity, but instead they serve only to erode her knowledge and with it her sense of selfhood. Her wanderings through Wonderland and the Looking-Glass land render her Deleuze's *enfant quelconque*, any child whatsoever, a child of the people to come. A child, indefinite and stripped of the markers of subjectivity and fixity. Her size and shape become fluid; even her name, as her conversations with the Gnat in the fourth square of the Looking-Glass land make plain, becomes redundant. Alice's selfhood dissolves; Alice is no more. The paradoxical changes Alice undergoes lay bare the very nature of becoming that literature offers us: that change inheres within itself; that becoming is never uni-directional, but pulls us in two directions at once. In what appear to be the mutually exclusive actions of growing up and down, in getting bigger and smaller at the same time, Alice reveals that the only being is that of pure becoming.

How do we grow up? This all-pervasive, molar question of children's literature fixes us in a linear, uni-directional movement through time, towards another molar state: adulthood. Aware that we are conditioned into thinking about growing up in such a way, and that we require an alternative, Deleuze and Guattari offer us the concept of becoming. Becoming undoes all subjectivity in its process of double capture, of assembling with a heterogeneous other. Becoming-other helps us break free of the molar categories and socially imposed classifications and subjectivities that arrange us (adult-child, male-female, human-animal, etc.), and opens us to new possibilities. To become is to abandon one's discrete subjectivity and to be contaminated on a truly other level, animal or plant, as the texts of Virginia Woolf, J.-M. Gustave Le Clézio and Miguel Angel Asturias show. Pushed to the extreme, our becomings allow us to embrace otherness at a molecular level beyond the limitations of human perception. Without such restrictions, we are able to grow otherwise, like Alice, up and down, rhizomatically, through the middle, without a fixed starting or end point. To read Deleuze in children's literature is to pursue, then, characters like Alice who shake our fixities; characters who take us beyond an evolutionary and bodily growth to involution and incorporeal growth; characters who put us on the path towards becoming.

To grow incorporeally is to grow in the temporality of Aiôn, as Alice does when she descends the rabbit hole or passes through the drawing room looking-glass. In these movements, Alice suspends her normal, everyday time, her Chronos, and enters the unhinged time of Aiôn. In Aiôn, the obligation to move in a uni-directional, linear fashion is removed. On the labyrinthine line of Aiôn, time may be bent backwards and forwards and around itself. The temporality of Aiôn that pervades many children's texts and to which Ionesco's *Contes* and Pierrette Fleutiaux's Trini novels attest, captures the bi-directionality of the molecular child, of the child who becomes, who is pulled in two directions at once – up and down – simultaneously towards child and adult. Aiôn, which holds past and future at any point on its line, draws together the supposed sequential periods of childhood and adulthood and sweeps them up into a childhood block that exists at all moments in time and that allows 'adult' and 'child' to contaminate each other. Child and adult become contiguous, as they do in Alice's sister's imaginings where the young and older Alice are drawn together. When children's authors play with varied and diverse temporalities, they are shaking the fixity and linearity of a pre-defined pathway towards adulthood. Their stories carve out new possibilities for the people to come: the possibility of growing otherwise.

When Alice descends the rabbit hole or heads through the looking-glass, she embarks on a journey across the curious lands she finds there. Much children's literature concerns, as we have seen, journeying; the venture away from and the return home. Reading Deleuze in children's literature shifts the focus away from journeying to and from somewhere, and even beyond the larger journey of growing up, of moving from childhood to adulthood. Rather, journeys with Deleuze bring other supple, molecular lines to the fore. These lines traverse us, push us to move through the middle, and help us compose maps and cartographies. The most dynamic of these lines is the line of flight which creates possibilities for deterritorialisation and for nomadic slippages between the strata of the regime.

These molecular lines or lines of flight in children's literature propel their characters to the faraway landscapes of desert islands or elusive countries that always remain somewhat beyond reach. With Deleuze any 'return home' is a liberating one: one that through trajectories and their subtending becomings takes us to landscapes in Aiôn which are unfixed in time and space. Dhôtel's elusive *grand pays*, like Tournier's desert island or Alice's Looking-Glass land, are home to the creative and capricious molecular surface-child, whose ageing is no longer a concern.

Alice's adventures are as much about language as the curious creatures she meets there. Initially she tries to demonstrate her knowledge of the majoritarian norm, but the landscapes of Wonderland and the Looking-Glass land deterritorialise her words. Alice begins to stutter. The addition of French and Latin create further distortion and her speech begins to seep out on its own line of flight from the corners of her mouth, creating its own inimitable style. Alice's voice, which in the world she leaves behind is often silenced, is now rich and expressive.

Elaborated from Deleuze's notion of the fourth person singular, my plea to call out a zeroth voice in children's literature is perhaps the wildest trajectory in my readings of Deleuze in children's literature. The zeroth voice is not simply a child voice or an adult voice, but one that allows both child and adult to coexist in a pure moment of time and in one voice stripped of distinct subject positions: it is the voice of the molecular child that emerges in the space of children's literature. The zeroth voice emerges as language begins to speak itself, freed from the limitations of its organs of production and perception. It emerges at the zero point of thought, as the double sidedness of sense is revealed. It is the voice of the dissolved self of becoming which exists in the flow of assemblage: it is what we hear when the encounter that is reading works for us.

L'Oiseau philosophie: *Molecular Text*

If Alice is a molecular child par excellence, then *L'Oiseau philosophie*, Deleuze in picture-book form, is the perfect molecular text for this child of the people to come. *L'Oiseau philosophie* is molecular in so much as it cannot be subsumed into a distinct category: it is a children's book, a picture book, and yet a book of philosophy at the same time. Its readers can be the most learned of scholars or the most ingenuous – a young child who has not yet learnt to read may still be attracted to and amused by the imagery of the text. *L'Oiseau philosophie*'s molecularity continues within the book: like Deleuze and Guattari's own *A Thousand Plateaus*, it is a rhizome book, composed of plateaus and lacking any linear impetus. Reading may start at any point and progress to any other; it is malleable and fluid, devoid of beginning and end, caught up in a flux of ceaseless becomings.

There is no eponymous character in this text, no fictional child to watch grow and mature. There is only the molecular child and the character of childhood itself. Peopled with ambivalent yet playful figures, which like the child who plays, unbind time from its linear impetus and push simultaneously towards childhood and maturity, *L'Oiseau philosophie* reminds us that childhood inheres throughout life and that 'the child is the becoming-young of every age. Knowing how to age does not mean remaining young; it means extracting from ones age the particles, the speeds and slownesses, the flows that constitute the youth of *that* age' (ATP 277E/340F, original emphasis). *L'Oiseau philosophie* calls out the youth in its readers. This youth, as Ronald Bogue suggests, 'is its newness, its power of setting in disequilibrium the codes, conventions and practices of fixed power structures' (Bogue 2010: 99).

This is what we should hope the encounter with children's literature to be: an invigorating ride on a witch's broom which defies a reader's age but celebrates youth. To read Deleuze in children's literature is to liberate readers from the codes that contain them and to invent new possibilities for the people to come.

Note

1. Woolf's *Nurse Lugton's Curtain* was translated as *Le Dé en or* in 1983 by Frédéric Armel (see Barai 2014); Joyce's *The Cat and The Devil* appeared in French as *Le Chat et Le Diable* in 1966, translated by Jacques Borel.

References

Albrecht-Crane, Christa (2007) 'Style, Stutter', in *Gilles Deleuze: Key Concepts*, ed. Charles J. Stivale, Stocksfield: Acumen, pp. 121–30.

Appleyard, J. A. (1994) *Becoming a Reader: The Experience of Fiction from Childhood to Adulthood*, Cambridge: Cambridge University Press.

Asturias, Miguel Angel (1999) *L'Homme qui avait tout, tout, tout*, trans. Aline Janquart, Paris: Éditions du Seuil.

Bankston, Samantha (2017) *Deleuze and Becoming*, London and New York: Bloomsbury.

Barai, Aneesh (2014) 'Modernist Repositionings of Rousseau's Ideal Childhood: Place and Space in English Modernist Children's Literature and Its French Translations', Dissertation, Queen Mary, University of London, at <https://qmro.qmul.ac.uk/xmlui/handle/123456789/7903> (accessed May 2020).

Barker, Keith (1998) 'Animal Stories', in *International Companion Encyclopedia of Children's Literature*, ed. Peter Hunt, Routledge: London and New York, pp. 282–94.

Barrie, J. M. (1995) *Peter Pan*, London: Penguin Popular Classics.

Barthes, Roland (1977) *Image, Music, Text*, London: Fontana.

Baudrillard, Jean (1994) *Simulacra and Simulations*, trans. S. F. Glaser, Ann Arbor: University of Michigan Press.

Baugh, Bruce (2000) 'How Deleuze Can Help Us Make Literature Work', in *Deleuze and Literature*, ed. Ian Buchanan and John Marks, Edinburgh: Edinburgh University Press, pp. 34–56.

Beaulieu, Alain and Ord, Douglas (2017) 'The Death of Gilles Deleuze and a Composition of a Concept', *Deleuze Studies* 11:1, pp. 121–38.

Beckett, Sandra L. (1997) *De grands romanciers écrivent pour les enfants*, Montréal: Les Presses de l'Université de Montréal.

Beckett, Sandra L. (2009) *Crossover Fiction: Global and Historical Perspectives*, New York and Abingdon: Routledge.

Beckett, Sandra L. (2012) *Crossover Picture Books: A Genre for All Ages*, New York and Abingdon: Routledge.

Beckman, Frida (2017) *Gilles Deleuze*, London: Reaktion Books Ltd.

Bergson, Henri (1927) *Essai sur les données immédiates de la conscience*, Paris: Presses Universitaires de France.

REFERENCES

Bergson, Henri (2000) *Time and Free Will: Essay on the Immediate Data of Consciousness*, trans. F. L. Pogson, Mineola, NY: Dover.

Bettelheim, Bruno (1991) *The Uses of Enchantment: The Meaning and Importance of Fairy Tales*, London: Penguin.

Bogue, Ronald (1989) *Deleuze and Guattari*, New York and London: Routledge.

Bogue, Ronald (2003) *Deleuze on Literature*, New York and London: Routledge.

Bogue, Ronald (2010) *Deleuzian Fabulation and the Scars of History*, Edinburgh: Edinburgh University Press.

Bohlmann, Markus (2012) 'Moving Rhizomatically: Deleuze's Child in 21st Century American Literature and Film', PhD thesis, University of Ottawa, at <https://ruor.uottawa.ca/handle/10393/23140> (accessed April 2020).

Bohlmann, Markus (2014) 'In Any Event: Moving Rhizomatically in Peter Cameron's *Someday This Pain Will Be Useful to You*', *Children's Literature Association Quarterly* 39:3, pp. 385–412.

Bohlmann, Markus and Hickey-Moody, A. (eds) (2019) *Deleuze and Children*, Edinburgh: Edinburgh University Press.

Bond Stockton, Kathryn (2009) *The Queer Child, or Growing Sideways in the Twentieth Century*, Durham, NC: Duke University Press.

Boundas, Constantin V. (1994) 'Deleuze: Serialization and Subject-Formation', in *Gilles Deleuze and the Theater of Philosophy*, ed. Constantin V. Boundas and Dorothea Olkowski, London: Routledge, pp. 99–118.

Bourassa, Alan (2015) 'The Analyst and the Nomad: Lacan, Deleuze and Coetzee's *Life and Times of Michael K*', in *Deleuze and the Schizoanalysis of Literature*, ed. Ian Buchanan, Tim Matts and Aidan Tynan, London and New York: Bloomsbury, pp. 137–53.

Bradley, Joff (2015) 'The Eyes of the Fourth Person Singular', *Deleuze Studies* 9:2, pp. 185–207.

Braidotti, Rosi (2000) 'Teratologies', in *Deleuze and Feminist Theory*, ed. Ian Buchanan and Claire Colebrook, Edinburgh: Edinburgh University Press.

Braidotti, Rosi (2008) *Metamorphoses: Towards a Materialist Theory of Becoming*, Cambridge: Polity Press.

Braidotti, Rosi (2011) *Nomadic Subjects: Embodiment and Sexual Difference in Contemporary Feminist Theory*, New York: Columbia University Press.

Bryden, Mary (2007) *Gilles Deleuze: Travels in Literature*, Basingstoke: Palgrave Macmillan.

Buchanan, Ian (2000) *Michel Certeau: Cultural Theorist*, London: SAGE.

Buchanan, Ian (2009) 'Is Anti-Oedipus a May '68 book?', in *Deleuze and History*, ed. Jefferey A. Bell and Claire Colebrook, Edinburgh: Edinburgh University Press, pp. 206–24.

References

Buchanan, Ian (2015) 'The "Structural Necessity" of the Body without Organs', in Buchanan et al. (eds), *Deleuze and the Schizoanalysis of Literature*, London and New York: Bloomsbury, pp. 25–42.

Buchanan, Ian, Matts, Tim and Tynan, Aidan (eds) (2015) 'Introduction: Towards a Schizoanalysis of Literature', in *Deleuze and the Schizoanalysis of Literature*, London and New York: Bloomsbury, pp. 1–22.

Burns, Lorna (2012) *Contemporary Caribbean Writing and Deleuze: Literature Between Postcolonialism and Post-Continental Philosophy*, London and New York: Continuum.

Butts, Bruce (2003) '"He's behind you!": Reflections of Repetition and Predictability in Lemony Snicket's *A Series of Unfortunate Events*', *Children's Literature in Education* 34:4, pp. 277–86.

Carroll, Lewis (2008) *The Complete Illustrated Lewis Carroll*, London: Wordsworth.

Carroll, Lewis and Gardner, Martin (2000) *The Annotated Alice: Alice's Adventures in Wonderland & Through the Looking-Glass: The definitive edition*, New York: W. W. Norton and Company.

Colebrook, Claire (2002) *Gilles Deleuze*, London and New York: Routledge.

Cummins, June (1997) 'The Resisting Monkey: "Curious George," Slave Captivity Narratives, and the Postcolonial Condition', *ARIEL: A Review of International English Literature* 28:1, pp. 69–83.

Czarnecki, Kristin (2011) 'Who's Behind the Curtain? Virginia Woolf, "Nurse Lugton's Curtain," and the Anxiety of Authorship', *Selected Papers from the 21st Annual International Virginia Woolf Conference: Contradictory Woolf, University of Glasgow, 10 June 2011*, ed. Derek Ryan and Stella Bolaki, Clemson University Digital Press, pp. 222–8.

Davis, Colin (2010) *Critical Excess: Overreading in Derrida, Deleuze, Levinas, Žižek and Cavell*, Stanford: Stanford University Press.

De Bolle, Leen (2010) 'Deleuze's Passive Syntheses of Time and the Dissolved Self', in *Deleuze and Psychoanalysis: Philosophical Essays on Deleuze's Debate with Psychoanalysis*, ed. Leen De Bolle, Leuven: Leuven University Press, pp. 131–55.

Delessert, Étienne (2015) *L'Ours bleu: Mémoires d'un créateur d'images*, Geneva: Éditions Slatkine.

Deleuze, Gilles and Parnet, Claire (2004) *L'Abécédaire de Gilles Deleuze*, directed by Pierre-André Boutang, Paris: Éditions Montparnasse.

Dhôtel, André (2015) *Le Pays où l'on n'arrive jamais*, illustrated by Julia Wauters, Paris: Flammarion Jeunesse.

Dosse, François (2010) *Gilles Deleuze and Félix Guattari: Intersecting Lives*, trans. Deborah Glassman, New York: Columbia University Press.

Downey, Glen Robert (1998) 'The Truth about Pawn Promotion: The Development of the Chess Motif in Victorian Fiction', PhD thesis, University of Ottawa, at <https://dspace.library.uvic.ca/handle/1828/8275> (accessed May 2020).

REFERENCES

Duhême, Jacqueline (1986) *Line et les autres*, Paris: Éditions Gallimard.
Duhême, Jacqueline (1998) *Passion Couleurs: Entretiens avec Florence Noiville*, Paris: Éditions Gallimard Jeunesse.
Dusinberre, Juliet (1999) *Alice to the Lighthouse: Children's Books and Radical Experiments in Art*, Basingstoke and New York: Macmillan.
Éluard, Paul (1997) *Grain-d'Aile*, Paris: Éditions Pocket Jeunesse.
Faulkner, Keith W. (2006) *Deleuze and the Three Syntheses of Time*, New York: Peter Lang.
Ferlinghetti, Lawrence (2001) *How to Paint Sunlight: Lyric Poems and Others (1997–2000)*, New York: New Directions.
Fleutiaux, Pierrette (1997) *Trini fait des vagues*, Paris: Éditions Gallimard Jeunesse.
Fleutiaux, Pierrette (1999a) *Trini à l'île de Pâques*, Paris: Éditions Gallimard Jeunesse.
Fleutiaux, Pierrette (1999b) *L'Expédition*, Paris: Éditions Gallimard.
Foucault, Michel (1980) *Language, Counter-Memory, Practice*, trans. Donald F. Bouchard and Sherry Simon, Ithaca: Cornell University Press.
Foucault, Michel (2001) *Dits et écrits I, 1954–1975*, ed. D. Defert and F. Ewald, Paris: Éditions Gallimard.
Frankart, Roland (2012) '*Le Pays où l'on n'arrive jamais*, encore et toujours Le Prix Fémina d'André Dhôtel', in *André Dhôtel, entre archaïsme et modernité*, Amsterdam and New York: Édition Rodopi, pp. 39–56.
Freud, Sigmund (1986) *The Essentials of Psycho-Analysis*, trans. J. Stratchey, London: Penguin.
Freud, Sigmund (2015) *Beyond the Pleasure Principle*, trans. J. Stratchey, Mineola, NY: Dover.
Gaarder, Jostein (1995) *Le Monde de Sophie: roman sur l'histoire de la philosophie*, trans. Hélène Hervieu and Martine Laffon, Paris: Les Éditions du Seuil.
Gannon, Susan (1987) 'One More Time: Approaches to Repetition in Children's Literature', *Children's Literature Association Quarterly* 12:1, pp. 2–5.
Garnier, Marie-Dominique (2003) 'The Lapse and the Lap: Joyce with Deleuze', in *James Joyce and the Difference of Language*, Cambridge: Cambridge University Press, pp. 97–111.
Gelas, Bruno and Micolet, Hervé (eds) (2007) *Deleuze et les Écrivains: Littérature et Philosophie*, Nantes: Éditions Cécile Defaut.
Gobard, Henri (1976) *L'Aliénation linguistique: Analyse tétraglossique* Paris: Flammarion.
Gubar, Marah (2013) 'Risky Business: Talking about Children in Children's Literature Criticism', *Children's Literature Association Quarterly* 38:4, pp. 450–7.
Henky, Danielle (2012) 'De quelques romans-jeunesse d'André Dhôtel:

References

prendre l'enfance au(x) mot(s)', in *André Dhôtel, entre archaïsme et modernité*, Amsterdam and New York: Édition Rodopi, pp. 71–86.

Hickey-Moody, Anna (2013) 'Deleuze's Children', *Educational Philosophy and Theory* 45:3, pp. 272–86.

Hildick, Wallace (1965) 'Virginia Woolf for Children?', *Times Literary Supplement*, 17 June 1965, p. 496.

Hodgkins, Hope Howell (2007) 'High Modernism for the Lowest: Children's Books by Woolf, Joyce and Greene', *Children's Literature Association Quarterly* 32:4, pp. 354–67.

Honeyman, Susan (2005) *Elusive Childhood: Impossible Representations in Modern Fiction*, Columbus: Ohio State University Press.

Hume, David (2008) *An Enquiry Concerning Human Understanding*, New York: Cosimo.

Hunt, Peter (1984) 'Questions of Method and Methods of Questioning: Childist Criticism in Action', *Signal* 45 (September), pp. 180–200.

Hunt, Peter (1995) *Criticism, Theory, and Children's Literature*, Oxford: Blackwell.

Ionesco, Eugène (1968) *Présent passé, Passé Présent*, Paris: Éditions Gallimard.

Ionesco, Eugène (2009) *Contes 1, 2, 3, 4*, Paris: Éditions Gallimard Jeunesse.

Jardine, Alice (2001) 'Woman in Limbo: Deleuze and his Br(others)', in *Deleuze and Guattari: Critical Assessments of Leading Philosophers, Volume III*, ed. Gary Genosko, London and New York: Routledge, pp. 1397–413.

Joyce, James (1965) *The Cat and the Devil*, illustrated by Gerald Rose, London: Faber and Faber.

Joyce, James (1966) *Le Chat et le Diable*, illustrated by Jean-Jacques Corre, trans. Jacques Borel, Paris: Gallimard.

Joyce, James (1975) *Selected Letters of James Joyce*, ed. Richard Ellmann, New York: Viking.

Joyce, James (1990) *The Cat and the Devil*, illustrated by Roger Blachon, St. John's, Newfoundland: Breakwater Books.

Kaufman, Eleanor (2012) *Deleuze, The Dark Precursor: Dialectic, Structure, Being*, Baltimore: Johns Hopkins University Press.

Keeling, Kara (2007) *The Witch's Flight: The Cinematic, the Black Femme, and the Image of Common Sense*, Durham, NC: Duke University Press.

Knapp, Bettina L. (1998) 'Entretien avec Pierrette Fleutiaux', *The French Review* 71:3, pp. 436–41.

Kohan, Walter (2015) *Childhood, Education and Philosophy: New Ideas for an Old Relationship*, London and New York: Routledge.

Kümmerling-Meibauer, Bettina and Meibauer, Jörg (2011) 'On the Strangeness of Pop Art Picturebooks: Pictures, Texts, Paratexts', *New Review of Children's Literature and Librarianship* 17:2, pp. 103–21.

REFERENCES

Lambert, Gregg (2007) 'Expression', in *Gilles Deleuze: Key Concepts*, ed. Charles J. Stivale, Stocksfield: Acumen, pp. 31–41.

Laplanche, Jean and Pontalis, Jean-Bertrand (1967) *Vocabulaire de la psychanalyse*, ed. D. Lagache, Paris: Presses Universitaires de France.

de Lauretis, Teresa (1984) *Alice Doesn't: Feminism, Semiotics, Cinema*, Bloomington: Indiana University Press.

Le Clézio, Jean-Marie Gustave (1978) *Voyage au pays des arbres*, Paris: Éditions Gallimard.

Lecercle, Jean-Jacques (1985) *Philosophy through the Looking-glass: Language, Nonsense, Desire*, La Salle: Open Court.

Lecercle, Jean-Jacques (1994) *Philosophy of Nonsense: The Institutions of Victorian Nonsense in Literature*, London and New York: Routledge.

Lecercle, Jean-Jacques (2002) *Deleuze and Language*, Basingstoke: Palgrave Macmillan.

Lecercle, Jean-Jacques (2012) *Badiou and Deleuze Read Literature*, Edinburgh: Edinburgh University Press.

Lesnik-Oberstein, Karin (1994) *Children's Literature: Criticism and the Fictional Child*, Oxford: Clarendon Press.

Levy, Michelle (2004) 'Virginia Woolf's Shorter Fictional Explorations of the External World: "closely united . . . immensely divided"', in *Trespassing Boundaries: Virginia Woolf's Short Fiction*, ed. Kathryn N. Benzel and Ruth Hoberman, New York and Basingstoke: Palgrave Macmillan, pp. 139–56.

Lewis, C. S. (1980) *The Lion, The Witch and The Wardrobe*, London: Collins.

Leysen, Annemie (2010) 'Four Impressive Nominees: Analyzing the Andersen Illustrator Finalists', *Bookbird: A Journal of International Children's Literature* 48:4, pp. 15–20.

Livesey, Graham (2010) 'Assemblage', in *The Deleuze Dictionary*, Revised Edition, ed. Adrian Parr, Edinburgh: Edinburgh University Press, pp. 18–19.

Lorraine, Tamsin (1999) *Irigaray and Deleuze: Experiments in Visceral Philosophy*, Ithaca: Cornell University Press.

Lorraine, Tamsin (2000) 'Becoming-imperceptible as a Mode of Self-Presentation: A Feminist Model Drawn from a Deleuzian Line of Flight', in *Resistance, Flight, Creation: Feminist Enactments of French Philosophy*, ed. Dorothea Olkowski, Ithaca: Cornell University Press.

Loti, Pierre (2013) *Île de Pâques*, Paris: Magellan et Cie.

Lundy, Craig (2012) *History and Becoming: Deleuze's Philosophy of Creativity*, Edinburgh: Edinburgh University Press.

McGillis, Roderick (1984) 'Calling a Voice Out of Silence: Hearing What We Read', *Children's Literature in Education* 15:1, pp. 22–9.

McMaster, Juliet (2001) 'Adults' Literature by Children', *The Lion and the Unicorn* 25:2, pp. 277–99.

References

Martin, Ann (2006) *Red Riding Hood and the Wolf in Bed: Modernism's Fairy Tales*, Toronto: University of Toronto Press.

Massumi, Brian (1992) *A User's Guide to Capitalism and Schizophrenia: Deviations from Deleuze and Guattari*, Cambridge, MA: MIT Press.

Milne, A. A. (1973) *Winnie-the-Pooh*, London: Methuen Children's Books Ltd.

Mortimer, Robert G. (2000) *Physical Chemistry*, San Diego: Academic.

Muehrcke Philip C. and Muehrcke Juliana O. (1974) 'Maps in Literature', *Geographical Review* 64:3, pp. 317–38.

Necman, Sylvie (2009) 'Dessiner l'absurde, Le Temps Samedi Culturel', at <http://www.etiennedelessert.com/documents/Contes_LeTemps.pdf> (accessed May 2020).

Neimanis, Astrida (2007) 'Becoming-Grizzly: Bodily Molecularity and the Animal that Becomes', *PhaenEx* 2:2, pp. 279–308.

Nell, Victor (1988) *Lost in a Book: The Psychology of Reading for Pleasure*, New Haven and London: Yale University Press.

Newland, Jane (2009) 'Toward a Zeroth Voice: Theorizing Voice in Children's Literature with Deleuze', *Jeunesse: Young People, Texts, Cultures* 1:2, pp. 10–34.

Newland, Jane (2013) 'Repeated Childhood Pleasures: Rethinking the Appeal of Series Fiction with Gilles Deleuze', *International Research in Children's Literature* 6:2, pp. 192–204.

Newland, Jane (2016) 'Jacqueline Duhême, l'imagière des poètes: une vie de rencontres hors pair', *French Cultural Studies* 27:1, pp. 73–84.

Newland, Jane (2019) 'Temporalities of Children's Literature: Chronos, Aion and Incorporeal Ageing', in *Deleuze and Children*, ed. Markus P. J. Bohlmann and A. Hickey-Moody, Edinburgh: Edinburgh University Press, pp. 162–78.

Nikolajeva, Maria (1998) 'Exit Children's Literature?', *The Lion and the Unicorn* 22:2, pp. 221–36.

Nikolajeva, Maria (2000) *From Mythic to Linear: Time in Children's Books*, Oxford: Scarecrow Press.

Nikolajeva, Maria (2010) *Power, Voice and Subjectivity in Literature for Young Readers*, New York and Abingdon: Routledge.

Nodelman, Perry (1985) 'Interpretation and the Apparent Sameness of Children's Literature', *Studies in the Literary Imagination* 18:2, pp. 5–20.

Nodelman, Perry (1988) *Words About Pictures: The Narrative Art of Children's Picturebooks*, Athens: University of Georgia Press.

Nodelman, Perry (2008) *The Hidden Adult: Defining Children's Literature*, Baltimore: Johns Hopkins University Press.

Noiville, Florence (2009) 'Contes 1, 2, 3, 4, d'Eugène Ionesco: Choucroute et rhinocéros', *Le Monde des livres*, at <http://www.lemonde.fr/livres/article/2009/10/22/contes-1-2-3-4-d-eugene-ionesco_1257210_3260.html?xtmc=delessert&xtcr=14#> (accessed May 2020).

REFERENCES

Novak, Barbara (1970) 'Picture Books', *New York Times*, 24 May 1970, p. 224.

Olkowski, Dorothea (2008) 'After Alice: Alice and the Dry Tail', *Deleuze Studies* 2 (Supplement), pp. 107–22.

Opie, Peter and Opie, Iona (1997) *The Oxford Dictionary of Nursery Rhymes*, Oxford: Oxford University Press.

Ord, Douglas (2014) 'Differentiations of "Enfant/Child" in the Achievement of Gilles Deleuze' MA thesis, Laurentian University, at <https://zone.biblio.laurentian.ca/dspace/handle/10219/2236> (accessed May 2020).

O'Sullivan, Emer (2010) *Historical Dictionary of Children's Literature*, Plymouth: Scarecrow Press.

O'Sullivan, Simon (2007) *Art Encounters Deleuze and Guattari: Beyond Thought and Representation*, Basingstoke: Palgrave Macmillan.

Palmer, Helen (2014) *Deleuze and Futurism: A Manifesto for Nonsense*, London and New York: Bloomsbury.

Parnet, Claire (2014) 'Jean-Pierre Bamberger, le prince des agents secrets est mort Libération', at <http://www.liberation.fr/societe/2014/10/06/jean-pierre-bamberger-le-prince-des-agents-secrets-est-mort_1116221> (accessed May 2020).

Pavlik, Anthony (2010) '"A Special Kind of Reading Game": Maps in Children's Literature', *International Research in Children's Literature* 3:1, pp. 28–43.

Pebesma, Evan A. (2017) 'Doubles: The Duality of Humour', Electronic Thesis and Dissertation Repository, at <http://ir.lib.uwo.ca/etd/4686> (accessed October 2017).

Peraldo, Emmanuelle and Calbérac, Yann (2014) 'How to Do Narratives with Maps: Cartography as a Performative Act in *Gulliver's Travels* and *Through the Looking-Glass*', *Reconstruction: Studies in Contemporary Culture* 14:3, at http://reconstruction.eserver.org/Issues/143/PeraldoCalberac.shtml (accessed October 2016).

Perrot, Jean (1991) 'Jacqueline Duhême et l'illustration des poètes', *Argos: revue du CRDP de Créteil* 7, pp. 25–31.

Perrot, Jean (1999) *Jeux et enjeux du livre d'enfance et de jeunesse*, Paris: Éditions du Cercle de la Librairie.

Philippopoulos-Mihalopoulos, Andreas (2012) 'Law, Space, Bodies: The Emergence of Spatial Justice', in *Deleuze and Law*, ed. Laurent de Sutter and Kyle McGee, Edinburgh: Edinburgh University Press, pp. 90–110.

Pisters, Patricia (2003) *The Matrix of Visual Culture: Working with Deleuze in Film Theory*, Stanford: Stanford University Press.

Preece, Rod (2011) *Animal Sensibility and Inclusive Justice in the Age of Bernard Shaw*, Vancouver: University of British Columbia Press.

Propp, Vladimir (1994) *Morphology of a Folktale*, trans. L. Scott, Austin: University of Texas Press.

References

Ramey, Joshua (2012) *The Hermetic Deleuze: Philosophy and Spiritual Ordeal*, Durham, NC: Duke University Press.
Ransome, Arthur (2012) *Swallows and Amazons*, London: Vintage Books.
Ratelle, Amy (2015) *Animality and Children's Literature and Film*, Basingstoke: Palgrave Macmillan.
Reimer, Mavis, ed. (2009) *Home Words: Discourses of Children's Literature in Canada*, Waterloo: Wilfrid Laurier University Press.
Reimer, Mavis (2014) *Seriality and Texts for Young People: The Compulsion to Repeat*, ed. M. Reimer, N. Ali, D. England and M. Dennis Unrau, Basingstoke: Palgrave Macmillan.
Renou-Nativel, Corinne (2009) 'L'Esprit d'enfance d'Etienne Delessert', at <https://www.la-croix.com/Archives/2009-11-26/L-esprit-d-enfance-d-Etienne-Delessert-_NP_-2009-11-26-358747> (accessed May 2020).
Reynolds, Kimberley (2007) *Radical Children's Literature: Future Visions and Aesthetic Transformation in Juvenile Fiction*, Basingstoke: Palgrave Macmillan.
Rohman, Carrie (2013) 'A Hoard of Floating Monkeys: Creativity and Inhuman Becomings in Woolf's Nurse Lugton Story', *Deleuze Studies* 7:4, pp. 515–36.
Rose, Jacqueline (1994) *The Case of Peter Pan or the Impossibility of Children's Fiction*, Basingstoke: Macmillan.
Rudd, David (2005) 'Theorising and Theories: How Does Children's Literature Exist?', *Understanding Children's Literature: Key Essays from the Second Edition of the International Companion Encyclopedia of Children's Literature*, ed. P. Hunt, London and New York: Routledge, pp. 15–29.
Rudd, David (2013) *Reading the Child in Children's Literature: An Heretical Approach*, Basingstoke and New York: Palgrave Macmillan.
Saldanha, Arun (2013) 'Introduction: Bastard and Mixed-Blood are the True Names of Race', *Deleuze and Race*, ed. Arun Saldanha and Jason Michael Adams, Edinburgh: Edinburgh University Press.
Salinger, J. D. (1994) *For Esmé – with Love and Squalor and other stories*, London: Penguin Books.
Sartre, Jean-Paul (1981) *The Words: An Autobiography of Jean-Paul Sartre*, trans. Bernard Frechtman, New York: Random House Inc.
Sendak, Maurice (1963) *Where the Wild Things Are*, New York: Harper Collins.
Sigler, Amanda (2008) 'Crossing Folkloric Bridges: The Cat, the Devil and Joyce', *James Joyce Quarterly* 45:3–4, pp. 537–55.
Somers-Hall, Henry (2013) *Deleuze's Difference and Repetition: An Edinburgh Philosophical Guide*, Edinburgh: Edinburgh University Press.
Sotirin, Patty (2007) 'Becoming-woman', in *Gilles Deleuze: Key Concepts*, ed. Charles J. Stivale, Stocksfield: Acumen, pp. 98–109.
Stengers, Isabelle (2009) 'Thinking with Deleuze and Whitehead: A Double

Test', *Deleuze, Whitehead, Bergson: Rhizomatic Connections*, ed. Keith Robinson, Basingstoke and New York: Palgrave Macmillan, pp. 28–44.

Stevenson, Robert Louis (1908) 'A Gossip on Romance', *Memories and Portraits*, London: Chatto and Windus.

Stivale, Charles J. (2008) *Gilles Deleuze's ABCs: The Folds of Friendship*, Baltimore: Johns Hopkins University Press.

Susina, Jan (2010) *The Place of Lewis Carroll in Children's Literature*, Abingdon and New York: Routledge.

Thurston, Luke (2004) *James Joyce and the Problem of Psychoanalysis*, Cambridge: Cambridge University Press.

Tournier, Michel (1972) *Vendredi ou les limbes du Pacifique*, Paris: Gallimard.

Tournier, Michel (2012) *Vendredi ou la vie sauvage*, illustrated by Jean-Claude Götting, Paris: Gallimard Jeunesse.

Trites, Roberta Seelinger (2000) *Disturbing the Universe: Power and Repression in Adolescent Literature*, Iowa City: University of Iowa Press.

Tynan, Aidan (2012) *Deleuze's Literary Clinic: Criticism and the Politics of Symptoms*, Edinburgh: Edinburgh University Press.

Watson, Victor (2000) *Reading Series Fiction: From Arthur Ransome to Gene Kemp*, London and New York: Routledge Falmer.

Williams, James (2003) *Gilles Deleuze's Difference and Repetition: A Critical Introduction and Guide*, Edinburgh: Edinburgh University Press.

Williams, James (2008) *Gilles Deleuze's Logic of Sense: A Critical Introduction and Guide*, Edinburgh: Edinburgh University Press.

Williams, James (2011a) *Gilles Deleuze's Philosophy of Time: A Critical Introduction and Guide*, Edinburgh: Edinburgh University Press.

Williams, James (2011b) 'Never Too Late? On the Implications of Deleuze's Work on Death for a Deleuzian Moral Philosophy', in *Deleuze and Ethics*, ed. Nathan Jun and Daniel W. Smith, Edinburgh: Edinburgh University Press, pp. 171–87.

Wise, J. Macgregor (2007) 'Assemblage', in *Gilles Deleuze: Key Concepts*, ed. Charles J. Stivale, Stocksfield: Acumen, pp. 77–87.

Woolf, Virginia (1988) *The Widow and the Parrot*, illustrated by Julian Bell, Afterword by Quentin Bell, Harcourt Brace Jovanovich: San Diego.

Woolf, Virginia (2004) *Nurse Lugton's Curtain*, illustrated by Julie Vivas, Harcourt Books: San Diego and New York.

Yin, Jing (2013) 'Becoming-animal: Becoming-wolf in *Wolf Totem*', *Deleuze Studies* 7:3, pp. 330–41.

Zanger, Jules (1982) '"Habours like Sonnets": Literary Maps and Cartographic Symbols', *The Georgia Review* 36:4, pp. 773–90.

Zepke, Stephen (2005) *Art as Abstract Machine: Ontology and Aesthetics in Deleuze and Guattari*, Abingdon and New York: Routledge.

Zipes, Jack (2001) *Sticks and Stones: The Troublesome Success of Children's*

References

Literature from Slovenly Peter to Harry Potter, New York and London: Routledge.

Zourabichvili, François (2003) *Le Vocabulaire de Deleuze*, ed. J.-P. Zarader, Paris: Ellipses Éditions.

Index

L'Abécédaire de Gilles Deleuze, 1, 5, 149, 150
À la recherche du temps perdu (Proust), 59
A Thousand Plateaus (ATP, Deleuze and Guattari)
   Aiôn, 41, 66, 67
   becoming, 47, 48, 49
   becoming-animal, 49–50, 51, 53, 55, 56
   becoming-imperceptible, 60, 62
   becoming-molecular, 59, 61, 63
   becoming-plant, 58
   birds, 138
   Body without Organs (BwO), 148
   books, 7, 63
   cartography, 78, 80, 82, 102n
   The Cat and the Devil (Joyce), 111
   chessboard movements, 85
   Chronos, 67
   lines of flight, 22n, 76–7, 78, 140
   Moby Dick, 145
   molar lines, 21–2n, 76
   molecular child, 5
   molecular lines, 22n, 76
   nomads, 89, 92
   and *L'Oiseau philosophie*, 133–4, 160
   rhizomes, 75–6, 153n
   ritournelle, 34, 35, 38
   trees, 142
agencements, 20n, 48; *see also* assemblages
agency, 48; *see also* voice
Aiôn, 41–4, 45
   becoming, 144
   death, 150, 151
   growing up / growth, 66–71, 92, 158
   journeying, 159
   molecular child, 99–100
   nonsense, 124
   rhizomatic childhood, 143
Albrecht-Crane, Christa, 108
Alice Doesn't (de Lauretis), 120

Alice's Adventures in Wonderland (Carroll), 13, 15–16
   language, 107–9, 111–12, 115–18, 127–8, 130–1
   molecular child, 157–60
   pure becoming, 64–6, 67, 68, 71
   see also Through the Looking-Glass (Carroll)
aliquid, 116–17, 118, 121, 128
alterity (otherness), 3, 4; *see also* Other
animals
   Oedipal, 51–2, 55
   see also becoming-animal
Anti-Oedipus: Capitalism and Schizophrenia (AO, Deleuze and Guattari), 112, 145–6
Appleyard, J. A., 25–6
Artaud, Antonin, 110–11, 146
assemblages, 8, 20–1n, 48, 52, 125
Asturias, Miguel Angel, 9
   L'Homme qui avait tout, tout, tout, 12–13, 42–3, 58, 61–2, 63, 156
authors, 9
authorship, 7, 105, 124–5

Bamberger, Jean-Pierre, 134, 148–50
Bankston, Samantha, 144
Barker, Keith, 51
Barrie, J. M., 47
Barthes, Roland, 130
Bartleby, 120
Baugh, Bruce, 48
Beaulieu, Alain, 151
Beckett, Sandra L., 98, 99
Beckman, Frida, 6, 150, 152
becoming, 11, 47–9, 71, 81, 95, 144, 147
   pure, 13, 64–71, 157–8
Becoming a Reader (Appleyard), 25–6
becoming-animal, 11, 49–56, 72, 144–5
becoming-imperceptible, 12–13, 60, 62–4, 72
becoming-molecular, 59–60, 61, 63
becoming-plant, 11–12, 57–9
Bellsybabble, 110, 111

Index

Bergson, Henri, 38, 39
Beyond the Pleasure Principle (Freud), 26–7
bird, 136–41
Body without Organs (BwO), 145, 146–8
Bogue, Ronald
  adult neurosis, 69
  becoming, 72
  becoming-animal, 52
  language, 114, 124
  lines of flight, 77
  maps, 82
  molar lines, 76
  nonsense, 124
  power relations, 53, 160
  time, 42, 43, 66–7, 143–4
Bohlmann, Markus, 3, 116
books, 7–8, 63, 129; *see also* picture books
Boulez, Pierre, 66
Boundas, Constantin V., 97
Bourassa, Alan, 99
Boy with Machine (Lindner), 146
Bradley, Joff, 125
Braidotti, Rosi, 53, 89, 90, 109, 144
Bryden, Mary, 80, 93, 94, 95, 96, 99
Buchanan, Ian, 8, 19, 27, 120, 124, 129
Butts, Bruce, 26

Calbérac, Yann, 83, 84, 85
Capitalisme et Schizophrénie: L'Anti-Œdipe Nouvelle édition Augmentée (Deleuze and Guattari) *see* Anti-Oedipus: Capitalism and Schizophrenia (AO, Deleuze and Guattari)
Capitalisme et Schizophrénie 2: Mille Plateaux (Deleuze and Guattari) *see* A Thousand Plateaus (ATP, Deleuze and Guattari)
Carroll, Lewis, 9
  Alice's Adventures in Wonderland, 13, 15–16: language, 107–9, 111–12, 115–18, 127–8, 130–1, 159; molecular child, 157–60; pure becoming, 64–6, 67, 68, 71
  Through the Looking-Glass, 1, 16–17: death, 151; language, 112–13, 118–20, 121–3, 130–1, 159; molecular child, 157–60; movement, 75, 83–6; time, 41–2
cartographers, 78–83
cartography, 102n
The Case of Peter Pan (Rose), 3

The Cat and the Devil (Joyce), 17, 23n, 70–1, 109–12
causality, 38–9
'Causes and Reasons of Desert Islands' (Deleuze), 93
child emotion, 6
child figure, 141–8
childhood, 5–6
  rhizomatic, 142–3
childhood blocks, 70, 71
childist criticism, 4
children's literature, 1–2
  authors, 9
  paradox of, 3–5, 18
Children's Literature (Lesnik-Oberstein), 3
Chronos, 41, 42, 43, 67, 100, 150, 158
Cinema II (C2, Deleuze), 70, 143, 157
circulating words, 122
Colebrook, Claire, 47, 61, 62–3, 64, 77, 125–6
comparative difference, 10, 26, 28, 30
compulsion to repeat, 27, 45n
Contes 1, 2, 3, 4 (Ionesco), 10, 46n, 156
  pure repetition, 29–30, 31–4
  repetition, 28
  ritournelle, 37–8
  time, 40, 42, 43–4
  zeroth voice, 130
contracting words, 121
contraction, 39
Criticism, Theory, and Children's Literature (Hunt), 3–4
Critique et Clinique (Deleuze) *see* Essays Critical and Clinical (CC, Deleuze)
Cummins, June, 54
Curious George (H.A. and Margaret Rey), 53–4

danger, 51
Davis, Colin, 8
De Bolle, Leen, 28, 89
de Lauretis, Teresa, 120
The Dead (Joyce), 126–7
death, 150–1
death drive, 27, 28
decalcomania, 102n
deferred action, 69
definite article, 54–5
delay, 69
Delessert, Étienne, 29, 30, 31–2, 33, 37–8
Deleuze and Futurism (Palmer), 60

INDEX

Deleuze and Language (Lecercle), 117–18
Deleuzian child *see* molecular child
Desert Islands and other texts (DI, Deleuze), 12–13, 93
desire, 146
deterritorialisation
  becoming, 48, 54–5
  bicycle assemblage, 21n
  childhood blocks, 70
  lines of flight, 77
  molar lines, 86
  nomads, 89, 91
  repetition, 33
  ritournelle, 36, 44–5
  see also reterritorialisation
Deux Régimes de Fous (Deleuze) *see* *Two Regimes of Madness* (TRM, Deleuze)
Dhôtel, André, 9, 58
  Le Pays où l'on n'arrive jamais, 14, 87–92, 156
Dialogues II (D, Deleuze and Parnet)
  assemblages, 128
  authorship, 7, 124–5
  Baruch Spinoza, 19
  becoming, 48, 68
  Body without Organs (BwO), 146–7
  books, 141
  Jean-Pierre Bamberger, 148
  journeying, 76
  lines of flight, 77, 91
  maps, 75, 80
  memories, 70
  minor literature, 105
  L'Oiseau philosophie (LOP, Deleuze), 18, 133, 150
  reading, 157
  rhizomes, 142
difference, 30–1, 44
  comparative, 10, 26, 28, 30
  pure, 38
Difference and Repetition (DR, Deleuze), 10
  death, 150
  nonsense, 124
  repetition, 25, 28, 34: Andy Warhol, 31; and expectation, 38, 39–41; and variation, 30
  time, 69
disempowerment, 16, 65
distance, 69
Disturbing the Universe (Trites), 47
Dodgson, Charles, 127
Dosse, François, 156

Downey, Glen Robert, 85
Duhême, Jacqueline, 9
  career, 134–5
  Grain-d'Aile (Éluard), 50
  L'Homme qui avait tout, tout, tout (Asturias), 13
  mother's description of, 153n
  L'Oiseau philosophie (LOP, Deleuze), 1–2, 18, 133, 136: friendship, 148, 149; molecular child, 142, 144, 145; philosophy bird, 137–9
  Passion Couleurs interviews, 152–3, 153n
Dusinberre, Juliet, 16

l'école buissonnière, 14
Éluard, Paul, 50, 134, 135, 137
empiricism, 63
encounter, 6–8, 150
endpaper maps, 78, 80, 81–2, 83–5, 86, 101
Enquiry Concerning Human Understanding (Hume), 38–9
environments *see* milieus
esoteric words, 121
Essays Critical and Clinical (CC, Deleuze)
  becoming, 50, 54, 58, 81
  Body without Organs (BwO), 147
  language, 105–6, 108, 109, 111, 112, 114, 120
  maps, 82, 83, 86
  Miguel Angel Asturias, 12
  milieus, 77, 80, 91
  molecular child, 141
  witch's broom, 18–19
expectation, 38–9
L'Expédition (Fleutiaux), 36–7
experience, 63

faire l'école buissonnière, 14
Faulkner, Keith W., 122
Ferlinghetti, Lawrence, 128
Fleutiaux, Pierrette, 9, 156
  L'Expédition, 36–7
  Histoire du gouffre et de la lunette, 21n
  Trini à l'île de Pâques, 10–11, 36, 80–1, 82
  Trini fait des vagues, 10–11, 35–6, 42
  zeroth voice, 130
For Esmé – with Love and Squalor (Salinger), 26
Foucault, Michel, 30–1

Index

'fourth person singular' *see zeroth* voice
Francis Bacon: The Logic of Sensation (FB, Deleuze), 152
free-indirect style, 125–7
Freud, Sigmund, 26–8, 69, 102n
friendship, 148–50

Gannon, Susan, 25
Gardner, Martin, 115
Garnier, Marie-Dominique, 111
Gavi, Philippe, 60
gluttonous readers, 26
'A Gossip on Romance' (Stevenson), 64
Grain-d'Aile (Éluard), 50, 137
Grindel, Eugène *see* Éluard, Paul
growing up / growth, 11, 13, 47, 64, 66, 67–71, 92, 158; *see also* becoming
Guattari, Félix, 136; *see also A Thousand Plateaus* (ATP, Deleuze and Guattari); *Anti-Oedipus* (AO, Deleuze and Guattari); *Kafka: Toward a Minor Literature* (K, Deleuze and Guattari); *What is Philosophy?* (WP, Deleuze and Guattari)

haecceity, 61
Henky, Danielle, 14, 92
Hickey-Moody, Anna, 70
The Hidden Adult (Nodelman), 4–5
Histoire du gouffre et de la lunette (Fleutiaux), 21n
home-away-home motif, 34–5, 36, 45, 76, 100
L'Homme qui avait tout, tout, tout (Asturias), 12–13, 42–3, 58, 61–2, 156
Hume, David, 38–9
Humpty Dumpty, 16–17, 118–20, 121–2, 131
Hunt, Peter, 3–4, 5

Île de Pâques (Loti), 36–7
L'île déserte et autres textes (Deleuze) *see Desert Islands and other texts* (DI, Deleuze)
indefinite article, 54–5
interpretation, 8
involution, 11, 47, 68–9, 71, 100, 142
Ionesco, Eugène, 9
   Contes 1, 2, 3, 4, 10, 46n, 156: pure repetition, 29–30, 31–4; repetition, 28; ritournelle, 37–8; time, 40, 42, 43–4; *zeroth* voice, 130

Jabberwocky poem, 121–2
journeying, 13–15, 76, 100–1, 159; *see also Le Pays où l'on n'arrive jamais* (Dhôtel)
Joyce, James, 9
   The Cat and the Devil, 17, 23n, 70–1, 109–12
   The Dead, 126–7
Joyce, Stephen, 17, 70–1
The Jungle Book (Kipling), 144–5

Kafka, Franz, 109
Kafka: Toward a Minor Literature (K, Deleuze and Guattari)
   becoming-animal, 51, 52
   bent and straightened heads, 140
   childhood memory, 70
   lines of flight, 77
   minor literature, 105–6
   repetition, 32
   voice, 125
Kaufman, Eleanor, 68
Kohan, Walter, 143
Kümmerling-Meibauer, Bettina, 31, 33

Laffon, Martine, 135–6
Lambert, Gregg, 125
language, 16, 105–6, 114
   Alice's Adventures in Wonderland (Carroll), 107–9, 111–12, 115–18, 127–8, 130–1, 159
   The Cat and the Devil (Joyce), 109–12
   nonsense, 123–4, 126–8
   Through the Looking-Glass (Carroll), 112–13, 118–20, 121–3, 130–1, 159
   Voyage au pays des arbres (Le Clézio), 57
   see also zeroth voice
Laplanche, Jean, 69
Lawrence, D. H., 147
Lazareff, Hélène, 149
Le Clézio, Jean-Marie Gustave, 9, 11–12, 57–9, 58, 156
Lecercle, Jean-Jacques
   free-indirect discourse, 126–7
   Gilles Deleuze, 135
   Humpty Dumpty, 119, 122
   nonsense, 123, 124
   sense, 113, 114–15, 116, 117–18
Lesnik-Oberstein, Karin, 3, 5
Levy, Michelle, 61
Leysen, Annemie, 31–2
Lindner, Richard, 146

INDEX

lines of flight, 19, 22n, 76–7, 78, 140, 159
Nurse Lugton's Curtain (Woolf), 54
Le Pays où l'on n'arrive jamais (Dhôtel), 91
Where the Wild Things Are (Sendak), 52
The Lion, the Witch and the Wardrobe (Lewis), 68
literary studies, 2
literature, 8, 63, 105–6; *see also* children's literature
'Literature and Life' (Deleuze), 82
Logic of Sense (LOS, Deleuze)
  Bellsybabble, 111
  esoteric words, 121
  Lewis Carroll, 16
  nonsense, 124
  portmanteau words, 121, 122–3
  psychoanalysis, 27
  schizophrenic language, 110
  sense, 1, 112, 113, 114, 116–17, 120
  sense of self, 65
  temporality, 67: Aiôn, 41, 42
  Vendredi ou la vie sauvage (Tournier), 15, 95–6, 97, 98, 99
  Vendredi ou les limbes du Pacifique (Tournier), 102–3n
  zeroth voice, 128, 129
Lorraine, Tamsin, 60, 63–4
Loti, Pierre, 36–7
Lundy, Craig, 67

McGillis, Roderick, 129
McMaster, Juliet, 2
major literature, 105, 106
majoritarian adults, 53, 72
majoritarian language, 107–8, 109, 120
majoritarian norms, 106
majoritarian positions, 105
majoritarian reading, 53–4
map-making, 78–83
maps, 88
  endpaper maps, 78, 80, 81–2, 83–5, 86, 101
Martin, Ann, 56
Massumi, Brian, 5, 134
Matisse, Henri, 134
meaning, 112–18
  Humpty Dumpty, 118–20
  see also nonsense
Meibauer, Jörg, 31, 33
memory, 69, 70
metaphors, 60
milieus, 77–8, 80, 82, 91, 101, 102n

minor literature, 105–6; *see also Kafka: Toward a Minor Literature* (K, Deleuze and Guattari)
minoritarian position, 53, 105, 106, 108
molar child, 5, 99
molar dog, 50
molar lines, 21–2n, 76, 77, 85–6, 101
molecular child, 5, 6, 8, 11, 13, 69–70
  Alice's Adventures in Wonderland / Through the Looking-Glass (Carroll), 157–60
  L'Oiseau philosophie (LOP, Deleuze), 18, 141–2, 144–5, 151
  Stephen Joyce, 71
  Vendredi ou la vie sauvage / ou les limbes du Pacifique (Tournier), 99–100
molecular dog, 50
molecular elephant, 61
molecular lines, 22n, 76, 86, 101, 159
molecular text, 160–1
Le Monde de Sophie (Gaarder), 135, 153n
monkeys, 52–5
Les Mots (Sartre), 83
Muehrcke, Philip C. and Julian O., 79, 84

Nachträglichkeit, 69
Nancy Drew and the Hardy Boys, 26
Narnia chronicles, 67–8, 71
Negotiations (N, Deleuze), 7, 129, 138
Neimanis, Astrida, 52
Nell, Victor, 26
Nietzsche and Philosophy (NP, Deleuze), 143, 144, 151
Nikolajeva, Maria, 16, 65, 67–8, 119, 120, 126
Nodelman, Perry
  becoming-animal, 51, 53
  children's literature, 4–5, 26
  home-away-home motif, 34
  picture books, 133
  repetition, 44, 45n
Noiville, Florence, 29, 152
nomadism, 89–92
nonsense, 15–17, 123–4, 126–8, 131
Novak, Barbara, 33
Nurse Lugton's Curtain (Woolf), 11, 52–3, 54, 59–61

Oedipal animals, 51–2, 55
Oedipal childhood memory, 70
L'Oiseau philosophie (LOP, Deleuze), 1–2, 18, 133–4, 135–53, 156

Index

bird, 136–41
  child figure, 141–8
  death, 150–1
  friendship, 148–50
  molecular text, 160–1
Olkowski, Dorothea, 64–5, 115–16
Opie, Peter and Iona, 119
orchids, 48
Ord, Douglas, 151
O'Sullivan, Emer, 16, 76
Other, 97, 98–9
otherness (alterity), 3, 4

Palmer, Helen, 60, 121
paradox, 2
  of children's literature, 3–5, 18
  of repetition, 10, 25–6
Parnet, Claire, 1, 148, 149; see also *Dialogues II* (D, Deleuze and Parnet)
Passion Couleurs interviews (Duhême), 152–3, 153n
Le Pays où l'on n'arrive jamais (Dhôtel), 14, 87–92, 156
Pebesma, Evan A., 124
Peraldo, Emmanuelle, 83, 84, 85
perception, 60, 62–3, 97
Perrot, Jean, 32, 137
Philippopoulos-Mihalopoulos, Andreas, 93
philosophy bird, 136–41
picture books, 133
Pisters, Patricia, 120, 145, 147
plants *see* becoming-plant
playgrounds, 77–8
pleasure principle, 27
Pontalis, Jean-Bertrand, 69
portmanteau words, 121–3
Pourparlers (Deleuze) *see Negotiations* (N, Deleuze)
power, 3, 54, 105, 120, 125; see also disempowerment
power relations, 53, 160
Le Procès-Verbal (Le Clézio), 12, 58
psychoanalysis, 19, 27–8, 69–70, 145–6
pure becoming, 13, 64–71, 157–8
pure difference, 38
pure repetition, 29–34, 40, 44

Qu'est-ce que la philosophie? (Deleuze and Guattari) *see What is Philosophy?* (WP, Deleuze and Guattari)
Quist, Harlin, 29

Ramey, Joshua, 139, 140
Ratelle, Amy, 144–5
readership, 3–4
reading, 48–9, 53–4, 63–4
reading gluttony, 26
Reading the Child in Children's Literature (Rudd), 4, 5, 156
Reimer, Mavis, 34
repetition, 10–11, 25–45, 84
  Aiôn, 41–4, 45
  compulsion to repeat, 27, 45n
  pure repetition, 29–34, 40, 44
  ritournelle, 10–11, 21n, 34–8, 44–5
  syntheses of time, 38, 39–40
resemblance, 60
reterritorialisation
  becoming, 50, 51, 54
  bicycle assemblage, 21n
  molar lines, 86
  nomads, 91
  ritournelle, 36
  see also deterritorialisation
Reynolds, Kimberley, 29, 123
rhizomatic childhood, 142–3
rhizomatic movement, 9–10, 13, 100–1
rhizomatic stories, 57
rhizomatic territory, 84
rhizomatic time *see* Aiôn
rhizomes, 75–6, 142, 153n
rhyme, 118–19
ritournelle, 10–11, 21n, 28, 34–8, 44–5, 57, 138
Robinson Crusoe (Defoe), 93
Rohman, Carrie, 52, 59, 60, 61
Rose, Jacqueline, 3, 5
Rudd, David, 4, 5, 118, 156
Ruy-Vidal, François, 29

Saldanha, Arun, 105
Salinger, J. D., 26
Sartre, Jean-Paul, 83
Scheler, Lucien, 137
schizophrenic language, 110–11
self, sense of, 64–5
Sendak, Maurice, 51
sens, 114
sense, 15–17, 112–18
  Humpty Dumpty, 118–20
  see also nonsense
sense of self, 64–5
'serial' series (Warhol), 31
series, 26, 113
Sigler, Amanda, 111
similarity, 60

INDEX

similes, 60
simulacra, 31, 32, 33, 43
simulacral voices, 126
Smith, Daniel W., 147, 152
Sophies verden (Gaarder), 135, 153n
Sotirin, Patty, 48, 146
Spinoza, Baruch, 18–19
Stengers, Isabelle, 19
Stevenson, Robert Louis, 64, 80
Stivale, Charles J., 6, 7, 149
stuttering, 33, 108–9, 111–12, 123, 131, 159
subjectivity, 54
surfaces of sense, 112–18
  Humpty Dumpty, 118–20
Susina, Jan, 65, 66, 108
Swallows and Amazons (Ransome), 78–80, 81–2
syntheses of time, 38, 39–40

territorialisation, 77; *see also* deterritorialisation; reterritorialisation
Theatrum philosophicum (Foucault), 30–1
thisness, 61
Through the Looking-Glass (Carroll), 1, 16–17
  death, 151
  language, 112–13, 118–20, 121–3, 130–1
  molecular child, 157–60
  movement, 75, 83–6
  time, 41–2
Thurston, Luke, 110
time
  Aiôn, 41–4, 45: becoming, 144; death, 150, 151; growing up / growth, 66–71, 92, 158; journeying, 159; molecular child, 99–100; nonsense, 124; rhizomatic childhood, 143
  Chronos, 41, 42, 43, 67, 100, 150, 158
  syntheses of, 38, 39–40
'To the Oracle at Delphi' (Ferlinghetti), 128
Tournier, Michel, 9, 14
  Vendredi ou la vie sauvage, 15, 93–100, 103–4n, 156
  Vendredi ou les limbes du Pacifique, 15, 93, 99, 100, 156
transcendental empiricism, 63
translation, 110
travelling *see* journeying

Trini à l'île de Pâques (Fleutiaux), 10–11, 36, 80–1, 82
Trini fait des vagues (Fleutiaux), 10–11, 35–6, 42
Trites, Roberta Seelinger, 47, 106
Two Regimes of Madness (TRM, Deleuze), 10, 21n, 148
Tynan, Aidan, 28

variation, 30, 44
Vendredi ou la vie sauvage (Tournier), 15, 93–100, 103–4n, 156
Vendredi ou les limbes du Pacifique (Tournier), 15, 93, 99, 100, 156
vision, 82–3, 101, 147
Vivas, Julie, 52, 59, 60, 61
voice, 3, 105, 106, 125, 126–8
  zeroth voice, 17, 128–30, 131, 159–60
Voyage au pays des arbres (Le Clézio), 12, 57–9, 156

Warhol, Andy, 31
wasp-orchid, 48
Watson, Victor, 25, 44, 84, 85
'What Children Say' (Deleuze), 77, 81, 86, 91
What is Philosophy? (WP, Deleuze and Guattari), 133, 153n
  André Dhôtel, 58
  art, 140
  becoming, 144, 147
  deterritorialisation, 36
  philosophy bird, 137
  witch's flight / line, 18, 139, 155
Where the Wild Things Are (Sendak), 51–2
The Widow and the Parrot (Woolf), 11, 12, 55–6
Williams, James, 39, 40, 43, 65, 113, 150
witch's flight / line, 18–19, 139, 140–1, 155, 156–7
Woolf, Virginia, 9
  Nurse Lugton's Curtain, 11, 52–3, 54, 59–61
  The Widow and the Parrot, 11, 12, 55–6

Yin, Jing, 54

Zepke, Stephen, 31
zeroth law of thermodynamics, 129, 132n
zeroth voice, 17, 128–30, 131, 159–60
Zourabichvili, François, 36

EU representative:
Easy Access System Europe
Mustamäe tee 50, 10621 Tallinn, Estonia
Gpsr.requests@easproject.com

www.ingramcontent.com/pod-product-compliance
Lightning Source LLC
Chambersburg PA
CBHW070358240426
43671CB00013BA/2547